ADVANCE PRAISE FOR

Black Hands in the Biscuits Not in the Classrooms

"Sherick A. Hughes has reversed the presumed story of Black America. In the usual story, struggles of African Americans end up presumably in despair and become social problems to be dealt with by public policies. What Dr. Hughes reveals to us is that racial struggle can also be understood in the contexts of hope and faith. Indeed, this book demonstrates that hope is the pedagogy used by African Americans in this southern community to survive the turmoil of desegregation and slow and violent pace of cultural and social change. Hope is the pedagogy that families use to prepare their African American children to survive racism and to prepare them for the challenges to come. Dr. Hughes's analysis has the potential for more racial uplift than any governmental policy could effect."

George W. Noblit, Joseph R. Neikirk Distinguished Professor, School of Education, The University of North Carolina

"*Black Hands in the Biscuits Not in the Classrooms* creates a picture that is rich in complexity, but simple in its poignancy and ability to capture the story of desegregation. The multiple lenses add power to the perspectives. This book masterfully weaves the local stories and knowledge of individuals and families with the broader discussions of desegregation as a national social and political event. The same is true of the way the local/personal narratives are woven with the theoretical constructs.

The way the narratives are presented and critiqued provides a compelling analysis of schooling, social hierarchy, and power embedded in social structures. The use of 'pedagogy, struggle, and hope' in the conclusions is particularly compelling for understanding the complexity and messiness of the social, political, and historical moments."

Van Dempsey, Associate Professor of the College of Human Resources and Education, and Director of the U.S. Department of Education acclaimed Benedum Collaborative, Benedum Center for Educational Renewal, West Virginia University

"Sherick A. Hughes captures my soul with this book. I see my story in his story, his elders are my elders, and his family is my family. The narratives presented in this book represent the many narratives of hope, promise, and uplift many Black folks receive from their elders. In many ways this book is a "homecoming" because you can feel the love, pride, and energy that are present in each family's quest for education. This book is appropriate for students and scholars alike because it represents the space between hope and struggle."

Robert Berry, Assistant Professor, Curry School of Education, University of Virginia

Black Hands in the Biscuits Not in the Classrooms

Studies in the
Postmodern Theory of Education

Joe L. Kincheloe and Shirley R. Steinberg
General Editors

Vol. 286

PETER LANG
New York • Washington, D.C./Baltimore • Bern
Frankfurt am Main • Berlin • Brussels • Vienna • Oxford

Sherick A. Hughes

Black Hands in the Biscuits Not in the Classrooms

Unveiling Hope in a Struggle for *Brown*'s Promise

PETER LANG
New York • Washington, D.C./Baltimore • Bern
Frankfurt am Main • Berlin • Brussels • Vienna • Oxford

Library of Congress Cataloging-in-Publication Data

Hughes, Sherick A.
Black hands in the biscuits not in the classrooms:
unveiling hope in a struggle for Brown's promise / Sherick A. Hughes.
p. cm. — (Counterpoints; v. 286)
Includes bibliographical references.
1. School integration—North Carolina—Albemarle Sound Region—Case studies.
2. Discrimination in education—North Carolina—Albemarle Sound Region—
Case studies. 3. African Americans—Education—North Carolina—
Albemarle Sound Region—Case studies. I. Title.
II. Series: Counterpoints (New York, N.Y.); v. 286.
LC214.22.N66H85 379.2'63'0916348—dc22 2004015770
ISBN 0-8204-7431-2
ISSN 1058-1634

Bibliographic information published by **Die Deutsche Bibliothek**.
Die Deutsche Bibliothek lists this publication in the "Deutsche
Nationalbibliografie"; detailed bibliographic data is available
on the Internet at http://dnb.ddb.de/.

Cover design by Lisa Barfield

The paper in this book meets the guidelines for permanence and durability
of the Committee on Production Guidelines for Book Longevity
of the Council of Library Resources.

© 2006 Peter Lang Publishing, Inc., New York
29 Broadway, New York, NY 10006
www.peterlangusa.com

Printed in the United States of America

Contents

Acknowledgments

Those who are mentioned in this section provided direct assistance to the creation, implementation, and conclusion of this dissertation. For fear of excluding indirect influential beings, I want to take this opportunity to direct my most sincere personal regards to those who are not mentioned—thank you and forgive me. The acknowledgment section is a dedication, in a sense, a recognition and expression of appreciation to the hearts, minds, and helping hands of those who assisted me directly on the road to "Book Complete."

It is necessary for me to first thank spirituality, religion, and all of the celestial spirits who carried me when I was weary. I wish to acknowledge the highest omnipotent beings who have been present in my soul. I have learned to call upon these almighty entities by the names Jesus and God. It is through Jesus and God that I am trying to understand and to fulfill the promise of *Brown* through research, teaching, and community service as I seek a glorious dwelling place that harbors refined shells from the formerly developing and unconsciously eroding shores of the academy.

To my mother and father, I owe an extreme expression of gratitude. I appreciate my parents, Jessie Hughes, Sr., and Maiseville Gregory Hughes, as icons who represent antioppressive Christian fellowship, team parenting, hard work ethic, and community service. When I search for social causes in which to believe, they always believe in me. I want to thank my six older siblings who reinforced the spirituality and tutelage of our parents and emerged as personal role models, teachers, and friends. Jessie Hughes Jr., Theresa Hughes Figgs, Elvese Hughes McLean, Janifer Hughes Sykes, Kent O'neal Hughes, and Shelia Hughes provided consistent support and love without limitation.

I am grateful for my mother- and father-in-law, Trish and Don Hoert, and my brother- and sister-in-law, Devin and Jennifer Hoert. Mom, Dad, Dev, and Jen Hoert are thoughtful and esteemed critical thinkers who have supported me in one way or another from the project's inception to its conclusion. I want also to thank the Cooper, Vails, and Vachon families who supported me, sheltered me in their homes, and allowed me to use their personal computers as I continued research and writing, while visiting the Detroit Metropolitan area of Michigan.

This book would not appear in its present form at this time without my wife, Megan Erin Hughes. She helped to give this project breath and life eleven years ago, when she first acknowledged me as her boyfriend. Her devotion and love protects our bundle of hope and optimism during the difficult times of book writing. Thank you for being my wife and a devoted expecting new mother to Baby Hughes. And thank you for being a wonderful foster caregiver to our puppy. Raleigh pup, thank you for your patience and a love that embraces our hearts and protects our spirits.

Before I move away from family acknowledgments, I must thank my extended family, particularly the extended family members of my wedding party. I was married in the middle of my research for this book and these extended family members helped me to maintain my sanity. Thank you Vasana Hemvong, Melissa Vachon, Angelica and John Butte, Maura Tierney, Cindy Vails, Jakob and Erik Osmundson, and Dr. Nitasha Clark—all highly knowledgeable young intellectuals who dribble ideas with me.

I sincerely appreciate the insight of the following black professors, teachers, and friends of mine who are associated with the University of North Carolina at Wilmington: Dr. Deborah Brunson, Dr. Nitasha Clark, and Tayaka Mathis Daniels, MA. I am also grateful for the first university to which I was introduced in person, Elizabeth City State University (ECSU). As I was engaging in initial research, ECSU's G.R. Little Library and its staff offered a comfortable and comprehensive research station. ECSU is certainly a consistent "rising star in the Northeast" and a historically Black university with unlimited potential. I owe much thanks to the wonderful stewards of state historical records in Raleigh, North Carolina: William Brown, David Chiswell, Chris Meekins, and Earl Ijames.

Of course, this book would not have been plausible without my excellent dissertation project committee: Dr. George Noblit, Dr. Ben Reese, Dr. Deb Eaker Rich, Dr. Mary Stone Hanley, Dr. William Malloy, and unofficial committee member, Dr. Charles Thompson. I also must thank other alumni, colleagues, peers, and friends of the University of North Carolina at Chapel Hill for engaging me in productive discussions about my project: Former Dean, Madeleine Grumet; my mentor, Dr. Robert Berry; Beth Hatt-Echeverria; Luis Urrieta; Joe Mosnier; John Dye; Darrell Cleveland; Trey O'quinn; my mentee, Rita Joyner; Dr. Katherine Marshall; and last but not least Dr. Van

Dempsey who urged me to consider Black Hands in the Biscuits as part of the title after hearing Dora Erskin's story at AESA.

I thank UNC staff members Clint Kale and Doug Edmunds for their technical support. In addition, I owe much gratitude to the following UNC School of Education staff members: Nancy Hodgin, Ann McCrimmon, Sharon Marlowe, Cady Blalock, Janet Carroll, Janice James, Tim Eldred, Cheryl Kemp, Cherry Marsh, Mary Herndon, Steve Michael, John Axt, Adrianna Domingos, Kate Willink, and Mona Vance. Also, I wish to thank our hired transcriptionists for their tireless, timely, and detailed work: Linda Brown and Laura Altizer.

I appreciate the Institutional Review Board, its chair Dr. Barbara Goldman, and the University of North Carolina at Chapel Hill who allowed this project to reach the final stages of implementation and completion. I thank the Spencer Foundation for its generous grant to Dr. George Noblit and Dr. James Leloudis who funded this dissertation as one portion of their larger grant project. I thank each of the families of the northern plains in the Albemarle area of Northeastern, North Carolina, who allowed me a space in their lives, homes, and schools. These folks participated in the study and taught me as much about myself as they did about themselves. I chose not to reveal their names here in order to protect them from any negativity that could arise for them due to the intimate and sensitive nature of the information they shared. To all informants: May your hopes and determination persist and continue to inspire people today and for generations to come. Your wisdom provided necessary sparks for me to create an educational nonprofit agency named G3, Inc.—Graduates opening Gateways for future Graduates. As founder and president of G3, Inc., I work to implement a mission and vision where *graduates* represent formal as well as informal educational settings and to maintain an agency that is dedicated to social justice and peace through family–school–community partnerships.

I could not have come to represent the rich and complex stories of those participating families without my adviser, Dr. George Noblit. I return here to express additional gratitude to George after thanking the families, because he helped me hone my own voice in a manner that also allowed me to better hear theirs. George helped transform my ideas into funded learning opportunities coupled with pragmatic intellectual dialogues. I will always cherish my adviser for extending his role to mentor, sponsor, and friend. George, I thank you for believing in me and for leading me to a prophetic pragmatism that helps me to maintain the dignity of my humanity.

I wish to thank both Melissa Jeter, executive director of G3, Inc., and Gui Lin, UT-Toledo Foundations of Education doctoral student, for their excellent proofreading and copyediting work. Finally, I wish to acknowledge the following members of the Peter Lang Publishing family for their excellent work: Dr. Shirley Steinberg; Chris Myers, and Bernadette Shade.

This book is dedicated to the Hughes family, and written with additional inspiration from a woman I never met named Pauli Murray. Pauli Murray was a graduate of Durham, NC's, Hillside High who in 1938 was denied admission to graduate school at the University of North Carolina at Chapel Hill. A letter to Murray from the former dean replied, "Members of your race are not admitted to the University" (Crow, Escott, & Hatley, 2002, p. 162). Pauli Murray returned to North Carolina in 1977 as an ordained priest to administer the Holy Eucharist at the Chapel of the Cross in Chapel Hill, an Episcopal house of worship in which her slave grandmother, Cornelia, had been baptized in 1854 (Crow, Escott, & Hatley, 2002, p. 162).

In memory of lifelong learners and educators,
Mr. Whittier Crockett (W. C.) Witherspoon and Mrs. Leronia Witherspoon

Prologue
Unveiling Hope in a Struggle
for *Brown's* Promise

In this world, the optimists have it, not because they are always right, but because they are positive. Even when wrong, they are positive, and that is the way of achievement, correction, improvement, and success.
> —David Landes, *The Wealth and Poverty of Nations*

Each time a man [or woman] stands up for an ideal or acts to improve the lot of others, or strikes out against injustice, he [or she] sends forth a tiny ripple of hope.
> —Robert F. Kennedy

Part of the promise of *Brown v. Board of Education* was to eliminate active malice against young black students and their families in northeastern North Carolina. Prior to *Brown*, Jerry "Woody" Winston[1] recalled feeling subjected routinely to a racist rhyme as a youngster, as one of several white high school buses passed by him and his peers who shared only one school bus in his county:

> The white high school had a bus! They used to pass by us, and say, "Nigger, nigger, black as tar, can't go to heaven on a motor car." And we would run and try to catch them and throw dirt in there.
>
> See, we couldn't run and keep up with the old bus, you know. But yeah, they used to holler at us, "Nigger, nigger, black as tar, can't go to heaven on a motor car." I'll never forget that.

Such early malice provides a backdrop for understanding how Winston and his peers began and continue to struggle for hope through formal and informal education within their families. Alongside education, they seek refuge in God, hard work, and democracy to remedy the legal and social inequities in all the spaces where black students learn.

The U.S. Department of Education's *Fulfilling the Promise of* Brown, by Judith Winston (no relation to Woody Winston), reminds us of civil rights enforcement activities and the administration of targeted funding programs by the Department of Education (DOE) to address black–white school inequities. Judith Winston (1995) claims a multifaceted mission and vision to fulfill this portion of *Brown*'s promise, which included efforts to:

1. Achieve desegregation at all education levels
2. Eliminate within-school segregation, that is, placement of minority children in lower tracks, including special education, and the exclusion of minorities from higher achievement level courses
3. Ensure that diversity goals of *Brown* are met after integration, by encouraging affirmative recruitment efforts and seeking to eliminate hostile environments
4. Expand the guarantees of equal protection of the laws specified in *Brown to* limited-English-proficient students and to women and girls
5. Provide funding, technical assistance, and training in the areas of "race," sex, and national-origin discrimination. (p. 761)[2]

In 1972, President Nixon sought a Southern strategy that had the effect of reducing the number of federal resources available to black plaintiffs pursuing the implementation of court-ordered school desegregation. Winston argues that this political move changed "our ability to place more students in desegregated educational settings—albeit an important and significant factor in the achievement of equal educational opportunity" (p. 762). She details efforts after the decisions of *Brown I* vs. *Brown II*. It was *Brown I* whereby "the Court in 1954 pronounced that constitutional imperatives could not be met by a separate but equal formulation, and *Brown II* where the Court in 1955 focused on guidelines for the lower courts to use in fashioning remedies with 'all deliberate speed'" (p. 761).

Brown speaks of the importance of education in our society as the "foundation of good citizenship" and as "a principal instrument in awakening the child to cultural values, in preparing him for later professional training, and in helping him to adjust normally to his environment" (p. 761). In fact, the call of *Brown I* and *II* includes as a "fundamental prerequisite to quality" an appreciation of the diversity that helps people have social contracts with other citizens (p. 761). In the context of today's America, this means that we must ensure that all of our nation's children, from all groups, have a realistic opportunity to achieve at high levels with or without busing.

Thus, as Winston alludes, fulfilling the promise of *Brown* necessitates having schools that are open and equipped to teach children of varying classes, creeds, and colors. However, it is insufficient "if the education they receive at the end of the bus ride will not prepare them for a competitive world, or to be good citizens, or to have an appreciation of people unlike themselves" (p. 765). To fulfill the promise of *Brown,* our education policy must sustain tailored needs to match those of "children in all of the education settings where we find them," which requires an understanding of the places that produce them—the home and the family (p. 765; also see Stewart & Allen-Smith, 1995; and Gutman & McLoyd, 2000).

Unfortunately, far too many educators, education researchers, media, and the general public have exaggerated the "needy" black family. Their image of black families downplays individuality and hope while distorting key residuals of history, where leftover structural conditions contribute to current educational needs in many black school communities. Typical dialogue failures involve dismissing the point that historically few (four to five) generations remove most black families from enduring complete social exclusion, and ignoring the evidence that suggests that public education is replete with white-only defined ways of being appropriate, normal, knowledgeable, and worthy. As the fiftieth anniversaries of *Brown I* and *II* come and go, some of the dismissal and exclusion of black voices in many northeastern North Carolina schools is as alive and well today as it was in 1954 and 1955. Even if black families wanted to lose their cultural heritage by completely assimilating, one generation is not long enough to close what I call the "appropriateness to success in a predominantly white educational organization" gap.

Perhaps, I was schooled about this appropriateness more thoroughly and at a younger age than my family at home could have imagined, because I was the youngest of seven children. My parents and siblings could draw from their experiences with the predominantly white desegregated school before my birth, to acquaint me with its hidden rules and norms of survival and success once I was born. Desegregated schooling forced upon others and me, those white middle-class school-defined measures of "appropriateness" in the classroom. Even blacks of a wealthier social class (see Hughes, 2003, situational wealth vs. generational wealth) have been unable to, have not been allowed to, or have been critically and conscientiously resistant to participate in all of the forms of speaking and acting that are deemed "appropriate" or 'useful" by the white educational regime at this point in North Carolina history.

So how does the fulfilling of *Brown* play out in the lives of the local families who must live with its negative consequence, albeit unintended, and maintain hope? The families in this book explain how they shun educational hopelessness and despair as they offer stories most consistent with the work of Kane (2000). Kane describes blacks viewing their families as warm, nurturing, expressive, and supportive of individual autonomy. These findings are also consistent with historically Afrocentric descriptions of black families. Kane does argue, however, that we shouldn't generalize, but keep in mind one simple rule: "Such findings must be used with an openness to variations among individuals and families" (pp. 699–700). Under this rule, I am reminded that all such portrayals of black families are "presented for the sake of contextual understanding only, never to justify stereotyping" (pp. 699–700). Members of the Biggs, Winston, and Erskin families, whose stories are included in this book, are past and present teachers, cafeteria workers, and administrators, and are no exception to Kane's rule. Although all three families spoke of educational struggle and hope, their experiences are highly individualized.

For example, unlike other members of his family, Woody Winston did not force his children to attend schools with whites prior to mandatory desegregation. His children remained in the Marian Anderson School for Blacks during the freedom-of-choice period and therefore were not subjected to some of the early backlash from retaliatory whites. His brother-in-law, however, experienced cross burnings at the hands of angry white Ku Klux Klan (KKK) members, who were not going to allow blacks the freedom to choose their schools without a fight. Woody Winston labels such reactionary white racists "mean ones." He notes that some of the cross-burning whites are alive and well today. (I learned later from his son, Ross Winston, that some of those cross-burning whites serve on influential education and commerce boards in the area today.)

> Well, I'll tell you. When they first integrated the schools, all right, my kids, they didn't want to go. And I didn't force to send them. But the kids that did go, even down to my brother-in-law went, you know they burned a cross in every one, all the people's yards?
>
> Because then my brother-in-law worked with me. I was supposed to pick him up. He was right there. I said, "What you doin'?" He said, 'They burned a cross in my yard this morning." They didn't burn one in mine because my kids didn't go.
>
> Yes, sir. There's some mean white folks around here, living here right now. I can tell you that right now.
>
> Yeah. They're living. Oh, yeah. Burning a cross in the yard. The ones that started going to these high schools.

Just as his father recalled, Ross Winston discussed the cross burnings by reactionary whites in the yards of the northeastern four who desegregated the school—who merely exercised the so-called freedom of choice. Ross's elegant brick home lies across a rural paved road from what appears to be an abandoned shack. I soon learned that the abandoned, dilapidated green structure was once home to one of the first families to desegregate schools in northeastern North Carolina. Parents and promising grade-school children lived there. All of them endured at least one sleepless night at the hands of the KKK. Ross Winston recalled:

> I remember the house right across the road there, you know, where they came
> and burned crosses in their yard. . . . Yeah, they burned a cross. . . . That was
> Lucas. Um hum. He lived right across the road, in that green house right across
> the road. . . . They burned a cross in his yard. They burned one in Walter Leir's
> yard. You know Walter Leir? . . . They burned one in their yard. They burned
> one in Laura Biggs' yard, and I'm trying to think of which other one. I do know
> that they burned one in those three yards. I bet nobody done told you that, did
> they?

Ross was correct. Other than from his father, who did not remember all of
the names of those who had crosses burned at their homes, I had heard of
only one cross burning. They told me about one of them. I didn't know the
whites had gone on a tirade, although one cross burning is enough. As noted
in the story of white teacher Barbara Needham, the Klan burned a cross in
her father's yard to scare him into joining them, so we at least have an idea
about the culprits. Ross claims to know who did the burnings and that they
are prominent citizens still living today.

> And I know the people that did it. Because [inaudible] people told me. I was at
> the telephone company and I had friends, and they told me exactly who the peo-
> ple were that did it. That's right. The people that did it, now they'll ride around
> and look at me [inaudible] but I know where they came from. . . . I know exactly
> the people that did it.
>   Um hum. It was in the newspaper. As a matter of fact, they had a picture of
> that cross over there. My granddaddy went out and threw a bucket of water on
> it. And they had a picture of that in the paper.

As I write this chapter over half a century after Woody Winston's "race"-
dominated childhood, I am watching a documentary on the History Channel
in which contemporary Klan members explain their cross-burning ritual. Klan
members view this ritual as a symbol of their hope for coming out of this time
of darkness with "niggers and Jews" (opposition to the "white race") into the
light of Jesus Christ. Strangely enough, the Jesus Christ that Klan members
use to justify their activity is the same Jesus Christ worshiped by the many of
the people they hate. Narratives presented throughout this book acknowledge
Christ as a provider of faith and hope to sustain the Civil Rights movement for
equitable education in northeastern North Carolina. "The Lord," as commonly referred to back home, has always comforted the same people the Klan
intended to terrorize.

Even in the face of continuous Klan activity and its oppressive form of
Christianity, Woody Winston is hopeful and thankful—hopeful because some
forms of racism-based harassment have clearly decreased, thankful because his
children, father, sister, brother-in-law, nieces, and nephews survived the early
cross-burning, "nigger"-slurred years of segregation and the early transition
into desegregation. He acknowledges the Lord as key to enhancing his own

quality of life and his ability to "pay it forward" by helping other blacks, including my own father.

> Well, I'll tell you, some people made it in a different way. You understand. Some worked on the farm, some didn't. See, that have a lot to do with it. You understand? Yeah, see, if your daddy hadn't worked down that local, he would never have been like he was today. See? He came down there, left the farm, and came down there with us. See, and all of us pulled together because we're from North Carolina, and looked after one another. Now you take a boy up there today, he farmed, he wasn't doing nothing. He asked me one day if he could come down there, and I said come on down there with us. He came. He stayed down there and retired. . . . Right. So your daddy would never have did nothing but working with those Sawyer and stuff on the farm. No, he couldn't.
>
> Right. I helped many people. I worked with people on my job who couldn't even buy nothing to eat when 12:00 come. I would come up there in my car and buy them something to eat. . . . Uh huh. The colored. So I helped many people [to realize post-*Brown* opportunities]. Thank the Lord I could do it!

In 2002, Woody attended a function for his granddaughter at the former Marian Anderson School for Blacks. His narrative shares his amazement and disappointment of seeing so few blacks in charge of educating the children. His narratives ring of the old adage that in the South, whites don't care how close you get as long as you don't get too high, while critiquing how close he actually wants to get to them and the inequity of the school structure for effectively educating black children.

> Well, you know what, I don't see. The change to me was the white folks were taking over the schools. You know that? One of my sons went down there. You know it was Dinah. Dinah's daughter was one of the most active one in there for colored or white. And she told me to go out there with her that day. And she hugged me and she graduated. There wasn't but one colored teacher up there on stage. All them were white. It knocked me down! . . . Yeah, it made me mad because there should have been a lot of colored people up there. That's our school. I'm going to tell you right now, we came a long ways, don't get me wrong, but we just stood up on the back row. We've got a long way to go. . . . A long way to go yet. See, our people think they love us. They don't love us. No. We've got a long way to go yet. We've just stood up on the back row. . . . I was surprised that there was only one colored teacher on the stage. That was our school, Marian Anderson, now, and see, it got to me. They ought to have had almost wide enough, but they didn't.
>
> That's right. Some of them is pretty good. Some of them was pretty good. But you've still got that racism in them, I'll tell you that right now. They don't want you to get too far. And if I hadn't worked down yonder, I'd be in bad shape. A lot of us who worked down there have come a long ways. I'll tell you that right now. We could make it around here.

In the 1980s, North Carolina's total population boomed, but the growth was concentrated in urban centers. Nineteen counties in the coastal plain and in rural areas lost population, as did rural areas everywhere (see Cecelski, 1994, and Stewart & Allen-Smith, 1995). Cecelski argues that "nothing hurt economies more than the farm crisis" (1994, p. 164). Black families, like mine, were disproportionately hit the hardest (p. 164). Black residents go to great lengths to find employment, often without schools hiring them, as Woody Winston alludes. The jobs they do find require commuting. The U.S. census data suggests that the average northeastern North Carolinian commutes approximately half an hour each way to travel to and from work by car. Like my mother, aunts, siblings, and I once did, many blacks still endure a commute from forty minutes to over an hour each way during the tourist season to wash dishes or clean motel or hotel rooms on the Outer Banks. More black folks have to move away, because fewer are hired in local-, state-, or government-based careers such as those available in the schools. As Celeski explains, "Only the annual family, and church, homecomings disclose that northeastern North Carolina remains the spiritual center for large numbers of its departed children" (p. 164).

I am one of those departed children, partaking in the exodus to the North. Specifically, I made the journey to the Midwest to pursue the plentiful leads for tenure-track university professor positions in Social Foundations and Sociology of Education, only to find continued signs of racism and racialization (i.e., focus on "race" as the driving device of humanity which can exist with or without the inferiorization, antipathy, and institutional power commonly ascribed to racism). In the middle of my neighborhood park, where many grade-school children learn and play, the word "nigger" is spelled out in plain view on the black asphalt. Because black folks often say and write "nigga," the "er" ending in the spray-painted word suggests that it was not written by blacks. The narratives that build the story of this book, in conjunction with my most recent Northern exposure to "race," provide a diverse, antioppressive education challenge for all of us. Much to my dismay, ignorance and insensitivity persists north of the Mason-Dixon Line. Recently I have heard such comments as: "I didn't know black people tanned"; "I don't know how to deal with black people because none were in my school"; "You made it; why can't other blacks?"; and "If they would just work hard like you and stop relying on the government. . . ." The myth of merit prevails. Yet, at my neighborhood meeting, I received reports of talks to add another trashcan and bins for "puppy poop" bags, but no discussion of erasing the "n" word on the playground. Irrespective of the ethnicity of the culprit, such an eyesore is a reminder of an ugly past and should offend all Americans. Blacks who have "made it" may be leery of moving to the neighborhood, as should anyone— whites, Latinos, and others—if the word "nigger" is okay for the park. I hesitate to take my visiting family to the park today after traveling from North Carolina to the "great white North." Why don't I paint over it? It was here when I arrived. I'm interested to see how much I can trust my predominantly white neighborhood watch to do the right thing. Only time will tell.

Jesse Jackson's now famous charge to the United States to move more blacks, particularly males, to "Penn State" and away from "the State Pen" was accompanied by messages of the existence of more Black males "incarcerated than in college." However, black families have never received such attention for producing more working, tax-paying males and college-bound females than incarcerated ones. This book is about a multiplicity of black family trials counterbalanced by their hope and success. This work is intended not only to offer a positive image but also to provide a clearer picture of rural Southern black life and education. All of the children of these families are "in work and/or in college (or formerly in college)" and none are "incarcerated." Even so, I do have cousins from back home who are incarcerated. One of my dearest relatives left for prison the fall that I left for college and we "graduated" at the same time, when I finished the first of two master's degrees. However, our family story, like those shared in this book, are replete with triumph. I begin each chapter of this book with a poem by author Kent Hughes. Hughes (2003), author of *4th Sunday in the Dirty,* was among the initial group of first-graders to desegregate his northeastern county elementary school. It is likely that if you run into a Hughes in northeastern North Carolina that he or she will be related to me. Kent Hughes is no exception. He is my brother, one of my six older siblings, who grew up with me only six miles from the Bartlett Plantation, where my ancestors were enslaved just four generations ago. Our yard is near a swamp and it floods with little warning. Such is typical of real estate sold to many black families in the area, somewhat due to affordability, much to do with racism and segregation.

Upon learning about this project, my mother offered two poignant early memories of the 1950s *Brown* era and the old Frizbee's Studio. Frizbee's used to travel to the segregated black schools to take pictures. The studio workers not only had to make the trek to another county and from the city to the country, but they also had to cross *Jim Crow's* ethnic boundaries for this photo shoot. Frizbee's was one of the few white photography studios to do so. My mother took their willingness to travel across multiple social and geographic boundaries in order to photograph blacks at the school as a sign of their alliance with us, but she was wrong. When she made the trip and traversed those boundaries with my eldest sister Theresa, a one-year-old at the time, the Frizbee's representative abruptly exclaimed, "We don't make [individual] appointments for nigras." When my mom shared more stories of struggle, I asked, "Mom, how in the world did you find hope before and after *Brown?*" She thought for a long while and then spoke. "My faith, my religious faith. Then I tried to pass it on to y'all." The pedagogy of struggle and hope and its passing along from one black generation to the next fills the bulk of the pages of this book.

You will read about grandmothers such as Dora Erskin, who speaks of her "black hands in the biscuit dough." She was my first interviewee and her statement was profound, as it foreshadowed stories of a perceived complicity to continue the domestication of blacks, while limiting our legitimate authority in grade schools. Black cafeteria workers, such as Margie Hines and my own mother, were among the first to desegregate the schools. This move closely follows a factory model in the exchange and placement of blacks, particularly black women, from the kitchens of white people's homes to the kitchens of the grade schools serving predominantly white students: limited promotion, little social mobility, and one assembly line after another. I pass these stories of school desegregation along to you, the reader, with hope that you will feel inspired to form social contracts and to find spaces where you can bring hope to your spheres of influence as we seek to fulfill the promise of 1954.

Notes

1. Pseudonyms are used throughout the rest of the book to protect the identities of the contributors.
2. The term "race" is written in quotation marks here and throughout the rest of this book in order (a) to avoid further reification of the term by alerting readers with actual marks that can immediately render the term different or even suspicious; (b) to remind readers to always be skeptical of the usage of the term; and (c) to suggest that the term is part of a critically conscious dialogue to be engaged internally and with others (see also Riggs, 1999).

References

Cecelski, D. S. (1994). *Along Freedom Road*. Chapel Hill: University of North Carolina Press.

Gutman, L. M., & McLoyd, V. C. (2000). Parents' Management of Their Children's Education Within the Home, at School, and in the Community: An Examination of African-American Families Living in Poverty. *Urban Review, 32*(1), 1–24.

Hughes, K. (2003). *4th Sunday in the Dirty*. Charleston, SC: Imprint Books.

Hughes, S. A. (2003). An Early Gap in Black-White Mathematics Achievement: Holding School and Home Accountable in an Affluent City School District. *Urban Review, 35*(4), 297–322.

Kane, C. M. (2000). African American Family Dynamics as Perceived by Family Members, *Journal of Black Studies, 30*(4), 691–702.

Riggs, F. (1999, January). Focus on Ethnicity. In *Intellectual Odyssey: An Autobiographical Narrative* (chap. 5). Retrieved December 28, 2004, from http://www2.hawaii.edu/~fredr/autobi05.htm#5

Stewart, J. B., & Allen-Smith, J. E. (Eds.). (1995). *Blacks in Rural America*. New Brunswick, NJ : Transaction Publishers.

Winston, J. (1995). U.S. Department of Education, *Fulfilling the Promise of* Brown. *Teacher's College Record, 96*(2), 757–766.

Hope, Struggle, and Education at "The Top of My Life"

THE TOP OF MY LIFE
by Kent Hughes

I climbed to the top of my life
To look back on what I had learned
I found that the flames inside me
As a child had never ceased to burn
I saw the drummer beating their drums
As I went toward the sound
I followed the footsteps of my forefathers
Their sweat and blood helped pave the ground
For me to walk upon the ground
I crawled before I would stand
Even when I thought I was ready
I wasn't close to being a man
An elder told me
About the path he had to cross
Even as a child I understood
How he helped pay the cost
I saw myself in my teenage years
I was infinity at the time
Until I saw my friends pass before me
And soon had a change of mind
Although I struggled through my teenage years
I made it from a boy to man
I saw myself being impatient
But later I would understand
I then climbed down from the top of my life

To look forward to what I can learn
And remember the flames inside me as a child
Were always meant to burn

Introduction

I am a hopeful black man, resonating with words spoken by my elders. Some of these wise words reflect experiences and a striking paradox in our nation's history:

> In the North, whites don't care how high you get as long as you don't get too close. In the South, whites don't care how close you get, as long as you don't get too high. (original author, unknown, n. d.)

It is a paradox that emerged from narratives in response to the seminal *Brown v. Board of Education* decision of 1954, which desegregated public schools. Fifty years later, I am grateful to be here, "at the top of my life" for the first time, with the resources and legitimacy to write a book honoring the stories of the elders who produced me and the educational fire that burns within us all. Here, on the fiftieth anniversary of *Brown,* I am grateful to share one story of school desegregation and some of the struggles and hopes it brought with it for the first day of school in my region of the "New" South. It is my time to climb down from the top of my life, looking back on what I have learned, looking forward to what is yet to be.

The experiences of elders such as Dora and Nolen Erskin, the seventy-seven- and eighty-four-year-old parents of nine living children, are most typical and yet most poignant as they narrate this story. The Erskin family accounts are part of a larger collection of narratives that include "voices" of retired grade-school administrators and counselors, as well as past and present parents, teachers, and students in the school community. These narratives, all together, tell a comprehensive story of trials and triumphs in the Southern rural schooling of black folks in the northern mainland of the Albemarle area in northeastern North Carolina (northeastern Albemarle). It is a story of a school community talking, as Noblit (2002) proclaims, "in the present, about the past, for the future"—a future of continuing the arduous work to fulfill the promises of 1954.

After 1954, all nine of the Erskin children finished high school and would be considered worthy citizens by U.S. standards—despite the challenges and obstacles they faced, as elaborated in the Erskins' narratives.

> DORA ERSKIN: I did tell the white lady that I was working for, I told her, I said, "Your husband's daddy, the granddaddy, took the children out of northeast Albemarle public schools and put them in private schools, so the children wouldn't be in school with the blacks." I told her, I said, "Well, he come here

and sit down to the table and eat," I said. "My black hands are in his biscuits. He eats them." I said, "What's the difference?" She said, "Tell him that." I said, "No. I'm not going to." I said, "You tell him." [laughter] I said, "You tell him." She said, "I will." I believe she will if it ever came up. She didn't like him either. No sir. He's sitting down and eating my food. I said, "My black hands are in his biscuits, and he'll eat them, but he didn't want his grandchildren to mix with the blacks."

QUESTION: Did he send them over to City Academy?

DORA ERSKIN: He most certainly did! He most certainly did and told his son he'd pay for half of them. "I'll pay for the other half." I was listening right at him when he said it. He didn't think I heard him, but I heard it. I heard it. I heard that.

QUESTION: So what do y'all think the white folks were so worried about?

DORA ERSKIN: Lord, I couldn't tell you, honey. I think, I don't know. But I heard a white man say—I was in his kitchen—I heard a white man say he cash a lady's check, black woman, black teacher's check, turn to the other man and said, "You ought to have seen that check she brought in here and we cashed it. Niggers has got money nowadays. See. Niggers has got money nowadays." So that's what they were afraid of, I guess. [I] Don't want the blacks to ask the white for nothing, like they used to. They don't have to go to them for everything.

NOLEN ERSKIN: They don't want the blacks on top.

DORA ERSKIN: Listen right at him [white store clerk] when he said that. I remember when [her daughter] Wanda was going to school; it was Wanda and a little white girl. Now they were the two smartest ones in the class. I got a letter saying that, what was it now. . . . Wanda and this girl were too smart to be in that grade, and they were going to put them in another grade, sent me a paper for me to sign. I signed it, and just 'cause Wanda was black, they didn't let neither one of them go to the next grade. I remember that. I remember that. The paper went to Raleigh [North Carolina's state capital]. I mean that's where it came from, Raleigh. Come to the school, and it was Wanda and [a] little white girl.

QUESTION: So the teacher that told you that, was the teacher black or white?

DORA ERSKIN: Yeah, she was black.

QUESTION: She was a black teacher?

DORA ERSKIN: If it had been a white one, I wouldn't have ever heard anything about it. She was the one that sent me the letter from the school. She got the letter from Raleigh. She sent me the letter from school and wanted to know did I want Wanda to pass on. If I did, sign that paper; so that's what I did. I signed it. I went out there and talked to her. Neither girl was skipped to the next grade

because Wanda was black. She told me that was why, because Wanda was black.
That's exactly what she told me.

Under the conditions portrayed in the Erskin narratives, and others, it seems that one would be hard-pressed to find more than struggle in post-*Brown* education for blacks of northeastern Albemarle. Yet I am here, like the Erskin children, writing and black, born and raised in the very same area within the Albemarle area of collective black struggle. My current social position (middle-class, black male; tenure-track professor) rings of something that comes with struggle, a complex, intangible force that refuses to allow struggle to be linked to despair. It is hope. These narratives are essentially telling *my* story as well. It is an educative story of how I, as a black person from a working-class background in northeastern Albemarle, became more academically, socially, and economically mobile through formal and informal education, when most of my counterparts did not. I credit my family's educational practices, particularly those that helped me cross the bridge connecting the rules and norms of home and school. Their ability to teach me how to cross that bridge was a crucial element that led me to my current social space. Actually, there are two other key issues for which to account in my telling of this story: (1) the constructions of my participants (families sharing their experiences) and (2) my appropriation of their constructions in my efforts to make them transfer to readers (writing what families shared with me, but organizing it while considering reader diversity). With this information in mind, I set out to tell the story of my people and myself—to understand how they (we) find hope and endure struggle and what differences the balance of struggle through hope makes in the educational experiences of the black residents of northeastern Albemarle, North Carolina.

Book Rationale

The northern mainland of the Albemarle area in northeastern North Carolina was chosen as the backdrop for my story due to (a) my familiarity with the schools as a former K–12 student in the region, (b) the smallness of the school communities—most have only three to four total schools even today, (c) the rural nature of the schools, (d) the ethnic and socioeconomic status of families and school personnel, and (e) the particular history of racialization and education problems after *Brown*. Lawrence Blum (2002) alludes to "racialization" as an exaggerated and misguided focus on "race" as the integral characteristic of human groups, which leads us to dismiss most other social factors and cues that influence knowledge capacity, human development, thought, and action. The rural northeastern Albemarle school communities represented in this story serve only a combined total of about 21,732 school-age youths (an average of fewer than 4,400 youths per county as of this writing). All of these schools pay lip service to an espoused mission to "work with parents and community to prepare their children to live well and prosper together in an ever-changing global society." Yet my experiences, growing up in the region, seem hauntingly similar to the North versus South paradox portrayed above in the wisdom of my elders. Nearly three decades and two generations of collective struggle for a sound global education separate my elders' introduction to school desegregation from my own. Still, the "New South," now composed of native southerners and northern transplants, faces the inherited dilemma of black–white structural mobility ("too high") versus black–white social proximity ("too close"). This dilemma seems to have rendered a situation where too many forced and faked "social contracts" proliferate (Rousseau, 1762).

Jean-Jacques Rousseau's (1762) notion of ideal social contracts involves authentic human participation, collaboration, reciprocation, and "welcomed" obligation. It seems that too many white and black adult stakeholders in the lives of northeastern Albemarle's school-age children live in contrast to this social ideal. Narratives of this book tend to portray blacks and whites as intimate strangers living a sort of default social contract. I describe the contract as "default" because many blacks and whites in the school communities of northeastern Albemarle seem to share unrealized social possibilities. Their educational stories seem to meet more often at the crosshairs of law and "unwelcomed" obligation and less often at the crossroads of love and social responsibility. Such default social contracts are known to come with social penalties (e.g., bias, suspicion, complicity, and civil unrest). In the cases of northeastern Albemarle, social penalties seem to exist in all of the forms above, all of which are capable of diminishing the educational preparation necessary for both whites and people of color to live well and prosper together, locally and abroad.

When combined, retellings of this history suggest that in action the northeastern Albemarle schools' missions become racialized at best, and presume a racial hierarchy at worst, where even poor whites are held above their black counterparts. Therefore, it seems more accurate to understand the mission in use as addressing the needs of *some* parents and *some* members of the community to prepare *some* students to live and prosper in a *limited, nonglobal* society replete with detrimental threats to achievement (Steele, 1998). Recent data from the U.S. Census Bureau (http://quickfacts.census.gov) and the North Carolina Public Schools Statistical Profile 2003 (http://www.ncpublic-schools.org/fbs/stats/statprofile03.pdf) support my arguments about the real life of the mission of northeastern Albemarle's public schools. The area's public schools are local beacons to black youth, who make up from over 7 to 40 percent of the school-age population in a given county. However, presently, at a typical rural northeastern Albemarle public school, there is an abundance of black teaching assistants but not enough black teachers to match the percentage of the black school-age population. One county has no black teachers at the secondary level at all. With nearly 360 black school-age children looking at high school as the pinnacle of their school lives, this imbalance and lack of educational role models is shocking. Four of the five counties have no black guidance counselors on guidance staffs with three to seven members. All five counties have school psychologists and librarians, but none of them is black. All of the counties hire a larger proportion of black service workers than black teachers, but the opposite is not true for whites. Students can see as many as five black service workers before seeing one black teacher in school, while they may see thirteen white teachers before seeing one white service worker. School administration offers an equally abysmal outlook for aspiring black school personnel in the area. Two of the five counties have no black principals and two of them have no black assistant principals; one county has neither. At the top levels of administration, there is usually only one black voice to represent the entire black community of a given county—a community weary and leery of the waning support they feel from hired and elected school officials in a dichotomous (black–white), racialized environment.

There is only one Native American student in a typical school setting and usually less than 1 percent of the students identify themselves as Hispanic or Asian. In my own recounting of K–12 school experiences in the area, I remember that even "others" were pressured by peers at school to choose either "honorary" black in-groups or "honorary" white in-groups for purposes of gaining social status along with a sense of belonging. Although black parent and student populations have decreased very little, black educators in northeastern Albemarle began dwindling when schools desegregated. It is not unusual to find a maximum of one black principal, school board member, or county commissioner in northeastern Albemarle school communities that once thrived on the tutelage of black educators. Once their term as administrator or elected official ends, they are likely not to try again, after fighting a token identity and finding limited success in brokering for and with their black community. This disappointing fact must be considered along with the family and school personnel narratives that relay stories regarding the continuously unfair rejection of highly qualified blacks wh surface in grade school faculty applicant pools. I was provided some evidence supporting the notion that few white northeastern Albemarle school officials seem to care that there are no longer enough black teachers or administrators in the area. With the loss of so many black educators, there are limited numbers of school personnel who can lead, mentor, sponsor, and negotiate in order to offer optimal educational opportunities to the region's black students, while helping white students fulfill the mission of learning to live in a "global society" (see also Clark, 1983; Ladson-Billings, 1994; O'Connor, 1997; Reis & Diaz, 1999; O'Connor 1999; & Mickelson, 2001).

Arguably, schools in northeastern Albemarle have been plagued with black–white desegregation tension since the inception of *Brown*. During an assembly I attended in the 1992–93 school year, one staff member of a north-eastern Albemarle school declared, "Our school doesn't need these problems," alluding largely to black–white dating relationships argued as the root of strife between many black and white students at that time. I remember that no one disagreed publicly or even argued that the root of the problem seemed to be connected more to the detrimental influences of racialization than to teen dating. Consequently, except in the context of this study, no one has yet to acknowledge in a public medium that any current northeastern Albemarle school conditions are connected to school desegregation and its elimination of black schools and black educators. So, consideration of the problems I inherited from the way schools were desegregated in my area is apparently absent from the public sphere that can spark policy changes.

Without a complete circuit, how can we attempt to spark change? Born in this context of inherent, hidden school agendas and racial discrimination, I was still able to obtain a Ph.D. in education from the state's flagship public university, the University of North Carolina. And a small disproportionate number of other blacks who went through northeastern Albemarle schools before and after me have also garnered such positive educational outcomes. Despite racism and concerted efforts to control blacks' distribution of power in school decision making, some of us came to see broader individual possibilities, to live out the aspirations of our ancestors, and to embrace education as the vehicle. The fact that these triumphs happened, even as blacks lost a large degree of control over the education of their children, means something was going on in the black family to compensate for missing links at school. This story, then, reverses the stigma of the black family as deficient, and reclaims the distribution of power in the form of black family support systems and hope and optimal achievement (see also Luster & McAdoo, 1991; Bempechat, 1991; Bempechat & Wells, 1989; Bempechat & Drago-Severson, 1999; Bempechat & Ginsburg, 1989; Baker & Stevenson, 1986). Families have endured political and educational turmoil with these mechanisms of hope. Thus, we have a story of the experiences of black families who prevailed with limited support from allies, even when the heaviest distribution of power to schools was largely surrendered to some disgruntled whites under the guise of school desegregation (see also Edwards, 1976; Epstein, 1989; Delpit, 1993; Delpit, 1995; Gutman & McLoyd, 2000). Along with my relatives and other young adult people of color from the area, I not only inherited problems, but I also inherited privileges from the blood and sweat, aches and pains, tears and triumphs of my elders. Now, northeastern Albemarle's intriguing school desegregation story can be told in public again by a person of color to an audience of color, and yet, for the first time to a white audience by a black native son.

Several notable scholars discuss the happenings in school and the relationship to black communities in other regions of North Carolina (e.g., Noblit & Collins, 1981; Noblit, 1999; Cecelski, 1994; Siddle Walker, 1996; Phillipson, 1999). These scholars offer some useful information through narratives and stories about the social consequences of school desegregation for black families and communities as they experience K–12 schooling. The dialogue about this matter has been largely a hidden transcript (Scott, 1990), veiled from official public discourse for at least the following reasons posited by Lemert (1999): (1) the powers-that-be (persons assuming the heaviest distribution of power) want them concealed; (2) either those persons assuming more power or those assuming less power may resist talking about them because they are too threatening and are too much to deal with; or (3) people need time and experience to learn how to put into words the reality in which they live (but not everyone has the time or resources to reach this point in life) (p. 2).

Yet the folks featured in this book, whether retired or still struggling with public schools, dare to speak now, to share some of their private transcripts. I felt honored to be invited into their homes to listen to and share collective struggles of school desegregation for the purposes of synthesizing transferable information to readers, to audiences, to you. This book was written with the blessings of those families and their past and present school allies. In fact, it is with their insistence that I share their little-known stories—stories of struggle and hope to make school a better place for rural, black, southern families (see also Anderson, 1988; Stewart & Allen-Smith, 1995). Thus I am obligated to tell their stories well, speaking as close to their words as possible.

The setting for this black educational his story-telling is a rural, Southern deciduous forest nestled in the counties known collectively as the "northern mainland" of the Albemarle area of North Carolina: Pasquotank, Camden, Perquimans, Currituck, and Chowan (ICW-NET, LLC, 2004). The southern edges of these five counties form the jagged northern shoreline of the Albemarle Sound, located in the northeastern corner of the state. The retelling of this history portrays how pre- and post-*Brown* school histories from this northern mainland Albemarle area involve (a) understanding and enduring education struggles; (b) constructing and reproducing education hopes through relational ties; and (c) handling struggle, education hopes, and relationships in a manner that is connected to the black families' educational outcomes. Most narratives of the book refer to three of the five counties; however, by the end of the book readers will have learned from informants whose stories and experiences of school, to varying degrees, span all five counties. In order to protect the informants and the integrity of individual counties throughout the rest of the book, these counties shall be referred to most often as the collective phrase "NE Albemarle." Additional references to the counties and the area include "northeastern Albemarle," "northeastern Albemarle (counties)," "the northeastern Albemarle (area), (county), or (region)," and "County (A), (B), (C), (D), or (E)."

Intellectual Framework

The goals of this book are influenced largely by the work of the late Brazilian educator Paulo Freire in his book *The Pedagogy of Hope*. Pedagogy is understood here as the art of teaching while learning and learning while teaching— (a) sculpting model units and lessons for a collage of school, community, and university settings; (b) painting a multilayered, multicolored, culturally relevant portrait for connecting teachers and students who strive to reach their highest potential; and (c) performing critical pedagogy that is rich with deeper meanings, emotional content, and methods to engage some degree of critical consciousness with each teaching and learning opportunity. This critical temper of pedagogy and learning may allow students and teachers to recognize and alleviate oppression of self and others while balancing life with thoughts and actions that breathe hope.

Freire explains the pedagogy of hope and oppression as necessary concomitant forces working toward an education that is strong in social justice, where the adequately educated can transcend social oppression without reproducing it. In arguing that hope is a fundamental human need, Friere warns us against separating it from action. Freire ties all of this to education, much in the ways that black families and their school allies in northeastern Albemarle counties do. He depicts the union of hope and struggle:

> The idea that hope alone will transform the world . . . is an excellent route to hopelessness, pessimism, and fatalism. [T]he attempt to do without hope, in the struggle to improve the world, as if that struggle could be reduced to calculated acts alone, or a purely scientific approach, is a frivolous illusion. . . . Without a minimum of hope, we cannot so much as start the struggle. But without the struggle, hope . . . dissipates, loses its bearing, and turns into hopelessness. One of the tasks of the serious progressive educator, through a serious, correct, political analysis, is to unveil opportunities for hope, no matter what the obstacles may be. (Freire, 1996, pp. 8–10)

Like Freire, I want my work to further the process of unveiling educative opportunities for hope in black families like my own, by studying how they construct their educational experiences to find hope in post-*Brown* northeastern Albemarle schools. My work speaks particularly to school personnel and families—when school desegregation happened and how it played out in their lives. The narratives in this book continue to offer hope today, as they trace the change and constancy in the struggle for educational opportunities.

I now understand that my family and other black families in northeastern Albemarle endured some denial of educational and economic success due to the highly racialized structure of schooling in our community, state, and nation. I originally returned to the region focused on the past and longing for a better future for blacks in the integrated school setting. Yet the possibility for improving education for black folks in the northeastern Albemarle counties may rest in our understanding of the present as well, and how we use the past and an imagined future to construct the present for blacks and whites, as Noblit and Dempsey (1996, pp. 29, 48) suggest so well. They write, "in our sense, ideas are not great because of what they say about our past or our future but because of how they help us construct our present" (p. 75). Noblit and Dempsey (1996) correctly foreshadow that black folks of northeastern Albemarle "are not the pawns of the ideas promoted by the intellectuals. . . . [T]hey are participants in . . . life, using relationships, narratives, each other, situations, and ideas to construct virtue with their experiences of schooling" (p. 75). Like Noblit and Dempsey, John Dewey (1938) alludes to the importance of seizing present educational experiences:

> What, then, is the true meaning of preparation in the educational scheme? In the first place, it means that a person, young or old, gets out of his present experience all that there is in it for him at the time in which he has it. When preparation is made the controlling end, then the potentialities of the present are sacrificed to suppositious future. When this happens, the actual preparation for the future is missed or distorted. The ideal of using the present simply to get ready for the future contradicts itself. It omits, and even shuts out, the very conditions by which a person can be prepared for his future. We always live at the time we live and not at some other time, and only by extracting at each present time the full meaning of each present experience are we prepared for doing the same thing in the future. This is the only preparation which in the long run amounts to anything. (p. 49)

According to these perspectives, the best time for black families and their white school allies to reclaim their place in northeastern Albemarle County schools is now with home as a co-equal partner in the education of youth (see also Prom-Jackson et al., 1987; Scott-Jones, 1987). As the rest of this text will reveal, I learned of massive transgenerational efforts to come together in order to transform, or to find openings, or to resist—ultimately to balance educational struggle with hope.

Two fellow native North Carolinians, Dr. Vanessa Siddle Walker and Dr. David Cecelski, also contribute to this book's intellectual framework of struggle and hope. Both authors share my conviction of "speaking well" through the school segregation and desegregation stories we share with the world. Siddle Walker's (1996) book, *Their Highest Potential,* tells the segregation story of the Caswell Training School in Caswell County, North Carolina. Far west of the Albemarle area, the setting of Siddle Walker's book illuminates the positive aspects of black segregated schools. She argues that to focus solely upon those schools as sites of poor resources offers an incomplete picture at best. She offers evidence that the "environment of the segregated schools had affective traits, institutional policies, and community support that helped black children learn" despite the rejection and neglect those schools received from all-white school boards (Siddle Walker, 1996, p. 3). Siddle Walker's seminal work suggests that after *Brown* in North Carolina, blacks were more "schooled" or taught to reinscribe the social hierarchy, power differentials, and oppression of white standards than educated. This "schooling" was not indicative of the "education" that she found to occur quite often in the segregated black Caswell County Training School. Such an "education" included cultural learning about context, inequality, and social justice (see also Shujaa, 1994; Brunson & Vogt, 1996).

David Celeski's (1994) book, *Along Freedom Road,* discusses the plight of two historically black schools in northeastern Albemarle's Hyde County. Hyde County is located south of the Albemarle area featured in this book. Hyde's school desegregation experience appears to be quite different from Albemarle's. O. A. Peay and Davis Schools were the pride of the town. When federally mandated school desegregation came to Hyde in 1967, the white elite planned to consolidate by closing O. A. Peay and Davis Schools. This would have meant, as it meant already in many northeastern Albemarle towns, the massive loss of black teaching and administrative jobs, the dissolution of a center for the black community (Phillipson, 1999), and trust that teachers would care with genuineness, understanding, valuing, and acceptance (Siddle Walker, 1996) and know how to teach and work with black students and parents (Noblit & Dempsey, 1996). The black citizens decided to fight and, as a result, they were among the few in the South who won the battle to keep their schools open. With the activism of Golden Frinks and the Southern Christian Leadership Conference, beginning in 1968, the Black Hyde County citizens staged several protest rallies, including the March On Raleigh (the North Carolina state capital) in 1969.

After three years of black protest and national exposure in Hyde County, two plans were put to a referendum. The white leadership was initially confident that Plan 1, to close the two black schools and desegregate blacks into the existing Mattamuskeet School, would win. Plan 2 involved leaving the two black schools open and integrating whites as well as blacks. Although the town had more whites than blacks, Plan 1 failed. Cecelski (1994) explains that whites reportedly voted against Plan 1 for several key reasons, reasons that seem half astonishing and half self-serving.

1. Whites began to sympathize with blacks because whites previously had lost neighborhood schools in the county due to consolidation.
2. Whites began to understand what the black schools meant to the community.
3. Whites had grown to distrust the white leadership.
4. Whites had grown tired of the years of negative local, state, and national exposure.

5. Whites did not want the increased taxes that would have been levied to renovate the Mattamuskeet School in order to accommodate blacks.
6. Whites wanted shorter bus rides for their children.

Unfortunately, the struggle that kept the O. A. Peay and Davis Schools as instrumental centers for black families in Hyde County was not enough to keep most black school communities intact. Cecelski, a white historian, does not discuss the continued educational struggles and hopes of the blacks of Hyde County after desegregation. The triumph of 1970 was better for the black school community of Mattamuskeet than it was for their neighbors in the counties to the north. In the end, questions linger about whether school desegregation in any form in northeastern Albemarle is still a Pyrrhic victory, as now white middle-class rules and norms can influence black schooling from the inside out and the outside in.

It is not by design but by consequence that my school desegregation story seems to provide support and continuity to the accounts "spoken" by Siddle Walker (1996) and Cecelski (1994). As you read the rest of this story, remember that I am not the first to tell some of it from the native history/native ethnography perspective. I am, however, the first to tell some of it that may not be familiar. I have come to understand my book as a third part, a kind of missing link in a trilogy. When read all together, the books of this trilogy provide a comprehensive story of segregated and desegregated schooling that is arguably transferable to multiple regions in North Carolina and the rest of the South.

It is important to remember that there has been no other time in history that the unfamiliar parts of this story could have been shared by the families, only to be told to you by an author from my black experience. I was one of the early in-practice (not just legalized) desegregated kindergarteners in northeastern Albemarle and I was a kindergartener in 1980 (partly because kindergarten didn't reach all of northeastern Albemarle counties until the late 1970s and partly due to local white resistance). I am a first-generation college graduate, the first male university graduate, and the only doctorate (this side of the Atlantic, anyway—my African ancestral history is largely unknown) from my large, rural, working-poor class family (see Gutman & McLoyd, 2000). I don't note this information because I believe university degree attainment to be the "pinnacle" (Noblit & Dempsey, 1996) of life. Instead, I offer this to highlight the fact that, while several generations of men in my family aspired to obtain college degrees pre- and post-*Brown*, I was the first to have the opportunity to turn this aspiration into a reality. I feel privileged (as opposed to entitled), blessed, and grateful to tell more of the school desegregation story to you through this historical, native ethnography of northeastern Albemarle.

The book shares some potentially harmful, volatile, and sensitive historical material. Part of my obligation, then, involves protecting the anonymity of the individuals, entities, and families who provided such materials. Therefore, pseudonyms are substituted for the real names of key informants. You will note that the rest of the book mentions no particular names of counties, only references to the region. Additionally, the only names of learning institutions presented in the rest of the book are those schools that no longer exist. Any actual former school names that remain in the text are there to offer readers a sense of the motives underlying the names of segregated black schools. My motives for noting the real names of former black schools are done purposefully and strategically with you, the reader, in mind. Former school names range from simple geographic demarcation, as with the Trotman Road School, to a desire for honoring black activists, as with the Marian Anderson Schools, to the need to convey community partnerships with wealthy white activist-donors, as with the Rosenwald Schools. I leave those former school names to honor them and to remind us of the silencing of black voices that once collaborated to give schools names that were intended to espouse and evoke community respect, honor, pride, and responsibility.

Throughout the book the terms "nigger," "Negro," and "colored," are written as offered by participants and archives to illustrate the historical context of describing black or African American people. "Black" and "African American" are used interchangeably for three reasons. First, "black" is generally one current race/ethnic identification of varying shades of brown-skinned American citizens with more traceable West African heritage who share a history of slavery and oppression in the New World. Second, "African American" often illustrates and/or embraces W. E. B. DuBois' (1903) notion of "double consciousness," an ambivalent and dynamic sense of self as having familial ties with African but yet distinctly American roots. Third, all but two of the participants whose experiences are interpreted in the book identify themselves as black and/or African American. The two exceptions are white teachers who identified themselves, when asked, as white rather than European, Irish, German, Greek, or French American, etc.

Such "white" identifications suggest a tie to a whiteness that is particular to the United States, where "white" assumes not only European American, but also American as the culture of white people. The white is American and nonwhite is "ethnic" notion also signifies that at least some whites are to a large degree removed from the double consciousness described by DuBois.

Subsequent Chapters

Chapter 2 pertains to the importance of the history of education and race in which power, agency, and identity affected educational hopes, struggles, and outcomes of black families in respect to their white counterparts. The chapter offers a history of school segregation, desegregation, and racial power distances that influenced and continues to shape the education of blacks in the rural South, and most pertinent, in the rural Southern school community of northeastern Albemarle. Much of the history in Chapter 2 is told from the perspective of current and retired grade-school teachers, counselors, and administrators.

Chapter 3 offers an in-depth introduction to the three black families highlighted in the book: the Biggs, Winston, and Erskin families. The introductions describe the family home and neighborhood environment. They also relay family memories of segregated schooling in northeastern Albemarle. The segregated school narratives provide a lens for seeing more clearly family experiences of desegregated schooling and the transition endured by these families.

Chapters 4 and 5 tell the school desegregation story of northeastern Albemarle from the perspectives of these three black families. The Biggs, Winston, and Erskin family cases comprise stories of desegregated schooling as experienced by two generations from each family. The two generations are labeled "first" and "second" to distinguish whether individual narratives speak to first- or second-generation family experiences of desegregated schooling (as either a primary caregiver, student, or school personnel member/parent in northeastern Albemarle). Although distinctly detailed, their perspectives reflect archetypal cases that speak to the ardor of blacks in the region who strive to unveil hope in the struggle for *Brown*'s promise.

Chapter 4 relays the narratives of the Biggs family. The stories of the Winston and Erskin families are presented together in Chapter 5 to offer readers a compact space for multiple comparisons of single, rural, black parenthood in a desegregated southern school community. In Chapter 5, readers will learn the story of widower Woody Winston and his trials and triumphs as a black, male, single parent early in the transition of school desegregation. Following the Winston narratives are those of the Erskin family, including the story of Candice Erskin, a contemporary, rural, single, black mother. Sadly, Candice Erskin still struggles today with the same racialized school system that plagued Woody Winston three decades before.

Chapter 6 focuses primarily upon incidents that weave the family stories together. This chapter offers a synthesis of family pedagogy from the case studies and multiple perspectives for theorizing about their experiences and how they shaped the future. Chapter 6 also reframes the cases and stories into information that is crucial for conversations on education policy issues. The Biggs, Winston, and Erskin families' journey to speak critically and candidly about how school desegregation and education policy shapes the educational lives of the often ignored black families in rural northeastern Albemarle counties of North Carolina. When taken all together, the families offer an important critique of education policy in northeastern Albemarle. It is a frustrating and all-too-familiar and story line for me. It is a reminder of broken promises, of negativity lingering in experiences of desegregated schooling, and presented to me as emotional, thoughtful, and spiritual cries for help. Cries for help pool on the one hand and yet messages of hope float from the other. If one reads my retelling of each family's story not only to listen to or hear them, but also to feel them as I do, one may understand how these families are silenced and how the vocalization of such stories is integral if we are ever to fulfill the promise of *Brown*.

Chapter 7 concludes the book by addressing my role as a northeastern Albemarle native historical ethnographer. Here I also discuss how each family sees me as a vehicle of hope for telling their story to others. It is my attempt to convey my feelings that this work represents the story of one community and is educative in that way. It is an educative story that turns away from a traditional "key figures" approach with its focus upon the Marshall, King, and Parks families of history to focus on the Biggs, Winston, and Erkin families in order to learn from these little-known "key figures" who also shaped the movement and who endure its consequences. The concluding chapter is also intended to enlarge understanding of the conditions of school desegregation and its influences on the struggles and hopes of rural, black, Southern families—the families that produce our families, our colleagues, our employees, our employers, our allies, our students, our teachers, our neighbors, our friends, our acquaintances, our policymakers, our enemies, and ultimately, ourselves.

References

Anderson, J. (1988). *The Education of Blacks in the South, 1860–1935*. Chapel Hill: University of North Carolina Press.

Baker, D., & Stevenson, D. (1986). Mothers' strategies for children's school achievement: Managing the transition to high school. *Sociology of Education, 59*, 156–166.

Bempechat, J. (1991). *Fostering High Achievement in African American Children: Home, School, and Public Policy Influences*. New York: ERIC Clearinghouse of Urban Education, Office of Educational Research and Improvement, U.S. Department of Education and Institute for Urban and Minority Education, Teachers College, Columbia University.

Bempechat, J. & Drago-Severson, E. (1999). Cross-national differences in academic achievement: Beyond etic conceptions of children's understandings. *Review of Educational Research. 69*(3), 287–314.

Bempechat, J., & Ginsburg, H. (1989). *Underachievement and Educational Disadvantage: The Home and School Experiences of At-Risk Youth*. Urban Diversity Series No. 99. New York: ERIC Clearinghouse on Urban Education and Institute for Urban and Minority Education, Teachers College, Columbia University.

Bempechat, J., & Wells, A. (1989). *Promoting the Achievement of At-Risk Students*. Urban Diversity Series No. 99. New York: ERIC Clearinghouse on Urban Education and Institute for Urban and Minority Education, Teachers College, Columbia University.

Blum, L. (2002). *I'm Not a Racist But . . . The Moral Quandary of Race*. Ithaca, NY: Cornell University Press.

Brunson, D. A., & Vogt, J. F. (1996). Empowering our students and ourselves: A liberal democratic approach to the communication classroom. *Communication Education,* 43, 73–83.

Cecelski, D. (1994). *Along Freedom Road*. Chapel Hill: University of North Carolina Press.

Cecelski, D. (2001). *The Waterman's Song: Slavery and Freedom in Maritime North Carolina*. Chapel Hill: University of North Carolina Press.

Clark, R. (1983). *Family Life and School Achievement: Why Poor Black Children Succeed and Fail*. Chicago: University of Chicago Press.

Delpit, L. (1993). The Silenced Dialogue: Power and Pedagogy in Educating Other People's Children. In L. Weis and M. Fine (Eds.), *Beyond Silenced Voices: Class, Race, and Gender in United States Schools* (pp. 119–142). Albany: State University of New York Press.

Delpit, L. (1995). The Silenced Dialogue: Power and Pedagogy in Educating Other People's Children. *Other People's Children: Cultural Conflict in the Classroom*. New York: New Press.

Dewey, J. (1938). *Experience and Education*. New York: Simon & Schuster.

DuBois, W. E. B. (1903). *The Souls of Black Folk*. Chicago: A. C. McClurg.

Edwards, O. (1976). Components of academic success: A profile of achieving black adolescents. *Journal of Negro Education* 45, 408–422.

Epstein, J. (1989). Family Structures and Student Motivation: A Developmental Perspective. In C. Ames & R. Ames (Eds.), *Research on Motivation in Education* Volume 3: *Goals and cognitions* (pp. 259–295). New York: Academic Press.

Freire, P. (1996). *Pedagogy of Hope*. New York: Continuum.

Freire, P. (1998). *Pedagogy of the Oppressed: New Revised 20th–Anniversary Edition*. New York: Continuum.

Gutman, L. M., & McLoyd, V. C. (2000). Parents' management of their children's education within the home, at school, and in the community: An examination of African-American families living in poverty. *Urban Review,* 32(1), 1–24.

Hughes, K. (2003). *4th Sunday in the Dirty [South]*. Charleston, SC: Imprint Books.

ICW-NET, LLC (2004). Welcome to the Albemarle. http://www.albemarle-nc.com/. Elizabeth City, North Carolina, June 12, 2004.

Ladson-Billings, G. (1994). *The Dreamkeepers: Successful Teachers of African American Children*. San Francisco: Jossey-Bass.

Lemert, C. (1999). (Ed.). *Social Theory: The Multicultural and Classic Readings* (2nd ed.). Boulder, CO: Westview Press.

Luster, T., & McAdoo, H. (1991). *Factors Related to the Achievement and Adjustment of Black Children*. Paper presented at the biennial meeting of the Society for Research in Child Development, Seattle, WA, April 1991.

Mickelson, R. (2001). Subverting Swann: First-and second-generation segregation in Charlotte schools. *American Educational Research Journal,* 38(2), 215–252.

Noblit, G. W. (1999). *Particularities: Collected Essays on Ethnography and Education*. New York: Peter Lang.

Noblit, G.W., & Collins, T. W. (1981). Cui bono?: White students in a desegregating high school. *The Urban Review,* 13(4), 205–217.

Noblit, G.W., & Dempsey. (1996). *The Social Construction of Virtue: The Moral Life of Schools*. New York: State University of New York Press.

Noblit, G. W. Personal Communication, August 15, 2002.

O'Connor, C. (1997). Dispositions toward (collective) struggle and educational resilience in the inner city: A case analysis of six African-American high school students. *American Educational Research Journal*, 34(4), 593–629.

O'Connor, C. (1999). Race, class, and gender in America: Narratives of opportunity among low-income African American youths. *Sociology of Education*, 72(3), 137–157.

Phillipson, M. (1999). *Values-Spoken and Values-Lived: Race and the Cultural Consequences of a School Closing*. Cresskill, NJ: Hampton Press.

Prom-Jackson, S., Johnson, S., & Wallace, M. (1987). Home environment, talented minority youth, and school achievement. *Journal of Negro Education*, 56, 111–121.

Reis, S., & Diaz, E. (1999). Economically disadvantaged urban female students who achieve in schools. *The Urban Review*, 31(1), 31–54.

Rousseau, J.-J. (1762). *The Social Contract*. London: Penguin (1953 Edition). Translated and introduced by Maurice Cranston.

Scott, C. (1990). *Domination and the Arts of Resistance*. New Haven, CT: Yale University Press .

Scott-Jones, D. (1987). Mother-as-teacher in the families of high- and low-achieving low-income first graders. *Journal of Negro Education*, 56(1), 21–34.

Shujaa, M. J. (Ed.) (1994). *Too Much Schooling, Too Little Education: A Paradox of Black Life in White Societies*. Trenton, NJ: Africa World Press.

Siddle Walker, V. (1996). *Their Highest Potential: An African American School Community in the Segregated South*. Chapel Hill: University of North Carolina Press.

Steele, C. M. (1998). A Threat in the Air: How Stereotypes Shape Intellectual Identity and Performance. In J. L. Eberhardt & S. T. Fiske (Eds.), *Confronting Racism: The Problem and the Response* (pp. 202–233). Thousand Oaks, CA: Sage.

Stewart, J. B., & Allen-Smith, J. E. (Eds). (1995). *Blacks in Rural America*. New Brunswick, NJ: Transaction Publishers.

"Moving My Mountain"
Rural, Black, Southern Schooling

MOVING MY MOUNTAIN
by Kent Hughes

Battered . . . but not broken
Fragile . . . yet concrete
No time for daydreaming
Dreamed already in my sleep
Too many dreams . . . left uncontested
Too many nightmares when I crash
Don't want anyone moving my mountain
Just move . . . so I may pass
Face me and you face my shadow
Keep up . . . I'm in overdrive
Question my life and how I'm living
The answer . . . I will survive
Staying tired as I keep on moving
Always thirsty for that . . . cool calm water
Following the footprints placed before me
Keeping each step I take in order
Claiming my destiny . . . when I'm praying
Staying true to who I am
Don't want anyone moving my mountain
God has given me the strength to climb

Prior to the Civil War, blacks in rural North Carolina, as elsewhere, were schooled primarily by three groups of people: nonreligious-affiliated sympathetic whites, religious-affiliated whites, and other blacks. Sympathetic whites ranged from fellow settlers or servants to white slave masters and their family members or workers, to abolitionists. Religious organizers ranged from the Society of Friends (Quakers) and Catholics to members of the modern Baptist, and other traditional Christian denominations (Crow, Escott, & Hatley, 2002, p. 153). Other blacks, slave and free, who taught their peers were generally schooled by one or two of the aforementioned groups. Of course, most of the early teachers of enslaved blacks taught privately or surreptitiously, since Southern statutes made it illegal to provide slaves complete literacy and mathematical skills. Early in U.S. history, then, there is evidence of educational mountains blocking North Carolina's blacks from a comprehensive education. Before they could even begin to claim their rightful place in American democracy, blacks endured the mountain climbing alluded to in the poem that opens this chapter. This climb was required to overcome heavy racism, discrimination, and terrorism.

Blacks, slave and free, were also largely responsible for completing the grueling work of the construction of rural northeastern Albemarle's Great Dismal Swamp Canal. The canal served as a major antebellum conveyer for trade from southeastern Virginia cities, such as the huge port of Norfolk, to eastern North Carolina. Free blacks were the captains of flat boats, key vehicles of trade from Virginia to North Carolina. With blacks, slave and free, becoming pilots and captains of sea vessels, some have argued that northeastern Albemarle's seafaring blacks were among the freest in the South (Cecelski, 2001). Moreover, in the 1800s there were approximately 900 free blacks in the area that engulfs northeastern Albemarle, which was more for one area than any other place in the South (Cecelski, 2001). The canal served a major function for business and trade until the advent of the steam engine and railroad during the Industrial Revolution.

So, overall, blacks tended to be educated on a need-to-know basis by whites or by white sympathizers or religious folks prior to the Civil War. Free blacks of northeastern Albemarle, especially seafaring people, learned much about education and politics during their travels that was shared secretly with northeastern Albemarle's other seafaring and landlocked blacks with whom they came into contact. Cecelski offers accounts of seafaring blacks in the area at the time who were not only literate and adept in math, but who also spoke several foreign languages (Cecelski, 2001).

After Lincoln's Emancipation Proclamation, all blacks were legally eligible for education. Many North Carolina blacks were able to take advantage of the Freedmen's Bureau's work in the South during the Reconstruction period of 1865–1877. During this time, the American Missionary Association of New York was the first and largest benevolent society to establish formal educational institutions for Southern blacks (Crow, Escott, & Hatley, 2002, p. 153). Likewise, Baptists, Presbyterian, Episcopalians, Methodists, and Roman Catholics opened black schools in North Carolina (Crow, Escott, & Hatley, 2002, p. 153).

In 1875, twenty-one years prior to *Plessy v. Ferguson,* an amendment to North Carolina's state constitution was adopted to make separate but equal educational facilities for white and black children. Crow, Escott, and Hatley (2002) explain how well the equal portion of the planned worked: "Poverty and the grossly unequal distribution of school funds meant that black students had fewer teachers, shorter terms, and inferior facilities and supplies" (p. 154). Although the plan was separate and unequal at best, segregated rural public schooling would remain intact for ninety-four more years. North Carolina established secondary schools for rural whites in 1907 and four years later some two hundred of them had been established in 93 percent of the counties. It was not until 1910 that the state allocated funds for black public elementary schools. Three years later, the office of supervisor of rural elementary schools was established to advance black rural education. Money from out-of-state philanthropies such as the Rosenwald Fund financed black rural school construction, while the Jeanes Fund made it possible to hire supervisors of these schools (Crow, Escott, and Hatley, 2002, p. 155). Secondary school courses were generally unavailable to black rural students at this time. Even between 1923 and 1929 public secondary schools for black rural students did not exist. All such schools were concentrated in "the more progressive counties of the state, including Durham, Forsyth, Guilford, Mecklenburg, and Wake [the capital county]" (Crow, Escott, & Hatley, 2002, p. 156). By the 1930s and 1940s, northeastern Albemarle counties did not have public secondary schools available for blacks, thus parents either sent their children to a private institution, if there was one nearby, or, as most opted, to simply forfeit the additional schooling. The largest city in the northeastern Albemarle area was home to P.W. Moore School, one secondary institution available for blacks during that time. For blacks who could afford it, there was also a parochial high school in that city known as Saint Elizabeth parish, which was established by the Catholic Church and operated by nuns.

At that time, there were also several well-established rural first-through-eighth-grade schools for blacks in northeastern Albemarle counties, such as Ivy Neck School, Trotman Road School, Wickham School, and the Rosenwald Schools. Along with the churches, these black schools were significant parts of the fabric that tied the black community together as it embraced the triumphs and challenges of segregated schooling. These schools would also contain the generations whose offspring fed into the few rural all-black schools that offered grades nine through eleven, such as Sawyer's Creek School, and later grades nine through twelve, such as Marian Anderson School. All of these black schools were either removed, or at best, reduced in both status and identity after *Brown.*

Black Rural Schooling and Desegregation in North Carolina

The year 1953 brought the Catholic Church into North Carolina's desegregated schools. Bishop Vincent S. Waters began the process of desegregating all parishes "in the Raleigh Diocese (which then encompassed all of North Carolina)" (Crow, Escott, & Hatley, 2002, p. 164). The following year, North Carolina began to face the challenge of desegregating all of its public schools in accordance to the Supreme Court ruling in *Brown v. Board of Education* (1954). *Brown* brought to the surface the harm that separate and unequal education brought upon black students:

> To separate them from others of similar qualifications solely because of their race generates a feeling of inferiority as to their status in the community that may affect their hearts and minds in a way unlikely ever to be undone. (Hesburgh et al., 1970, p. 9)

Writing for a unanimous court's decision, Chief Justice Earl Warren declared that in the field of public education "the doctrine of 'separate but equal' has no place. Separate educational facilities are inherently unequal" (quoted in Crow, Escott, & Hatley, 2002, p. 164). One year later in *Brown II,* the Court ordered states including North Carolina to proceed "with all deliberate speed" to integrate their public schools. It was here that blacks found yet another deceiving mountain. This time, with federal law on their side, it looked like the climb to a crest of equitability would neither be as cold or steep, and clearly much of it was already paved. Still, as DuBois proclaimed soon after the *Brown* decision, "long steps along freedom road lie ahead" (Cecelski, 1994, p. 174).

Members of North Carolina's power structure had no intention of "walking with purpose" into desegregated schooling (Patricia A. Hoert, personal communication, June 4, 2004). In August of the same year, Governor William Umstead examined potential problems associated with *Brown* as posited by his Special Advisory Committee of Education, which was created for the sole purpose of stalling desegregated schooling. The committee included chair Thomas J. Pearsall, a prominent farmer and businessman, and three hand-picked "black members: Dr. Ferdinand Douglas Bluford, President of A&T College; Dr. J.W. Seabrook, President of Fayetteville State Teachers College; and Mrs. Hazel Parker of Tarboro, home agent for Blacks in Edgecombe County" (Crow, Escott, & Hatley, 2002, p. 167). Umstead's committee recommended "that North Carolina [should] try to find means of meeting the requirements of the Supreme Court's decision within our present school system before consideration is given to abandoning or materially altering it" (Crow, Escott, & Hatley, p. 167). To this end, the state legislature moved to decentralize authority and to take it away from the State Department of Public Instruction. This action also would make it harder to litigate desegregation. Each school system would have to be addressed individually and not just as one case for the state as a whole.

In May 1955, at the urging of Governor Luther H. Hodges, the General Assembly passed legislation that "removed references to race from the state's school laws and granted to the respective county and city school boards of education responsibility for school administration, pupil assignment, enrollment, and transportation" (Crow, Escott, & Hatley, 2002, p. 168). Governor Hodges, who took the seat upon Umstead's untimely death, often spoke to discontented crowds of blacks after this political move. In fact, "booing students repeatedly interrupted the governor during a speech at A&T College in Greensboro [a historically black college] on November 4, 1955" (Crow, Escott, & Hatley, p. 169). Blacks such as Durham banker and attorney John H. Wheeler understood the strategy as a diversion tactic and spoke when the General Assembly held a hearing in February 1955: "We wish to point out that the proposed legislation affecting the public schools seeks by various means to slow down or retard the process of integration" (Crow, Escott, & Hatley, pp. 168–169).

The diversion plan, which came to be known as the Pearsall Plan, would be ratified. The plan had two major facets: (a) transferring from the State Board of Education to county and city boards complete authority over enrollment and assignment of children in public schools, and buses, and (b) stipulating that parents who did not wish to send their children to a school with children of another race did not have to do so. White parents could withdraw their children from the public schools and enroll them in private institutions with the aid of state grants to pay tuition (Crow, Escott, & Hatley, 2002, p. 170).

It is no coincidence that Resolution No. 69, Legislation Establishing Commission to study the public school education of exceptionally talented children was passed in 1959, when the Pearsall Plan was raising some concerns from the federal government and after the Russians launched Sputnik and defeated America in the race to outer space in 1957. Governor Hodges called the first meeting of the Commission to Study the Public School Education of Exceptionally Talented Children on Monday, October 5, 1959, at 10:00 a.m. There was statewide support for such a tailor-made program to locate "gifted" (white) children (NCDPI Superintendent's Correspondence Files, 1959). On November 19, Assistant DPI Superintendent J. E. Miller wrote to Dr. C. D. Killian, chair of this Talented Children Commission and affiliate of the Department of Education at Western Carolina College, to inform him that DPI Superintendent Carroll thought the proposed pilot studies for gifted programming was a "good idea" (NCDPI Superintendent's Correspondence Files, 1959). There is also evidence that the still-segregated black schools had

separate gifted programs, suggesting that from the beginning the state separated black "giftedness" from white "giftedness" (NCDPI Superintendent's
Correspondence Files, 1959). Unfortunately, this 1959 distinction spilled over
to integrated schools in North Carolina, and would forever put a question
mark on the nature of giftedness and the nurture thereof. UNC-Chapel Hill
professors Dr. William Darity, Domini Castellino, and Dr. Carolyn Tyson
(2001) and UNC-Charlotte professor, Dr. Rosalyn Mickelson (2000), suggest that even when the results of their previous assessments are at the same
high levels as white children, black children are excluded significantly from
K–12 "gifted" programs, advanced placement, and college tracks. So, while
Governor Hodges succeeded in controlling the discourse of giftedness to
some extent, maintaining the constitutionality of the Pearsall Plan ultimately
was less fruitful.

The earliest account of the Pearsall Plan being declared unconstitutional
suggests it was deemed so in 1966 (Etheridge, 1993, p. 26). Another source
claims "it was not until 1969, in the case of *Godwin v. Johnston County Board
of Education,* that a federal court ruled the plan unconstitutional" (Crow,
Escott, & Hatley, 2002, p. 170). Most of the state's urban school districts
were desegregated by 1965, yet many small rural districts, such as those in the
northeastern Albemarle counties, were not. It is likely that the end of the Pear-
son Plan fell closer to the year 1965, because it was in that year that the state
enacted the Freedom of Choice Plan, whereby local boards "opened doors to
previously all-white schools to black children and black schools to white children" (Crow, Escott, & Hatley, 2002, p. 170). Following the school choice
tenets of the Pearsall Plan, if reassignment was requested by a parent, the
school board held the power to deny each request. Thus, as Crow, Escott, and
Hatley (2002) suggest, the burden of implementing school desegregation fell
to blacks. Blacks were handed an awful burden to face such hatred, fear, and
intimidation in school: "Freedom of choice was neither free, nor much of a
choice for blacks in rural North Carolina schools" (George Noblit and Sherick
Hughes, personal communication, March 15, 2002). This assertion is supported by Crow, Escott, and Hatley's (2002) research: "[D]uring the three
years in which the freedom-of-choice was operative, 85 percent of the state's
black schoolchildren continued to attend all-black schools, and not a single
white child elected to attend such a facility" (p. 172).

In January 1965, the North Carolina state attorney general's office replied
to Superintendent Charles Carroll's inquiry regarding compliance with Title
VI of the Civil Rights Act of 1964 (nondiscrimination in Federally Assistance
Education Programs). Issued by the U.S. Department of Health, Education,
and Welfare (HEW), Title IV states:

> All plans based on freedom of choice mean that there must be complete, volun-
> tary freedom of choice with adequate notice of same. No forms of threats or any

forms of intimidation, economic or otherwise, can be used to influence any decision of parents or guardians. (Bruton & Moody, 1965, p. 9)

Of course, the North Carolina plan did not adhere to those requirements. No one was even investigated whenever black northeastern Albemarle students and their "parents or guardians" were "intimidated or threatened" while attempting to exercise their "freedom of choice." Searching for more time and justification to circumvent *Brown* and Title IV, the state superintendent of schools wrote a letter to the State Attorney General's office requesting legal expertise and savvy advice. North Carolina State Attorney General Bruton, and Deputy Attorney General Moody replied to the letter from State Superintendent Charles Carroll in 1965:

> The members of the office of the Attorney General of North Carolina did not promote or urge the passage of the Civil Rights Act of 1964 but the Congress did pass the Act. No county or city board of education in this state is required in mandatory fashion to accept any Federal funds to promote school programs but if the funds are accepted then the conditions must be complied with and administered in good faith and this means total and complete desegregation of all schools in the county or city school system. If the funds are not accepted then such manner of operation affords no protection because the Attorney General of the United States under Title IV of the Civil Rights Act of 1964 can institute legal proceedings to force the desegregation of any school or school system, and this is true whether the school unit receives Federal funds or not. In short, the whole Act contemplates total and complete desegregation of public schools whether Federal funds are received or not.
>
> Neither the State Board of Education nor the county and city boards of education asked for this situation, but they must live with it and they will have to work with such clay as it is handed to them. *No form of token compliance, clever schemes, chicanery or subtle or sophisticated plans of avoidance—no matter how crafty or cunning—will in the end prevail. No devices or plans whether ingenious or ingenuous will constitute any legal defense to the mandates of this Federal statute* .[emphasis added] (Bruton & Moody, 1965, p. 10)

Three years later, in 1968, freedom of choice was ruled unconstitutional and an ineffective means toward ending school segregation by a federal court in *Boomer v. Beaufort County Board of Education*. During the year 1965, there was also a resurgence of groups such as the Ku Klux Klan and affiliates in North Carolina. The National White People's Party admonished that school desegregation would ruin the white way of life. Members of the liberal media of the state's capital poked fun at the groups like the Klan, but their power and means of intimidation and ability to live above the law in rural North Carolina was anything but a laughable threat to rural blacks. One picture from *The News and Observer* illustrates two grade-school-age white male students whispering "His Dunce Cap Slipped," as a large white man in Klan robe and head garb approaches them (September 9, 1965, p. 4). One flier from the National

White People's Party in Asheville, North Carolina, plays on the fears of liberal and conservative whites:

> Awake! Busing will turn your neighborhood schools into a savage jungle. Busing brutalizes productive civilized students with a wave of crime, extortion, rape, cannibalism. Forced busing has led to an increase in interracial sex. Forced busing will result in a race of mulattoes. (Department of Cultural Resources Division of Archives and History, Human Relations Council Files, Klan, n.d.)

It was not until the 1970s that full desegregation of public schools in North Carolina was achieved, when there was no place left to run or hide constitutionally. There is some evidence, however, that fear tactics like those of the Klan and the White People's Party worked. An article by Kitty Terjen (1971), titled *White Flight: The Segregation Academy Movement,* explains that North Carolina witnessed "a steadily increasing private school enrollment, from 18,721 students in 1964 to 36, 470 student in 1970–71, an increase of approximately 18,000." Terjen also notes in 1971 that "eighty-one private schools have been created in the state since 1964, 31 in the last year" (p. 71). Yet figures compiled at the time by the state's education department boasts that its "white flight" had not exceeded 5 percent (Boyd & Dennis, 1972).

Apparently, whites' fears of desegregation were also fueled by the idea that schools would loosen standards and become "dumbed down," so to speak— sentiments that persisted for decades. Perhaps white fears about the quality of education depreciating were unfounded, as an article in *The News and Observer* from the very next year suggests. In 1972, Dr. Charles E. King, a North Carolina Central University sociologist, and Dr. Robert R. Mayer, an associate professor of city and regional planning at the University of North Carolina at Chapel Hill, explained that in contrast to dire predictions, desegregation seems to be accompanied by an increase in the quality of education. Their 150-page report of *Southern City,* (a pseudonym used to keep the name of the actual city anonymous), described a remarkably smooth transition into a completely desegregated school system (Boyd & Dennis, 1972).

There were also stories of rural desegregation triumphs, like that of the schools in Hyde County, North Carolina, as noted previously with reference to Cecelski's (1996) *Along Freedom Road.* Another triumphant but lesser-known story is that of the southern section of Nash County. Southern Nash desegregated schools are in an area known by some as "Klan Country," with a white–black ratio of 60:40. During this time, students came from poor rural counties with racial problems, but a wealth of school leadership helped the situation. The principal appointed two male teachers, one white and one black, to serve as "co-sponsors of the Student Cooperative Association, the student council" (Gaston, 1971, p. 20). These two men devised a whole new student council to scrap the old system and achieve total integration.

Through their scrapping of majority rule for the principle of equality, crises over issues such as the election of homecoming courts, the choice of cheerleaders, and the election of student delegates to a state conference were resolved smoothly. Louis Low, the white faculty cosponsor, would later say, "We did not achieve perfect racial harmony. . . . But on the other hand, we did attain an acceptance of integration and a willingness to work together for common interests" (Gaston, 1971, p. 20). Such efforts were commended by the federal government at the time. In September 1969, in its report on Federal Enforcement of School Desegregation, the U.S. Civil Rights Commission pointed out that this was:

> no time for giving aid and comfort, even unintentionally, to the laggards while penalizing those who have made commendable efforts to follow the law, even while disagreeing with it. If anything, this is the time to say that time is running out on us as a Nation. In a word, what we need most at this juncture of our history is a great positive statement regarding this central and crucial national problem where once and for all our actions clearly would match the promises of our Constitution and Bill of Rights (Hesburgh et al., 1970).

In the late 1960s, North Carolina and other Southern states formed Councils on Human Relations with ideas for helping to improve race relations in the state. Topics discussed included civil rights, desegregation, education, and employment opportunities in North Carolina. Some of the materials, however, actually reinforced racial problems. Although the intent may have been positive, documents such as "Human Relations Training: Reading Book" stopped short of being transformative. The limitation of these training materials and meetings led teachers such as Gean Whitehall, a white former English teacher, to interpret that after desegregation "we couldn't correct black English in the classroom" (North Carolina Council on Human Relations Records Inventory #4880, 1999).

High-Stakes Testing and Accountability in Rural Black North Carolina

Boger and Bower (2001) offer a comprehensive view of initial desegregation case results and their residuals on Black rural educational opportunities in North Carolina. The late 1970s, 1980s, and 1990s would also bring the wave of standardized testing and accountability movements. In 1977, only seven years after many rural blacks were allowed to receive the same education as whites, the state introduced a statewide testing program, consisting of annual testing (Etheridge, 1993, p. 27). Each student in grades one, two, three, six, and nine were given an annual comprehensive, standardized test selected by the State Board of Education with "full summative information being reported regarding the results of these tests" (Etheridge, 1993, p. 18). These tests were especially attractive to whites wishing to distinguish their youth as "gifted" as envisioned nearly two decades before by former Governor Hodges.

Soon after the propaganda of the 1983 report *A Nation at Risk,* North Carolina redoubled its efforts to make teachers and students accountable with standardized, end-of-course tests. These tests would be revisited to include multiple-choice and open-ended standardized test questions that would be issued to grades three through eight by 1993 (Etheridge, 1993, p. 28). The year 1985 would bring the General Assembly enactment of North Carolina's Basic Education Program and the End-of-Course Testing Program (Etheridge, 1993, p. 27). A statewide promotion program was implemented in 1986, which was soon followed by the School Improvement and Accountability Act (SIAA) of 1989, making local schools more accountable for student achievement. The SIAA was revised in 1992 to make teachers specifically more accountable for school improvement planning and performance. That same year, ninth-graders entering high school would face tougher graduation requirements (Etheridge, 1993, p. 28).

In 1996, high stakes would be attached to those tests in North Carolina's Accountability, Basics, and Local Control (ABC) legislation, which included (a) gateway test grades for subjects, which means a student can be held back if the one-shot test is failed, even with an above-average GPA; (b) principals having to vouch for a child to be promoted to the next grade if the test is failed; and (c) $800 to $1,500 extra to teachers at the end of the year at "schools of distinction" or "exemplary schools" (ABCs of Public Education Program Online, 2002). All of these accountability and high-stakes testing moves can be seen as part of the "excellence" backlash to school desegregation by whites who felt that school curricula had become, as retired Albemarle teacher Gean Whitehall said, "watered down."

Thus, as rural blacks entered rural white schools, they were still largely unwanted, misunderstood, silenced, and miseducated. Still today, they have been forced to pass high-stakes standardized tests issued according to white school standards. These tests have reigned primarily as diagnostic. Whites who primarily make the rules for North Carolina schools set schools to devalue assessment beyond multiple-choice testing. Under their rules, assessments are not descriptive in ways that lead to increased school resources for underserved children who are disproportionately black. The state has subsequently placed much public emphasis on decreasing the test score gap between black students and their white counterparts, irrespective of socioeconomic status, through a dominant discourse that focuses only on the problems of black people. Again, the educational burden of proof has been placed on the shoulders of rural black students and their families to act chivalrously in the position of a voiceless minority in such schools as those in rural northeastern Albemarle.

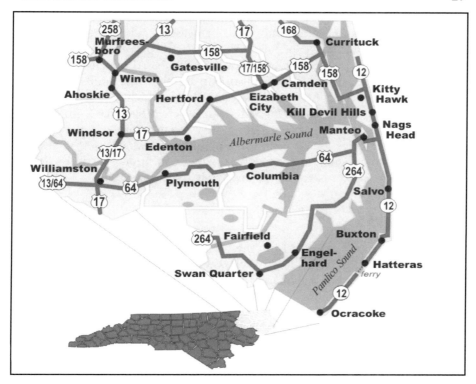

MAP 1: (http://www.carolinanow.com/inncarolina/norcoast.htm)

Oral History of Rural, Black Schooling in Northeastern Albemarle, North Carolina

The history of black education in northeastern Albemarle is largely oral. Indeed, an ancillary purpose of this book and the larger study of which it is a part is to document this history. I conducted interviews with five retired teachers (four black, one white), two present-day teachers, (one black, one white), and two retired black administrators with knowledge of this history. These narratives permit an understanding of both the events and the interpretations of these events as local lived experiences.

The narratives of Lois and Walker Whitmore are highlighted in each era, as one or both of them were a major part of northeastern Albemarle schools from the late 1940s through the 1990s. Other informative accounts from their colleagues span the 1940s through desegregation and the 1970s to the present. These former school personnel add much depth for understanding post-Reconstruction, segregated-to-desegregated schooling. And their narratives give a closer look at the history of northeastern Albemarle's black residents. Thus, their narratives span from World War II to *Brown* to today. These narratives include the great migration of blacks to Northern cities for industrial work, increased black military enlistment, and the Civil Rights Movement and Affirmative Action of the 1950s and 1960s, which ultimately pushed racial equality to the forefront of American issues. Narratives from the two white teachers illuminate another side of these racialized life experiences. The white teachers' stories serve to confirm and dispute illustrations of their black counterparts, thereby serving as complex, living educational histories. Again, pseudonyms are used to protect the anonymity of all narrators.

1940s–1950s

As the United States emerged from the bleak conditions of the Great Depression, it braced itself for World War II. It was during the war that a number of black male northeastern Albemarle residents were offered another venue for education, the U.S. military. Black northeastern Albemarle men, including my uncle, Winston Gregory, were schooled in the art of combat and went on to serve in both World War II and the Korean War. While these young men were on military tours of duty in Europe and Asia, things were evolving in black education back at home in northeastern Albemarle. The narratives of three black female former teachers, one black female cafeteria manager, and one black male administrator offer insight into northeastern Albemarle's segregated schooling during this period.

Eva Maryland Watson, a 71-year-old black former elementary school teacher in northeastern Albemarle, offered a list of crucial black schools that existed during segregation and prior to consolidation. (Note that eleven years was considered complete, and allowed high school graduation at the time Watson went through northeastern Albemarle's segregated schools.)

> There were five black schools in three parts of northeastern Albemarle county A: Rosenwald School, grades 1 to 11; Sawyer's Creek School, grades 1 to 11 near the middle of northeastern Albemarle; Trotman Road, grades 1 to 8; Wickham School, grades 1 to 11; and Ivy Neck School, some blacks went to school there, it is now a church near your momma's house. Black segregated schools were responsible for educating all kids. In the early 1950s, 1951 or 1952, the black schools were consolidated to three: Rosenwald, Sawyer's Creek, and Wickham School.
>
> Kids walked to school. We mostly went to school by horse and cart or walking. The first school bus for blacks came in the late 1940s. There was only one bus for the entire county.
>
> We got second-hand books, never new books. Up to the 1960s blacks had used books. One teacher taught two and three grades. My school started out as

a three-room school. Three were grades 1 to 11 and only three teachers. There were sometimes not enough teachers for each school.

(Watson claims to be a relative of Moses Grandy, formerly of northeastern Albemarle, who was noted as a remarkable tradesman and educated former slave in David Cecelski's [2001] book *The Waterman's Song: Slavery and Freedom in Maritime North Carolina*). She returned to school after a remarkable nineteen years away from the classroom to complete her teacher training at the urging of the late black principal Walker Whitmore. Whitmore had suggested, after Eva's five years of work as a secretary and accountant at his school, that she go back to school in order to apply then for an assistant teacher position. Heeding Whitmore's advice, she returned to the local State Normal College for Blacks, received a bachelor's degree in education, and taught at a public elementary school in northeastern Albemarle until her retirement.

One former student of Marian Anderson and cafeteria manager, Margie Hines, recalled the following fond and troubling memories about the 1940s and 1950s and black school culture in northeastern Albemarle:

> I think then parents had more time to spend with their children. Now a lot of blacks are going with single parents. Even if you're good in school they'll pick the ones with two parents. During segregated schools, single-parent status didn't matter. And if you did or grandparents raised them and the parents would go off to work, no one would know anything about it. [Now] it seems like they try to dog the single mother. . . . We'd have lunch on a big potbelly stove. You would bring your lunch or buy a ten-cent hot dog if you could.
>
> [When] I was going to school, it seemed like we [black families and schools] got along better. We always thought they [white schools and students] had better books, buses—we were walking and they were riding. I think if a lot of them knew what was going on it would have changed. They had better school buses; they would give us the old school buses. They only had one school bus for blacks; sometimes it was overcrowded and we'd rather walk. We would go home and pray and think that things would get better. Sometimes they would throw things at us and call us niggers. It really didn't matter to me whether I went to school with them or not. In 1946, when I started, they wanted equal rights. And they went on and fought for this until the 1950s and '60s, which were the worst times. . . . The main thing they wanted was better schools for us. We had two or three classes of kids in one classroom, whereas they didn't have one teacher teaching three classes.

Lois Whitmore, wife of Walker, taught at Marian Anderson High School until her retirement after more than fifty years (1945–1995) as a northeastern Albemarle teacher. During her time as a seventh-grade teacher, she was selected to represent the county in the 1972 competition for National Teacher of the Year after twenty-five years of service (*The Daily Advance*, October 7,

1971, p. 3). For this book, she recounted the struggles of black schools early in her career.

> They still tried to separate the blacks and the whites, and they would give the old books of the white students to the black children instead of giving them new ones . . . even when the buses were passed and Marian Anderson and northeastern Albemarle County High School, they had to let out ten minutes difference in time because they would cut up [act out] on the buses, the white kids, look out the window and call the black kids "nigger'"["Nigger, nigger, black as tar, won't get to heaven in a motor car"]. So the superintendent got together up here and said, one of these schools, said, "We'll have to let out about fifteen minutes earlier or ten minutes so we won't have that confusion." They did.

The late Walker Whitmore was a former principal of Marian Anderson High School. Whitmore was largely responsible for changing the name of the school from New Sawyer's Creek School. A fervent scholar and writer, Whitmore actually wrote the six-stanza "Alma Mater" for the new Marian Anderson High School in the early 1950s. He was interviewed with his wife only months before his death at ninety, and relayed the following sentiments about black schooling in northeastern Albemarle in the 1940s through 1950s:

> There were many times when black children had books that the white children had finished with and many of the sheets were torn out of the books, and they didn't look like anything at all. But we had to almost figure out what they said in the book, and of course, after that we were pretty well, we got along pretty well. But it wasn't to the extent that the white children were doing because of the fact that even then the whites were not close to us at all as black people. So we got along pretty well though as individuals like this.

The fond memories of segregated black schooling in northeastern Albemarle recalled by Harriet Talis seem to sum up the general sentiment of this time in black educational history. Talis was a teacher, counselor, and friend of the Whitmores. In fact, she is referred to in one narrative shared by Lois Whitmore. Talis also recalled positive elements about black segregated school life in northeastern Albemarle:

> The black segregated school was the center of training; center of culture. Great respect for teachers . . . principals looked up to teachers in a special way. There was great support. Back then there were May Day Programs, parents were very supportive. Basketball was a big thing for Marian Anderson, it would be a family affair. Fund-raising programs were brought in. . . . We worked real hard for little prayer. We had fundraisers for competition. Parents were working out ways to support us; it was a community affair. Teachers drove the players to the games and picked them up from the games [at] 1:00 and 2:00 in the morning. It's hard on veteran teachers who can't get parent participation now. Before, it was a community affair.

Ross Winston was another key narrator. Winston is a retired school official, and the first and only black elected to his position after schools desegregated in his northeastern Albemarle County. He first discussed the special things the black Rosenwald schools did for northeastern Albemarle. The segregated black schools of northeastern Albemarle were similar in some ways to those of Caswell County and Hyde County, as described in the works of Siddle Walker (1996) and Cecelski (1996) and here, in Ross Winston's account:

> Well, it was sort of like a meeting place for blacks. I guess it was something that the blacks controlled, you know what I mean, to a certain extent—their own PTA. It was just black-controlled, something that we controlled. You know what I mean? But when they integrated we lost that. And the black schools, we had all our black principals. And I remember Mr. Whitmore would give, we used to call it Chapel Day on Friday. And he would call the whole school together on Friday, and each class would do a play on Friday, and you could talk black on black in school together. And you could tell a white [inaudible] for a black kid to get an education, you know, what blacks had to look out for. You could get that black one-on-one. Now you can't.

The 1960s

The 1960s brought major changes to education to American schools. The state and northeastern Albemarle schools were no exception. Similar to the rest of rural North Carolina, northeastern Albemarle first deliberately ignored *Brown* and efforts to desegregate students with "all deliberate speed." In this effort, among the first school personnel to desegregate were the librarians. The idea was to first desegregate those with less responsibility for teaching children. For example, only two black female teachers went to the white high school in one northeastern Albemarle county. All of the black teachers and the one black administrator recalled that "attractive" black teachers with more "typical" white features were asked to desegregate that school.

> EVA WATSON: With Freedom of Choice, they moved some black teachers [to white schools]. They called [black] teachers out—everything with a light complexion. Mrs. Lois Whitmore [a light-skinned woman], refused to go [her husband was the principal of Marian Anderson]. There was also Ms. Betty Dorsey, who went to the high school, and Ms. Alice Reese went to kindergarten [she was the first black to teach kindergarten when it began; kindergarten wasn't in all North Carolina schools until 1979]. All light-skinned people were recruited to go to teach in white schools.

> LOIS WHITMORE: What they [white administrators during Freedom of Choice] tried to do was get the best [looking] black teachers. I refused to go and he said, "You go or quit." So I said, "I quit." My husband was the principal of Marian Anderson then. I was not fired. They didn't know the black man, then.

Three white males and one white female with no "attraction" criteria were the first to desegregate the former Marian Anderson School for Blacks. The first wave of desegregation stories in northeastern Albemarle involving white staff during the Freedom of Choice period were corroborated by the narratives from Ross Winston:

> But something else that I did experience in school in [northeastern Albemarle] North Carolina, and let me run this by you. Back in I think it had to be '66 or '67, we got some of our first white staff in school. Though our school wasn't fully integrated, but we got a white secretary, we had a white teacher, a couple of white teachers, and that was the beginning. And then we had some students, they had what they called "Freedom of Choice." And you could choose to go to any school you wanted to. And we had some students that left our [rural] school and went over to a northeastern Albemarle City High School, and my uncle was one of them, Lucas.

It was during the 1966–1967 school term that the two black teachers and four white teachers would cross the color line separating educators in that county. Some 707 students in the county were in desegregated schools, nearly all reflective of blacks going to white schools.

Because of the small size of the town and its relative seclusion, white flight to academies in neighboring cities was not immediate. There was simply no need for it, yet, and neither was there a need to utilize funds available to northeastern Albemarle whites by the Pearsall Plan. In the late 1960s, however, after the Pearsall Plan was deemed unconstitutional, northeastern Albemarle adopted the Freedom of Choice Plan. Although short-lived, Freedom of Choice would have a direct impact on the lives of northeastern Albemarle's black and white residents from 1967 through today.

The Black educators' narratives reflect a loss of intergenerational closure, representation, power, authentic voice, and to some extent, pride in their schools.

> HARRIET TALIS: It was 1968. I remember very few black students that year. There was Corey Penton, I remember him because he was one of my students. There was Wilford Leir. In 1968–69 I left because schools were reorganized and I went back to Marian Anderson. Then Mr. Whitmore left. They changed the name of the school. No more black high school students [high-school-age students in an all-black setting], just like that. It was done very quickly. It caught the community off guard and we didn't have much time to respond. There was some pressure, but they would make the effort and make it seem to do something, without much change actually occurring.

As mentioned, there are narratives from white former teacher Gean Whitehall. And there are also stories from white teacher Barbara Needham. Needham was a northeastern Albemarle student during the initial transition to school desegregation. She became a teacher trained at the local historically black state normal college. Needham now teaches at the former Marian Anderson High School for Blacks. Whitehall and Needham offer both different and similar views of school desegregation's influence on blacks and whites in the area. Whitehall seemed to misinterpret, perhaps from the 1970s human relations training, that black families or the state wanted relaxed "standards" for black students. Needham expressed words suggesting that blacks have more power than they may actually have. Both Whitehall and Needham agreed that blacks lost autonomy with school desegregation.

> GEAN WHITEHALL: I started out in [County D]. . . . During Freedom of Choice, the ones that wanted to, came. I didn't have any problems. I truly didn't see a difference in the kids. Everybody watched everyone else to see what was going to happen. Not many children came. There was more rumbling and mouthing than anything else. . . . From '59 on up we were told not to correct black students' English. We were told not to stress manners—shirt tails, prison style of wearing pants. We were told we had too strict of a dress code. We had to relax the dress code. Morals, values. There were no blacks as administrators. Mr. Roker I thought was good as an assistant principal, but I don't know what happened there.

> BARBARA NEEDHAM: Freedom of choice—I know the major court case was in 1954, but I can tell you that northeastern Albemarle was not affected until 1965. The first black students (two or three) came when I was a freshman. The 1954 ruling didn't extend to northeastern Albemarle until then. Those few students were paid to go. We as students felt sorry for them. We took them under our wing. Some of us, not all. My freshman, sophomore, and junior years were Freedom of Choice.

Former principal Walker Whitmore had left a rural northeastern Albemarle school in 1969 to teach at the local state Normal College for Blacks. At that time, he felt that it was better at the Normal College, because there was less hardship and more the school offered equitable compensation than rural grade-school administration.

> Do you know that there were people who did not give to the black man the same amount of money that they gave to the white man? I don't know where that money went. I have no idea. But this is what I think. When I left in '69, yeah, they had passed the segregation law there at that time. It was integrated because of the fact that we had, even before then we had, some white teachers. Miss uh, I can't think of her name. . . .

While Whitmore was trying to recall the white teacher's name, Lois Whitmore offered a more complete story about the white teacher her husband was trying to remember. The story seemed indicative of the era of the 1960s in northeastern Albemarle, in which librarians, secretaries, and "particular" teachers were the inaugural staff members to desegregate public schools. As the first few white teachers desegregated the all-black Marian Anderson High

School, they soon learned that black students could be even more kind and responsible than white students under the trying 1960s conditions. Lois Whitmore's story of an early black student–white teacher relationship is paramount in the portrayal of this era. She revealed the initial shock and later transformation experienced by a white teacher challenged by her own racial ideology, so much so that she wanted to claim a link to the support of black educators even at her death.

> I'm trying to think of her name, too, but [years before her death] she made me and Harriet promise her that when she died we would come to her funeral. She was white. She ran across the breezeway one day and fell. Two black girls went out there and picked her up. She was saying, "I had never seen anything like that in my life." So I went and got her some water, but she was going through a whole lot of things because her husband was sick. I think Harriet brought her some aspirins or something. She came, she was very [taken aback], she said, "I never knew this would happen. They picked me up!" And they brought her in on their own and put her in the chair. What was that woman's name? So, she made us promise her that when she died we would come to her funeral. . . . We did.

The 1970s

With the new decade came federally mandated full desegregation for northeastern Albemarle County schools. Community members of 1960s witnessed the consolidation of the black schools into one black school, Marian Anderson High. With Principal Whitmore at the helm, the school had reached prominence and had been a source of pride for the black community. The "Trojans" of Marian Anderson High, teachers, staff, and administrators alike, were educating black students who would be prepared for the workforce. Many became teachers and a several became clergy for the community. Two others, a man and a woman, went on to obtain doctoral degrees at the University of Cincinnati and Howard University. In fact, data from the superintendents correspondence papers in the North Carolina State Historical Records indicate that for several years prior to desegregation, Marian Anderson sent more blacks (eight) to college than the white northeastern Albemarle County high schools sent whites (five).

Mr. George Attix wrote a letter to Superintendent Charles F. Carroll of Elizabeth City, on February 2, 1960. Attix was manager of the Chamber of Commerce of a northeastern Albemarle City. In an effort to gather support for the creation of a community college for the Albemarle area to be housed in the city, a list of the number of white and Negro graduates from Albemarle area high schools was compiled, and the number of those graduates who proceeded to enroll in senior and junior colleges in trade, business, and nursing schools as well as military service was gathered. At the time, information was also obtained from high-school principals in several administrative units. Existing archival information from their study points toward the prowess of black segregated schools in the area. Even with inequitable school resources, one segregated school in the northeastern Albemarle area sent more blacks to college than whites during the years 1956 through 1959. (Box: DPI, Admin., Subject Files (State Superintendent) A-L January 1960–April 1960 Folder: A, Department of Cultural Resources Division of Archives and History).

It was both a tragedy and a blessing for the black community to witness the desegregation of successful black schools such as Marian Anderson. Desegregation of such community beacons came with utter disregard for pre-existing traditions. It was normal at the time for schools to undergo a complete name and mascot change to something like the "Northeastern Albemarle Middle School Bears." As the desegregated school buildings changed names, loyalties, and identities in the 1970s, white administrators were now at the helm of some formerly all black school buildings and they largely ignored the histories of honorable blacks within the school community who built academic and extracurricular strongholds, such as the mighty Marian Anderson School Trojans (1950s–60s). Indeed, school desegregation came on white terms, via an all-white school board and a "technical" compliance with HEW. Subsequently, black educators witnessed unemployment, drops in social status, and an increase of violence initiated by whites seeking to thwart school desegregation. When asked, these former black segregated school personnel described how they felt after witnessing black teachers, administrators, and control over the education of black children diminishing all at once.

> MARGIE HINES, black former cafeteria manager: They [white administrators] . . . changed the names of schools like Marian Anderson to Northeastern Albemarle Middle School. Then everybody went to the three schools: a Northeastern Albemarle Middle, a Northeastern Albemarle County High, and a primary. They had taken Mr. Whitmore's picture down and we had to go to the school board and protest to keep it up. . . . They would have the PTA meetings but they would always have everything set before we got there. They changed the name on their own. . . .

> EVA WALTON, retired black teacher: When black teachers retire, their positions are filled with whites. Out of nineteen teachers, there were only two blacks. And blacks were certified. Ms. Ellen Foress taught at a time without certification. When I went back, if blacks hadn't passed the NTE and didn't have a degree, they should look away. I was hired with the NTE stipulation. They said, "Finish in one year or you're fired." I got my NTE score in the mail and took it to her [the white administrator who questioned her ability to complete NTE] in 1971. I went in 1967 and I had been out for nineteen years and stayed twenty-four years to retirement.

Ross Winston discussed a loss of autonomy as he looked back on his schooldays from "the top of his life" as a retired school official. One source of frustration for him was loss of control over who would be lauded as black heroes. Winston recounted his experience of feeling as if whites told him and the black community whom to admire and mimic, and who would serve as mentors. Reverend Dr. Martin Luther King, Jr., was one of the few black males designated by white school officials and personnel for black students to admire, and Winston did, as he recalled: "And I also was in high school the time that Martin Luther King got shot. . . . And when Martin Luther King got shot, that was a damper, you know? That was a damper. All the stuff that you all have been fighting for now, it's gone now. You know." Winston argued that other black leaders were not given proper positive publicity for their efforts toward social justice. In Winston's eyes, white children also failed to benefit from what should have been a more concerted effort to portray blacks not as something that history "happened to," but as integral parts of building the America that whites know and praise.

> And they picked our heroes for us. You know what I mean? They picked our heroes, leaders for the time. And I guess the blacks were supposed to follow and listen to him. . . . A lot of people don't look at it, but they picked our leaders for us.
>
> You have to remember, some of that was taken out of context. "By any means necessary" was, I think, the phrase that you are referring to, and I think that phrase was taken out of context to mean shoot, kill, or whatever. But if you look at the context of what he said, that wasn't the intention of that phrase. But that was something that the white picked out of the speech, that "any means necessary."
>
> One day when I was in your [referring to his wife, a present-day northeastern Albemarle rural school teacher] classroom, and this was in Black History Week, and I was visiting the classroom, and you said, "Okay, students. Today we're going to talk about blah, blah, blah, and George Washington Carver did this," and a white boy did this right behind her. (Laughter.) He was like, "So what?" That wasn't all he was saying. (Laughter.) But to be honest with you, but not agreeing, but I was just looking at the other side and the way that they were reared. So what other way can you expect them to react? Because that's the way they have been taught.

In our discussion of integrated schools and curricula, Winston spoke at length of his disgust with Black History Month and how it plays out in northeastern Albemarle schools. For him, a former administrator, Black History Month was a source of problems, unnecessary problems. Although he believes that predominantly white schools "need it most," he seems to lament the way they pursue it in the classroom and its residual affects on learners. Similarly, he expressed his anger with the way the northeastern Albemarle schools acknowledge the work of the Reverend Dr. Martin Luther King, Jr. Similar to the narrative of Margie Hines, he offers a story of white students using the holiday for a fun time to be out of school, rather than an observance and praxis toward needed deracialization and harmony in northeastern Albemarle schools. From his account, far too many local white kids were leaving school that day and causing trouble, their form of boycotting a school that would informally celebrate a black man during the school day of the 1970s. It was the late President Ronald Reagan who, in 1986, declared the third Monday in January a federal holiday to honor Dr. King, although local pushes for the official observance had brewed for some time. And as many northeastern Albemarle white families supported Reagan, they seemed to disagree with his position as well as the notion of King's life as one worthy of such an honor.

> ROSS WINSTON: They're the ones that need it most. Now that's something, that I may see people get hot when they hear you say that, especially in the schoolroom. Black History Month, I think they should take that and throw it out of the school, because what it does, it causes more problems, I mean, you know, let's take a white history month. It cause a lot of problems, and I said what they need to do, they need to incorporate the curriculum, and that would alleviate the situation.
>
> And you know that Black History Month, I mean, you come around here, I mean, they say, "Oh, Martin Luther King's birthday is a holiday." Or they used to have it that if you didn't want to come to school that day, you didn't have to come to school. That's probably the way it was when you were in school.
>
> But now they found, and this was to the white kids, is that they was telling their moms that they were going to school that day, but they found out that they didn't have to go, they were taking off and going somewhere and getting into trouble. So now they went and made it a legal holiday. Not because they really want to make that thing a legal holiday, but of the problems it was causing their kids.
>
> I was a member of the administration, and you know [white] kids were going out there and getting into trouble and they were having wrecks and stuff, and telling their parents that they was in school, but they wasn't in school. Nobody, so hey, you know, we're going to make it a legal holiday, and then the parents will know where they are.
>
> And man, you know when I first got on the administration, the blacks didn't have no voice.

Black teachers and administrators worried about how to find a voice to patrol white accountability. And they wanted more control over school decision making in order to maintain the same high standards they had adhered to at the now dissolved segregated black schools. Paradoxically, many white teachers believed that both whites and blacks lost with school desegregation. For example, Gean Whitehall seemed concerned about intellectual losses in her formerly all-white high school due to a watered-down integrated curriculum—a new curriculum she believed to be a shoddy version of the past in that it catered to deficiencies brought into school by blacks. She also argued that blacks lost school pride and power, while along with a rigid school curriculum, whites lost cultural control of education.

> GEAN WHITEHALL, retired white teacher: From '67 to '71, Mr. Randall was the third [white] principal of one northeastern Albemarle County high school [and

he stayed through until about 1990; his wife was the school nurse who had a similar tenure at a northeastern Albemarle County High School]. It took that long to settle down. I'm not sure why. . . . Teachers never felt threatened and if one told you they did they're fibbing. Both times I felt threatened it was white boys. We had extra duty, we were told to check the restrooms. We stood in line at the lunch room and sat in the lunch room—we took turns.

Blacks lost pride in schools. Blacks lost control of schools and part of culture. Both sides lost. We don't teach as hard, we have watered it down. Textbooks are watered down. All of a sudden too many nonwhites are failing and we watered it down. We are too multicultural.

1980s–1990s

After a decade of the early transition into desegregated schooling, the 1980s were less turbulent in northeast Albemarle. Adults in the white community began to realize that their worst fears, that desegregation would turn northeastern Albemarle into a black-operated town, had been thwarted. Many white adults, although certainly not all, learned that black teachers could teach their children, and that they could be trusted to look out for their children's best interests. Black adults adjusted to their new places in the education of their children, private places called home and church. Black families, to some extent, lost trust in a public grade school's ability to meet their children's needs—and rightfully so, as they witnessed the "legal" weeding out of black school personnel.

Of course, this decade became one that showed decreasing numbers of black parents at school and the intergenerational closure between parent–teacher–child was largely severed for the black community. The students themselves seemed to relate better to one another. Lasting friendships formed, and much to the dismay of many, interracial dating relationships and marriages ensued.

> GEAN WHITEHALL: I was the last to know, but even the teachers figured out black and white dating. There was a lot of that at the beginning. I would not butt my nose in students' business. I tried to listen. We were one generation, you were another. I tried to give you your privacy. . . . Northeastern Albemarle County was fair in grades; if anything it was tipping [toward blacks]. I do think we messed up on discipline. I think blacks were treated unfairly with discipline; that was a bad mark on us.

Students still sat primarily in separate factions in the lunchroom and classroom, but there were bridges, partly influenced by sports and other extracurricular activities. The Whitmores offered a positive outlook on the 1980s and 1990s, yet Margie Hines, the former cafeteria manager and mother of seven children and fifteen grandchildren schooled in northeastern Albemarle, related a more painful story about this era.

In short, the 1980s and 1990s brought a larger focus on color-blindness and high-stakes testing to northeastern Albemarle public schools. The era also brought evidence that the few black teachers on staff could, in fact, help whites do well on the high-stakes tests. In addition, whites learned that some black students could do better on the tests than regional and state averages, and some blacks outperformed their white peers. Results of tests, however, like those of the Competency Test for one northeastern Albemarle school, still highlighted that gaps in reading and math competence separated blacks from whites. This particular school's white students in 1997–1998 outperformed their black classmates in third- through eighth-grade reading and math end-of-grade tests. Black fourth- and seventh-grade students, however, performed higher than whites on the end-of-grade writing tests that school term (ncpublicschools.org). These facts brought new challenges and triumphs in northeastern Albemarle County's school race relations in the 1980s and 1990s.

> LOIS WHITMORE, retired black teacher: After the kids got together and started knowing each other, it was a different story, and some of them had parents that were really, really great. Not only were they black parents but white ones, too. They had to rely on the black teachers to find out what their children were doing because they said some of them would come to us and say, "Mrs. Whitmore, I don't know anything about [black students] because they won't talk to us." Say, "They'll talk to you." I said, "Well, when they say some things I think you should know, I'll let you know," I said. "But I tell them [white teachers], 'You go tell your [student's] parents. I go tell your [student's] parents. Or we go together.' I said, 'Now you choose the one you want.' 'I think we'd better go together.' I said, 'Okay.'" So I would come down there and we'd sit around the table, and they were understanding, very cooperative. So we really didn't have the kind of problems that they had some places. We had plenty of them [problems], but we had the kind of [black] teachers that could solve issues. [Even some of] my [teacher] aides were white [in the 1980s and 1990s, including Barbara Needham].

> WALKER WHITMORE, retired black principal: They [blacks] gained everything when it comes to going to the same schools and believing, seeing what the whites had. Also they have learned that they can expect better schools.

All participants, except the Whitmores (who mentioned only gains) spoke candidly about how the figures above are indicative of what black northeastern Albemarle communities lost with the desegregation of schools. These thoughts, gathered during the summer and fall of 2002, are poignant examples of losses as the result of unequal schooling during segregation. The transition into desegregation continues in narratives from the black community. Stories of black notions of losses of black school identity, leadership, sponsorship, autonomy, and power are supported in the recollection of white teachers Gean Whitehall and Barbara Needham. Narratives pertaining to what northeastern Albemarle gained after over thirty years of school desegregation primarily focus upon the issues of equality, understanding, interracial collaboration, and friendship.

EVA WALTON, retired black teacher: Blacks gained equal rights. Kids are not denied choices. We gained equal rights for teachers, although we are not replaced with equal numbers when they retire.

Kids started school behind due to inequality during segregation, but we need more black teachers to help bridge this gap. There are twenty-seven teachers in K–5 and only six or seven are black. We have no power for voting—we'll never gain anything without that power in numbers in the desegregated. Our administration building has no black member. There are three schools, no black principals. We need equalization of staff; it would help bridge the gap in test scores. They now hire whites from the local [Historically Black Colleges and Universities (HBCUs)] and they used to not hire blacks from an [HBCU].

MARGIE HINES, black former cafeteria manager: We gained some of our rights. I know some of the teachers were prejudiced against blacks, though. Mrs. Bourgeois accused [one of my daughters] of stealing a quarter from a little white girl. I sent a letter to Mrs. Bourgeois explaining how we might be poor, but our kids don't steal, and though we might be poor I will send a quarter to the little girl and to her." She wouldn't take the quarter from my daughter. She knew I was right. I never had any other problems out of her. . . .

They got to use the same material as the whites, but I can't say they were all treated the same. It's been forty years and I think there's still a ways to go. Well, they did away with the black/white restrooms. I'm trying to think what else did we really gain. They really didn't. . . . We got new books.

HARRIET TALIS, retired black counselor: Black teachers lost, I can imagine, lost the same closeness that wasn't continued initially. Black teachers were made to feel that they were second-class. A white teacher would always be head teacher in a team. My husband was an agriculture teacher who was there and very experienced, having taught in Maryland and Virginia for several years. Rather than make them choose my husband or a white man who had been there as the head, they turned the whole team into Vocation and made Beatrice Meyer (a white teacher) the chair. She was home economics. They did that kind of thing.

We couldn't see a gain initially. I had some second-hand books. Blacks resented the fact that after teaching a number of years, and many with advanced degrees, they resented having to prove themselves. It subsided after a while; kids really made the difference.

GEAN WHITEHALL, retired white teacher: Both communities gained understanding and friendship. . . . Friendship, opening up educational resources. Careers have gone up. Without integrating I don't think your [blacks'] careers would be as diversified. I still think, though, that good segregated schools would have had the same results. Some will tell you that it's the materials, but it's not the materials, it's the teacher. You don't go into class unprepared. That's what made us weak. One teacher's strong point was her discipline; I'm not going to name any names [likely a reference to Mrs. Whitmore]. I think our discipline approach was different than segregated schools. . . .

Margie Hines, black former cafeteria manager: Northeastern Albemarle has always been a little sneaky with what they do. I've had students to tell me "I know he didn't get an A because his test scores were lower than mine." I know that's not right. I think they should be more strict about cheating. Because they did so much cheating they thought everyone did. A lot of them that did the cheating, they went off to college and flunked out. I've had some of the teachers come and hug me as if they feel like they are sorry. They thought some of the things you did that you were cheating. You've gone on to be very successful. The ones that I saw, I don't see anything like doctors, lawyers out of themselves. They were always taught that we were nothing and they taught us as nothing. My son always wanted to write like Mr. Whitmore [principal of Marian Anderson]. He went in her class and turned in something on how was his summer. She didn't accept his writing because she didn't believe he did it. He didn't do anything in her classroom. So I sent him to summer school. Her name was Mrs. Benson. It was his junior year, about 1980. He is now writing a book and I hope she would pick up his book. He would pretend he was asleep. I went out there, and I explained to her and Mr. Randall why he wasn't doing anything in her classroom. Then, they didn't do anything about it. I'm hoping now that would do something. I had to pay to send him to summer school in the city, $75 and with gas $150 or $200. I told him to put it in back of him, never look back, do your work and I think he went to Mrs. Whitehall [known to be fair to blacks] the next year. Lord help them if they went through what he did. She strutted around like she had no conscience. Karl always been good with writing.

Harriet Talis, retired black counselor: Course contract changes were made or reshaped to a degree. Northeastern Albemarle County high schools had a policy that each high school graduates had to have at least one vocation. Home economics, carpentry. I think there's a tendency for blacks not to choose carpentry. The teacher asked for my help with recruiting black students. Students said, "That's a white man's course." They would take agriculture, but not carpentry. The white students would regularly get jobs at the beach, but black students were not, I assume that was part of what I was not told by black students. There was concern about special education classes being unusually populated. In an LD class, there would be mostly white and EMH students would be mostly black. So we started looking at the test results differently. What shocked me was the idea was that white northeastern Albemarle County high schools didn't have and didn't need an EMH program prior to desegregation. At Northeastern Albemarle Primary School and Northeastern Albemarle High, white teachers with two years of training from a [regional historically White university]. Some even [teased and] called it EZ-TC. Every black teacher had [to have] a bachelor's degree. The two-year trained [white] teachers quietly went away, [largely because] black teachers were better trained. There are equal requirements now. In the late 1970s [1976 or so] a new superintendent came in to change things. Before then, to meet desegregation requirements, in so doing they would just place you anywhere.

Barbara Needham, current white teacher: Both communities lost identity. Now ask me if that was important. [I ask, "Was that important?"] No! I don't think that was important. We lost nothing. We gained great friends, insight, knowledge of what they [blacks] were going through. C and J Harrison came to meet me at the hospital when my husband was there. J prayed with him, C helped put him in bed. They used to eat with us in our home. One of the first times our black friends came to the house in 1961, I thought, "What would the neighbors thin?" They were my friends. So, I decided that we sit outside against our cars and talk. Frannie Sanders and her mother (Ella) were our friends. My daughter and Felicia are the greatest of friends.

Whites have always been dominant and majority. I think very few people get to experience what I did. I spend time as a teaching assistant for black teachers. Mrs. Whitmore in 1988–89. I love Mrs. Whitmore. I also worked under Mrs. Hensley and Mrs. Dora Marshall [former black teachers]. I think that they had the same attitude I did. I never even realized they were black and I was white. I was helping. We always worked as a team. Now my assistant is black. Most people probably would say, "Oh my, I work for a black woman. These three ladies were good, caring people. They didn't want to play a role reversal, but I got that from some of the white teachers. They were accepting. Someone in the system said, "How can you take orders from a black?" This was a teacher in the system who asked this question. She thinks she's above and beyond anyone. I enjoyed her the least. And she was white.

I had never been here [former Marian Anderson School, now an integrated northeastern Albemarle middle school] until my eldest daughter started school there. We [whites] had a beautiful Northeastern Albemarle County High School, which had the same amenities. Black students on the north side went to Southfield Hills High and the whites on the South went to Northeastern Albemarle High. Then, they said, "Let's build a new school (Northeastern Albemarle Primary School) and shut down Southfield Hills School (which was is great condition). During integration all white commissioners made the funding decisions. Ask me where did Marian Anderson get its funding? I don't know for sure. I came here and saw this school was run down in need of repairs. It blew my mind: leaky pipes, overgrown areas, no football field. White parents complained that they won't come to school here. I've never seen such inequality.

Also look at the location. None of the other school are off the beaten path [Highway 158]. So, it's like they [white school board members and county commissioners] said, "Let's hide them, so people can't see the inequality." Out of sight, out of mind. I saw this in 1981. This had become part of the white system then; it was still not up to par. When I look at the current construction, who's last? Us. I'm told we're last because it's a large project. . . . There is only one black board of education member out of five, and he's not running again this term. One-to-five doesn't seem to give the black community much power.

Ross Winston also spoke candidly about the lack of black representation in northeastern Albemarle's desegregated schools. Like their peers in the previous stories, he lamented the obliteration of black voices in black education, which came with integration. Winston spoke at length about the problem. As a former administrator during desegregation, he found the topic intense and emotional. His insider understanding of the issue added depth to my understanding of how black teachers and administrators were taken out of the picture of black education, from the 1980s to the present.

Winston offered a scenario whereby qualified blacks applying for school personnel positions were deemed either ill-prepared or overqualified. His words spoke volumes for the losses and gains conveyed in the teacher narratives.

> I know one thing that I can say, I remember one time that one thing that all the blacks wanted in northeastern Albemarle counties, and they was always hollering for a black on the school board, so they could have their access, and I think that was a positive for northeastern Albemarle. Something that we didn't have back in the '50s that we got now. And it's still continuing on. And one of the negatives was, you know, we had a lot of black administrators back in the '60s.
>
> So we lost those. We lost our black administrators. We lost black teachers because we probably had ten times more black teachers back then in the '50s and '60s than we do now. . . . But didn't they hide themselves on having interest, you know what I mean? They'll [white school hiring officials] say that they don't qualify. But one of the biggest things that I've heard, you know, and I've been [an administrator]. I would know a black come up for a principalship or something and he wouldn't get it, and I remember one time asking the superintendent, I say, "You know what, what happened to John Doe?" He said, "Well, he wasn't ready." And you know my question was, "You know, what does it take to get ready?" That's one thing that you hear a lot of, when it comes to black administrators that are qualified, "They're not ready." I've even had a black administrator tell me, because I had called soliciting information about black candidates, and I knew that they had people in there with their degrees and everything, and I would ask, and they'd say, "Well, they're not ready yet."
>
> You know, that was a phrase that is commonly used, "They're not ready yet." I don't know what they need to do, but "they're not ready." But I know we lost a lot of black teachers, and a matter of fact, you know, Sherick. Now during the changeover, they didn't fire none of them. All of them basically stayed in place, but there was just no replacement of them. . . . They didn't fire them or anything. We're just not going to replace you.

Former cafeteria manager Margie Hines supported Winston's claims and supported Cecelski's (1994) realization that blacks leave the area in search of careers. Her statements also spoke of the haunting inequities in school discipline that she felt could be eliminated with a return to more black teachers and other key school personnel, the traditional human resource of the segregated black schools (Siddle Walker, 1996).

> The government doesn't even know what's going on in the small schools. In northeastern Albemarle, they're not even hiring blacks. They hire whites. They told my daughter that she was overqualified. How can you be overqualified? Then she left from around here and went to Goldsboro and got a job. They lost their black teachers. Even one went out to apply. They wouldn't hire my daughter for a Teacher's Assistant saying she was overqualified. Soon after failure from this effort, three of her four daughters were hired in NE Albemarle County C and E [both have the largest degree of schools located in more city-like and less rural-type settings, both cater to ethnic minority population sizes that are among the highest in proportions of black families, and both have a recent history of

racially discriminatory tracking and other such in-school segregation inequities; see Hughes, S., 2003]. They lost having devotion, Bible verses, the prayers. They would send [one student, the white one] home for one day and one [student, the black one] home for a week. So if it had been a black principal he would wear both of them out [phrase for corporal punishment] and let them return to school. Black students began quitting and enrollment was so low. Northeastern Albemarle had so many dropouts the year you left or after 1993. Grades: whites do a lot of cheating [and get away with it]. I would see them with writing in their hands in the lunchroom.

Conclusion

In the substantial replies of the participants, we find deep history of the trials and tribulations associated with black–white schooling. The perspectives offered by these former school personnel should be considered as messages in the present, about the past, as narrators construct what the era meant to them then, seen through their current lenses. It is important to remember that these narrators served familial roles in northeastern Albemarle as well.

From a reading of their responses as not only school workers, but also parents and caretakers, we may gain some evidence to understand the experiences of black families. And readers may gain a preview, as I did, of how the black families participating in this study, some relatives of the school personnel, have come to socially construct education struggles and hope in a manner indicative of this small northeastern Albemarle community.

These narratives are also supported by documents suggesting increasing learning, teaching, and home-to-school gaps as well as decreasing college-track percentages contrasting northeastern Albemarle's black and white students. Overall, desegregation of schools may have been a Pyrrhic victory for northeastern Albemarle's black residents and a mere shift of methods of school control for their white counterparts. A more in-depth historical ethnography of northeastern Albemarle's black families' parents and grandparents followed the one-time interviews of former school personnel. The time spent with grandparents became equally as important, as 47.5% of northeastern Albemarle grandparents sampled were listed as "responsible as caregivers of school-age children" (U.S. Census 2000, http://censtats.census.gov/data/NC/05037029.pdf).

The subsequent chapters discuss the rich description gathered from days spent with these parents, grandparents, and other members of their families. There were some discrepancies between black–white, teacher–administrator, and home–school personnel understandings of school desegregation and its influence on the current state of black education. Thus the need to delve further into the topic was evident. In order to survive, two generations of northeastern Albemarle's black families had to find strength and stability in the midst of an ambivalent desegregated school. Gean Whitehall's perspective is crucial here because she was noted by all blacks as being one of few white allies in northeastern Albemarle. For example, Whitehall expressed previous feelings about standards and textbooks being "watered down" in order to cater to black families. Yet black school personnel lamented the loss of black school excellence and accountability during desegregation. Perhaps Whitehall is blaming the victim; perhaps her comments about deplorable shifts in learning standards should be directed to the whites who had the power in the state and county to (a) interpret school standard laws, and (b) implement any changes in texts or curriculum. The rest of this book is composed of social, historical, and critical ethnographic work intended to provide additional understandings of the social phenomenon known as school desegregation. Although the focus remains sharp, the lens shifts to view school desegregation from a black family-centered perspective. This perspective enables the third component in my effort to triangulate, to learn from similarities and contradictions within and between (1) teacher, (2) administrator, and (3) family narratives regarding this phenomenon. The stories illuminate hidden rules and norms of the times to create quite a real sense of school desegregation as something "bad," "better," and "good" for the education of Black citizens.

References

ABCs of Public Education Program Information. (2002). Online. March 13, 2002. http://www.ncpublicschools.org/Accountability/reporting/abcmain.htm

Berg, S. (1975). What's behind the N.C. 'earnings gap.' *The News and Observer,* Sunday, November 2, pp. 3, 8, Section IV.

Boger, J. C., & Bower, E. J. (2001). The future of educational diversity: old decrees, new challenges. *Popular Government,* 66(2), 2–16.

Boyd, B., & Dennis, B. (1972). Desegregation improves education, study shows. *The News and Observer,* Wednesday, January 19, n.p.

Bruton, T. W., & Moody, R. (1965). Reply to Dr. Charles Carroll, superintendent of public instruction concerning North Carolina school desegregation. Raleigh, N. C.: North Carolina State Archives, Gov. Dan Moore MSS, Box 26, Government, Federal–U.S. Commission on Civil Rights.

NE Albemarle Superintendent. (2001). NE Albemarle County Schools: Welcome to NE Albemarle County Schools. Online. http://www.NE Albemarle.k12.nc.us/index.html.

Cecelski, D. (1994). *Along Freedom Road.* Chapel Hill: University of North Carolina Press.

Cecelski, D. (2001). *The Waterman's Song: Slavery and Freedom in Maritime North Carolina.* Chapel Hill: University of North Carolina Press.

Crow, J.J., Escott, P. D., & Hatley, F.J. (2002). *A History of African Americans in North Carolina.* Raleigh: Office of Archives and History, North Carolina Department of Cultural Resources.

Darity, W., Castellino, D., & Tyson, K. (2001). *Increasing Opportunity to Learn via Access to Rigorous Courses and Programs: One Strategy for Closing the Achievement Gap for*

At-Risk and Ethnic Minority Students. Report prepared for the North Carolina Department of Public Instruction and submitted to the North Carolina State Board of Education. Raleigh, NC: NCDPI.

Etheridge, B. (1993). *The History of Education in North Carolina.* Raleigh: North Carolina Department of Public Instruction Office of the State Superintendent.

Gaston, P. M. (1971). The Region in Perspective. In *The South and Her Children: School Desegregation 1970–1971,* (pp. 5–20). Altanta, GA: Southern Regional Council Inc.

Hesburgh, Reverend T. M et al. (1970). *Equal Educational Opportunity: Statement of the United States Commission on Civil Rights Concerning the Statement by the President on Elementary and Secondary School Desegregation.* Washington, D. C.: New Community Press.

Hughes, K. (2003). *4th Sunday in the Dirty.* Charleston, SC: Imprint Books.

Hughes, S. (2003). An early gap in Black-White mathematics achievement: Holding school and home accountable in an affluent city school district. *Urban Review,* 35(4), 297–322.

Mickelson, R. A. (2001). Subverting Swann: First- and second-generation segregation in the Charlotte-Mecklenburg schools. *American Educational Research Journal,* 38(2), 215–252.

Mr. George Attix, Manager, Chamber of Commerce of Elizabeth City, Letter to Superintendent Charles Carroll. (1960). Box: DPI, Admin., Subject Files (State Superintendent) A–L January 1960–April 1960 Folder: A, Raleigh: Department of Cultural Resources Division of Archives and History.

NCDPI Superintendent's Correspondence Files. (1959). Raleigh: Office of Archives and History, North Carolina Department of Cultural Resources.

Noblit, G. W. (2002). *North Carolina School Desegregation: The Intersection Between Law, Tradition, and Transition.* Paper presented at the 2002 annual meeting of the American Educational Studies Association, Pittsburgh, PA.

North Carolina Department of Cultural Resources Division of Archives and History, Human Relations Council Files, Klan, n.d.

North Carolina Council on Human Relations Records Inventory #4880 (1999). Chapel Hill, NC: Manuscripts Department Wilson Library URL: http://www.lib.unc.edu/mss/ Processed by Teresa Church Encoded by Teresa Church.

Orfield, G. (2001). Schools more separate: Consequences of a decade of resegregation. *Rethinking Schools: An Urban Educational Journal,* 16(1), 14–18.

Siddle Walker, V. (1996). *Their Highest Potential: An African American School Community in the Segregated South.* Chapel Hill: University of North Carolina Press.

Terjen, K. (1971). *White Flight: The Segregation Academy Movement.* North Carolina Department of Cultural Resources Division of Archives and History, Human Relations Council Files, School Segregation.

The News and Observer. (1965). "His Dunce Cap Slipped." September 9, p. 4.

U.S. Census. (2000). Profile of General Demographic Characteristics: 2000. Geographic Area: NE Albemarle County, North Carolina. Online. http://censtats.census.gov/data/NC/05037029.pdf

"Always Remember"
Brown Lives in Black Family Pedagogy

ALWAYS REMEMBER
by Kent Hughes

Remember to appreciate family
And always honor a true friend
Be thankful and humble to those who help you
From beginning to end
Always love thy neighbor
As you should love yourself
Believe in your wildest dreams
And worry about nothing else
Never say you can't do it
Always give it a try
Before you decide to give up
Always question yourself . . . why?
If you remember nothing else
Remember what a friend told me
In life, never let anyone . . .
Rent a space in your head for free

The Biggs, Erskin, and Winston Families

Each family featured in this book is represented by at least two members representing a first generation (e.g., parents during the first *Brown* decision who are now grandparents) and a second generation (e.g., grade-school students during the first *Brown* decision who are now parents). Chapter 6 also presents narratives from a third-generation family member's perspective (e.g., any family member not born within twenty-one years of the first *Brown* decision and currently attending secondary or postsecondary schools in northeastern Albemarle). Generational time is understood here not as merely a viewpoint from which to begin apprehending history, but for exploring how the Biggs, Erskin, and Winston families maneuvered through history, and what each family did with their history. The idea is to begin understanding what it is about family pedagogy that shapes education outcomes and history.

The families here engage in this process of oral history that is understood to involve (a) recalling, (b) omitting, (c) bolstering, and (d) simply forgetting certain details of their schooling past. Family stories in the following chapters offer snapshots, not only into black family pedagogy, but also into educational life experiences. Let their messages inform us and warn us as we read. Let their stories challenge our taken-for-granted knowledge as we attempt to feel black family life at the crossroads of law, tradition, and transition. Follow me as we track how each Biggs, Erskin, and Winston family unit counterbalances a struggle for literacy, language, and culture with a family pedagogy of hope.

The Biggs Family

The Biggs family was the second black family to participate in this historical ethnography. Grandparents Larry Biggs, seventy-four, and Rena Biggs, seventy-two, who were married September 2, 1950, represent the first-generation experience of school desegregation for their family. Unlike the female-dominated dynamics of the first generation of the Erskin family, Larry Biggs offered the most stories from the first-generation standpoint in the family. Yet, as with the Erskin family, it was the spouse with the most formal education who largely told the family's story.

Larry and Rena Biggs

In 1952, Larry and Rena Biggs bought their first home. Larry discussed going as far away as Long Island, New York, to find work to help pay for the house, which was on the same land as the family home today. It was in Larry's story of finding and purchasing their first home that I began to gain a better understanding of my own family's reputation as an important factor for gaining rapport with the study participants. My late, beloved paternal grandmother, Amie Hughes, was credited with helping all three families represented in this book in some way. Of the Biggs, Erskin, and Winston family members, Larry Biggs was the first to acknowledge Grandma Amie in conversation with me:

> People used to go to Long Island and pick potatoes. Yeah. Long Island and pick up potatoes, went up there, we stayed six weeks up there and already I've got, this was an old house. Your grandmother, yeah, your grandmother was living on this lady's farm, and I was talking to somebody about a house, and she told me,

says this lady had a house. I can't even think of the man's name that used to live in this house, but anyway, sold me that house for five hundred dollars. Sold me the house for five hundred dollars. It was a three-story house that I had it taken down, and it cost me six hundred dollars to get it taken apart. Well, I took part of it down, but it was too high to move and boy, we were trying to get it so we could move it. I'd work all day, and folks would go there took my stuff away during the night until I started to bringing it home.

Like the Erskins, the Biggs family experienced a major house fire that destroyed their first home. They rebuilt on that land, however, and Larry and Rena raised eight children and a plethora of grandchildren there. Larry Biggs still works a full day, which is something I found quite impressive at his age and relative to some of the other black families that I had met and/or known in the area. Much of his day, in fact, is spent doing tasks such as mowing lawns for those who can no longer do it for themselves. Prior to the "official" interview questions during my first visit, Larry constructed a message from his experience that I later understood was meant as (a) an explanation for why he chose to participate in my study, (b) introspection—reminding himself of his goals, and (c) advice for me, my life's work, and more specifically what my intent should be for this study:

If I can help somebody along the way then I know my living is not in vain. I found that this world is too big for you to try to make it by yourself. We all need help from somebody. You don't care how much money you've got or what you've got. You're going to need somebody. A lot of people have got money and all but a lot of times the money's no good to them. That's my motto. Always do what you can for people.

Most of the first generation observed in this study remain active in the community, but at this age are not continuing to work full days as Larry is. His work schedule permitted me to visit the family only before 7:30 A.M. or after 7:30 P.M., when the sky is mostly dark in the fall on the northeastern Albemarle coastal plains. Larry Biggs seems to be a devout Christian and a twenty-year-plus veteran deacon of New Sawyer's Creek Missionary Baptist Church. I met with him after 8:40 P.M. for the second of three long visits because of his Bible study responsibilities. During my first two visits, Rena Biggs had already prepared herself for bed and did not wish to participate in those conversations, but her bed was close enough for her to hear us. The third, early morning visit better suited her routine, so she was able to participate then. During my first two visits to their home, the magnitude of a black, rural, Southern grandparent's perspective surfaced. It was clear from the beginning of my time with them that there was much to learn from gathering two generations of the Biggs family stories of schooling and how the family pedagogy of struggle and hope helps them endure northeastern Albemarle public schooling—from the early transition into school desegregation through today. Larry and Rena's two-story green house was cozy and warm. Trophies in their home are displayed for three generations who experienced desegregated schooling as parents, grandparents, or students. When I visited with them, there was an American flag on the outside of the screen door and a big pumpkin picture covering most of the outside of their front door, as Halloween was only a week away.

Willis and Virginia Biggs

Willis Biggs attended the same black segregated school that his parents did, originally named Sawyer's Creek, which was later changed to Marian Anderson largely due to the influence of Principal Whitmore. Willis began school in 1965 when there was no kindergarten and no integration, even though *Brown* had been decided eleven years earlier. It was a time where black parents urged their children to go to school to "not be in the fields, that's the main thing." Willis elaborated on this point:

> They wanted us to shy away from that, and do something. It was always pursued as do something like they did, you know, "they" as in white people, to kick back, so you can try to kick back, too. Have a decent job, you know, not like in the fields and farming or minimum-wage type jobs.

Willis recalled attending school from grades one through three before desegregation came during his fourth-grade year in 1968. This was the Freedom of Choice period. He, like his parents and the Erskin family, expressed fond memories of the segregated school and its activities for youth:

> Every Friday we had, what did they call it, Auditorium? We'd go to the auditorium and they would do a skit and yeah, they sure did. The whole school. We sure did. I remember that. Yeah. We used to go to Auditorium.
>   They had one [gospel choir] in the school. Yeah. It was funny. You know, you talk of first grade all the way to twelfth grade at one school. One school, that's the way we were. We were like this . . . everything you had to do you had to sit up front, you know, like if you were first grade, second grade, you had to sit in the first and second seats on the bus. In the auditorium you were up front.

For Willis, the segregated school was a special place for families to practice their faith and patriotism. His portrayal involved the faith, discipline, and patriotism that were a large part of black schooling. The segregated school discipline again seems synonymous to spanking, but its strong tie to faith, for Willis make this synonym useful and appropriate in school. He seems to lament the loss of those parts of Marian Anderson as he witnessed its change:

> Yes, morals within yourself, because we did the Lord's Prayer every day, the Pledge of Allegiance. Or we were going to get that paddle. We were going to get that that had holes in it. I never got it, but it used to have holes in it. He would turn the intercom on, you know, when they called you to the office and some-

body had to get some "licks," as they say. "Please don't hit me!" [laughter] and he would turn the intercom on the whole show. And in all the rooms you would hear them. It was a kind of "fear factor," I'll put it that way. He would put fear . . . but you respected that, and that's what it was all about. They had the respect of the community. That's why I didn't get into trouble.

Forty-three-year-old Willis Biggs is one of the oldest of the Biggs children. Upon entering his home, I encountered a tutoring session between his wife, Virginia, forty-six, and their elementary school-aged son. Willis, like his parents, lives in rural northeastern North Carolina, but in a different county. Although Willis' youngest child does not attend northeastern Albemarle schools, his eldest daughter attended them K–12, and she is now in graduate school. Willis and Virginia's home is situated beside a church and it lies between two recently harvested fields, likely corn, wheat, potatoes, cotton, and beans. I knew of Willis only from the legends about him in northeastern Albemarle about his abilities on the basketball court, and I learned that he was one of the few athletes from northeastern Albemarle's small 1A athletics to receive a college scholarship. Willis and Virginia graduated from college and they had a keen sense of their educational surroundings and opportunities. Upon graduation from northeastern Albemarle High School in 1977, Willis attended Chowan College for two years and then finished the last two years at Atlantic Christian College in Richmond. He received a bachelor of science degree in business administration.

Willis and Virginia recalled their time in school during integration as a time of change, when college became the new standard even for black students. Virginia first explained: "I think we were in the transition." And Willis clarified:

Yeah, we were in the middle, because we hit integration, and things started changing a little bit. And we started striving for a little higher, such as trying to get into college and finishing college.

They did claim, however, that the educational experience of the black family historically had an impact on college enrollment. Virginia, whose mother was one of few blacks in the area to attend college, did in fact rebel against the idea at first. Although Virginia ultimately became a college graduate, she delayed her entry. "I guess it would depend on the families, too," Virginia said. "Right. . . . How they pushed them," Willis added. With this early insight, it is no surprise that their son and daughter are known to be good students. Still, even with the good family status, both members of the second-generation Biggs family offered narratives of education struggle, distrust, and fear.

Willis and Virginia identify themselves as black, from a Christian background. The church is a strong part of their individual lives, so much so that they each retained their original church membership after marriage. Willis explains, "I'm a member of the Sawyers Creek Baptist Church, and I attend Green Chapel Baptist a lot more, which is my wife's church." Virginia, who is a lead teacher at a public school and is certified to teach children designated as gifted, offers this description of her identity: "I'm a black woman, teacher, Christian, and born-again, a leader, and mother, sister, daughter, grandmother. I didn't mention all of them." During my first two visits I met Willis and Virginia at their home after each had had a long day of work, which includes two jobs for Willis. I had them sit across from each other at a little-used dining table in a den section of their kitchen. They seemed to enjoy each other's company as they looked to each other for answers, questions, and support.

My observation of their parenting was indicative of this expression of unity. I observed Virginia working with their son on math homework. The couple affectionately called this "tutoring" time, and it seemed to be a regular educational activity in their home. Narratives of segregated and desegregated schooling here were quite useful for understanding the Biggs family experience and the generational history of messages of education struggle and hope. Although Virginia's comments are important, she did not attend northeastern Albemarle schools or teach in them. As stepmother to Willis' daughter, who did attend northeastern Albemarle schools, she did experience the system as a parent. But for this purpose, Willis' narratives are highlighted as we trace northeastern Albemarle school desegregation for the second and third generations of the Biggs family.

The Erskin Family

The Erskin family was the first black family to participate in this historical ethnography, after the pilot study and former school personnel interviews. Their family consists of two members representing the first generation and a single-parent daughter representing the second-generation, all of whom experienced school desegregation in northeastern Albemarle schools. The narratives of grandparents Dora Erskin, seventy-seven, and Nolen Erskin, eighty-four, were presented in the introduction of this manuscript. Dora and Nolen represent the first-generation experience of school desegregation for their family.

They are the proud parents of nine living children, six girls and three boys, and a host of grandchildren. Two of their daughters, along with one grandchild, were lost to a house fire in 1969. For the purposes of this ethnography, it was important to also spend time with at least one of their offspring who was (a) recommended by Dora and Nolen, (b) available, and/or (c) a parent of a child or children who attended northeastern Albemarle schools. The Erskin child who fit all of those criteria was Candice Erskin Brown. Like her parents before her, Candice, forty-one, works several jobs. She is a single mother of three boys currently attending northeastern Albemarle schools: one in elementary school, one in middle school, and one in high school. Candice vividly recalls the later years of desegregation.

Dora, Nolen, and Candice experienced exploitation with each attempt to get ahead through education and hard work. They also experienced the hopeful products of education, with new jobs and with family members graduating from college. It is evident in their portrayals, however, that the Erskin family not only experiences events of hope and struggle linked to education, but they also mentally and socially construct those experiences for themselves, their children, potential readers of this book, and me. At least, in part, the generational tones of these constructions surfaces in Candice's slight points of departure from her parents' pedagogy of struggle and hope. Generational ties also emerge in understanding how Candice's experiences of being a single, black parent differ from those of Woody Winston in contemporary northeastern Albemarle public schools.

Dora and Nolen Erskin

Dora and Nolen Erskin live in a modest pea-green two-story house on the mideastern end of northeastern Albemarle County A. Their home sits on less than an acre of land between a young pine forest in the back and an alternating wheat/corn field in the front. Their driveway is partly paved; three brown pups sit on the unpaved portion. Dora drives a compact car and Erskin drives a 1980s model Ford truck. I first met them when I was a child playing with their grandson, who moved from the North to live with them from tenth grade until graduation. Although I had known them as a boy, I had not spoken with them in over ten years. The conversation began as I entered through the front screen door, which led through a small screened-in porch to the wooden front door of their home.

All of our conversations occurred in the front room of the home, a living room where guests are generally escorted to sit and talk. Both the television in that room and one in a second room were playing as I entered each day, which reminded me of my grandmother. Nolen entered for conversation from the room farthest from the front door, where I presume he was watching television two of the three days I visited. Although he had less to say, he seemed as proud of me and proud to be invited to participate as Dora did. And although Dora frequently told me, "Baby, I don't know what else I can tell you," she offered a new lens into their lives for me and for them—a lens to their experiences of schooling that had been originally clouded by my childhood and their adulthood blinders. Dora and Nolen identify themselves as black people who "hadn't ever been in any trouble of any kind." Dora further identifies herself thus: "I call myself a nice housewife." These understandings of the Erskins' identities form the foundation for their discussions of segregated and desegregated schooling, educational struggles, and hopes.

The Erskins were married on September 27, 1942, and neither was able to complete high school. But like other black families of their generation in this manuscript, one spouse obtained considerably more formal education than the other. Dora, seventy-seven, and Nolen, eighty-four, both attended Sawyer's Creek school. Dora "finished the ninth grade" and Nolen "didn't get any further than second." At this time in northeastern Albemarle's history, the completion of eleventh grade was considered a good, sufficient formal education. Actually, at the end of eleventh grade was high school graduation. Dora explained at least part of the reason why they were unable to complete school: "He had to work, but I had to stay home and tend to a sick mother. I had a sick mother. I quit school to tend to her." Paradoxically, Dora's ill mother also constantly repeated one message during segregated schooling: "Get it now. Isn't any need to try to get it later because [that's] what they used to say. Get it while you can." Even now, Dora lamented, "Yeah twelfth, twelfth grade. When you go look for a job, that's the first thing they asked you." "Sure is!" Nolen added.

The couple had vivid memories of their segregated school and we discussed them at length during the first of my three visits. Both discussed inequality in building conditions, transportation, and student and teacher responsibilities. The Erskins seemed acutely aware of their school's inferior conditions compared to those of white northeastern Albemarle schools. Nolen provided verbal information, and a wealth of understanding and corroboration in nonverbal (nodding, sitting forward in his chair) responses to the stories his wife shared. Dora, who finished school in 1938, was quite vocal about this period and she seemed to want to share her recollection of her education struggles and how she experienced life as being second-class to whites in the 1930s.

> Well, when we were, when I first started school, we had one room like this here, from the first to the, I think, it was the seventh grade. Everything was in that one room. One teacher taught us all. . . . Well, one thing about it. We didn't have any school bus and they had a school bus, and we had to walk to school. They rode on the school bus. . . .
>
> We had to stay out of school and pick cotton. Both our daddies were farmers and we had to work [unlike most white children of northeastern Albemarle farmers]. . . . When I was going to school, it wasn't anything, go to school and back home and get up the next morning and go to school again. That was all, reading and writing and arithmetic. You didn't have anything special [like sports teams], anything. . . .
>
> When I was young, I said, "When I get grown, nobody gone [going to] ask me to pick a bale of cotton, pick a strawberry, or pick up a white potato." I wasn't going to do it. I did my share when I was young. ("I did mine too," Nolen added.)

Candice Erskin Brown

Candice Erskin Brown identifies herself as an "honest, dependable people person, going the extra mile, color-blind, black woman, with a guy friend." She was one of the youngest of the six living Erskin daughters. Her educational narratives of struggle and hope would link to her family in ways that both concur and critique. Candice was one of the two Erskin girls to be hospitalized for nearly a year following the house fire that the family endured in 1969. Burn scars are partly visible on one of her hands. She is as strong-willed as her mother, and is now the single mother of three school-aged boys. She is recovering from an abusive relationship and, like most northeastern Albemarle residents, she works more than one job. Candice holds down one full-time job at a neighboring county clerk's office and two part-time jobs at grocery stores. I was struck by her wisdom, ingenuity, and tenacity, as she seems to epitomize all of her parents' teachings and more. Candice speaks her truth candidly and articulately. She also rebukes some of her parents' supposedly timeless messages, yet her truth echoes others' experiences of struggle and hope in northeastern Albemarle's desegregated schooling.

Candice was seven years old when northeastern Albemarle schools were desegregated, and thus her memories of the first few transition years wax and wane. Her intense and frequent experiences of struggle, however, are unequivocal, as is her hope in education leading to a higher quality of life—of Christian life. Her home is a one-story, spacious double-wide trailer. There are four bedrooms: the two younger sons share one and the oldest son has his own. The boys share a bathroom; Candice has her own adjoining her master bedroom. The living room is complete with new-looking furniture and a new-looking wide-screen television. Separating the bedrooms and the living room is a spacious kitchen and dining-room table and seating area. It is clean and tidy and clearly a wonderful space for the boys to live. Less than one mile away from her parents, and on the same road, Candice has her own identity through her home and land, which is adjacent to a pine forest and a wheat/corn field. It was hard to meet with Candice due to her work schedule, so we met in the evenings. My visits to her home were perhaps the most inspiring of all. I began to understand her experiences of education struggles, hopes, and constructions thereof with her upbringing and messages for her own children. Those children would be the third generation of Erskin family members to experience desegregated northeastern Albemarle schools in some capacity.

Sadly, Candice currently experiences deskilling, devaluing, and infantilizing in the same northeastern Albemarle schools, the same things that plagued Woody Winston over thirty years ago. Candice speaks of the continuous and unnecessary struggles of single black parents with northeastern Albemarle public schools. It is continuous because over three decades separate Candice's parenthood from Woody's. It is unnecessary because help should be available. Margie Hines, child of a single parent, spoke in chapter two of her pre-*Brown* northeastern Albemarle school setting, in which being the child of a single parent didn't lead school personnel to brand her with a "scarlet letter," but instead brought extra tutelage from adults within the school community:

> MARGIE HINES: Even if you're good in school they'll pick the ones with two parents. During segregated schools, single-parent status didn't matter. [Now] it seems like they try to dog the single mother. . . .

Candice narrates a hauntingly familiar story of trials. She speaks from the standpoint of one who hopes for better working relationships with northeastern Albemarle schools. She cries as one who seeks a no-fault, collaborative approach to closing gaps in the education of her children and all children. As we learn more about her struggle to advocate for her three bright school-aged boys, there arises yet another painful reminder of the unfulfilled promise of *Brown*.

The Winston Family

Jerry "Woody" Winston

The first generation of Winston family members was represented by grandfather, Jerry "Woody" Winston. He lives on a dirt lane across the lane from one of his sons in a one-story red-brick home that he built. Mrs. Josephine Winston had passed away many years before I met Woody. His story of inequity, inequality, and inadequacy in the segregated school were poignant. His home is filled with pictures of his nine (eight now-living) children and many grandchildren. He has a shed that, when I visited him, had inside a large bucket of lard that he made from bear fat. An avid fisherman, he uses the lard to fry his fresh catch from the local waterways that surround the Coastal Plain town of northeastern Albemarle. "You can use this to rub on your hands for arthritis, too," Woody said with a smile. He appeared to be a thoughtful, caring, hardworking father who, for many years, had to compensate for the loss of his wife. When Mrs. Winston tragically died, she left behind her husband and several school-aged children. Woody often noted, "I had somebody here to have their meals ready for them," when he had to work. The children endured school segregation and desegregation in northeastern Albemarle with their father. When I visited, we first discussed Sawyer's Creek school and its evolution from the time Woody experienced it to the time his oldest children did so.

Like his peers, seventy-six-year-old Woody talked about being cold in the segregated school. But unlike the others, he linked his uncomfortable feelings at school with his performance. For Woody, the school should have, and could have, provided a place of warmth for learning. He told a story of a crooked white man who was at least partly responsible for the chilly segregated school. This message seemed salient in his mind, because it was the first he told upon being asked to describe his segregated school experiences:

> And when I got to school my hands would be so cold, I could not even get close to the heater [because the pain of having them thaw too quickly would be much worse than thawing them slowly and farther away from the heater]. They were just so cold. We had a wood heater.
>
> You see what happened, you got coal, but the man took and sold the coal, and got ripped off and the people he had working for him, he sent them in the woods to cut wood for us to burn. Old green wood stuff, and by the time the fire got warm, it'd be time to go home. How could you learn anything?
>
> I'm sitting there so cold I couldn't even put my hand to the heater. Be aching. Yeah, that's right. You see the coal come to northeastern Albemarle for us to burn in the heater. He would take the coal and sell it. You understand? And the people he had working on the farm, he would let them go into the woods and cut old green pine and gumwood for us to burn. And by the time you get all that stuff burning, it'd be time to go home.

Walking to school was a norm in the narratives of the first-generation family members. Along with remembering the one- to two-mile hike to school, the first generation also remembered walking about as far to catch the one bus allocated to them at the time. Regardless of the weather, blacks in the segregated school were walking to help their futures. Woody had a cousin who drove the bus who could offer some relief. In his stories about this experience, Woody argued that the school transportation conditions had an impact on his learning potential, before he even learned to write his name.

> Right. School was out. Then it'd be raining and we had to walk home and my parents had to come get us sometimes in a mule cart. We had to walk to school until we got that bus. And when we did get the bus, the bus had to come from Old Mill Lane.
>
> Then we had to walk two mile and a half to catch that. Then if it be raining, when they bring us home, we had to get off of that bus and walk home. Ron, my cousin, drove the bus, old man. He say, "Hell." He used to cuss all the time. He would tell me and my sister, "I ain't going to let you all walk in all this rain." It'd be raining so hard you couldn't hardly see. He would carry us home. I had a hard way before I even learned to write my name when I was going to school.

The hardship was not over once Woody entered the bus. Like Nolen Erskin and all of the other members of the first generation, Woody told a story about racial slurs coming from white students once he entered the bus system that took him to the segregated Sawyer's Creek school. I had heard parts of the rhyme when I began collecting stories for this book, but Woody was the first person to offer the full chant—a chant hollered by white grade-school students from the window of a moving school bus. Woody also repeated the story of how black students retaliated to these taunts.

> The high school had the bus. They used to pass by us, and say, "Nigger, nigger, black as tar, can't go to heaven on a motor car." And we would run and try to catch them and throw dirt in there. See, we couldn't run and keep up with the old bus, you know. But yeah, they used to holler at us, "Nigger, nigger, black as tar, can't go to heaven on a motor car." I'll never forget that.

Woody laughed and showed pride and nostalgia in spite of the pang of this memory. "Yeah, we had it hard coming up, let me tell you, but we made it," he said. He seemed most thankful for the achievements of his children, two of whom have become among the first black school administrators in northeastern Albemarle since schools desegregated, and his grandchildren. Woody's story is perhaps counterintuitive to our common beliefs about the capabilities of students placed "at risk," a category that Woody and his children would definitely fit. He is a widowed, black father of nine, who also happens to be a middle-school dropout. Certainly, there is much to learn from the Winston family's ability to survive and succeed against the grain of society and its low expectations of such nontraditional households. Woody alone adds to the complex history of how black, rural, male students have been placed among those not expected to complete grade school. (Consequently, black, rural, male students have among the highest dropout rates in the state even today.) Woody explained how early black–white working relationships may have influenced black male dropouts in northeastern Albemarle's public schools. When Woody was in grade school, white men would come to school to check out black males from the classroom to have them work on local farms. Around the same time, in the 1930s and 1940s, completing second grade, in Woody's words, made "you number one then, see. You get to the eighth grade, you did pretty good."

> I think I got up to like sixth grade. Yeah, like the sixth grade, and I quit because I had to stop and help farm and things.
>
> You be going to school and a white man would come out there and say, "Hey, children, your daddy said you could help me this evening." I'd go in there and tell the teacher and she'd tell me to go ahead. They wouldn't sign no paper or nothing. Just go ahead and go farm, and plow them mules. That's right.
>
> Yeah, we would go in there and tell the teacher, and the teacher would say, "Go ahead." There wasn't signing no papers and stuff. [Laughter.] Anybody could come to school and get you. You know? Especially if you knowed them, you know. Because you know you're going to blend. And then you'd get about fifty cents for half a day. Fifty cents for half a day. And you plowed them mules until the sun went down. That's right. And the next day it'd be the same thing. You go to school and half a day, and "Your daddy said you could help me plow this evening." I go tell the teacher and go on.

After the sixth grade, northeastern Albemarle had little to offer blacks like Woody and those of the first generation in this study. A good job for someone in his position in northeastern Albemarle with his level of formal education was working for wealthy whites in town. The industrial work of the area was limited to low-wage positions in local mills, as previously discussed by the Erskin and Biggs families.

> Well, a good job then, you go to work for some kind of well-to-do people, and a lot of times you would stay there. Either you would go to some of your people and stay and go to work there, you know.
>   Right. Well, they were so, you know, I don't know what to say. It was kind of hard. Most of the things we had to do then, went to a mill or something, or company coming in, and had a meal or something like that.

From Woody's experience, we find further evidence that black teachers faced arduous times finding northeastern Albemarle jobs not only during integration, but during segregation as well. A formal education could get you a job, but if you were black, that "good" job was not likely to be in northeastern Albemarle, or even the Albemarle area of North Carolina.

> Well, see, that was . . . if you had a little education you could get a little job, you know. It would help you get a job. See, used to [be], you couldn't go to college and teach school. We're a back county. You could go to New York. Most of the people left and went to New York or Norfolk somewhere, see. They left from around here.

With little formal education and dark brown skin, Woody used what ability he had to work as a foreman in one of the local mills. The mill eventually closed. Then, like many of the other men of this study, and like my father, he went on the commute to join the International Longshoreman's Association union in Norfolk, Virginia. Woody worked in that union for twenty-nine years until his retirement.

> Yes, sir. I worked down there twenty-nine years. I went back and forth. Yeah, about an hour or an hour and fifteen or twenty minutes. Then you worked there then, you worked about half day and then had to come home. Until we got in a good union.

After sharing his experiences of education and the limits for it to reach fruition in the life of a black student, Woody returned to discussing more details of life at the segregated Sawyer's Creek school. In the fashion and language of a grandfather, Woody offered a narrative of his difficulty in school and how it contrasts with the easier school experiences of later generations. He first offered the narrative of yet another person who retaliated against white students' racial slurs by shooting at their school bus. Similar to the story relayed by the first generation of Erskins, Woody recalled how the uncle of local Reverend Omar Battle aimed and fired at the bus of white students.

> A Battle boy [uncle of local Reverend Omar Battle] shot at the bus, too. Yeah, Charlie. For running over his dog and talking trash to him while driving the bus, Charlie shot at the bus.

Still, with resistance and the will to sometimes fight fire with fire (literally), most blacks chose a different, nonviolent path in northeastern Albemarle during this time. In another narrative Woody returned to the difficulty of actually getting to school to learn. He lamented additional constraints and barriers he faced in simply reaching the school by foot due to geography and ecological issues such as extremely humid, hot weather and certain poisonous animals, like snakes. To Woody, his grandchildren have a much easier time, and they should at least be thankful for that. He seemed disturbed at remembering what walking to school was like for some black students of Sawyer's Creek School for Negroes.

> But these children now, they've got it good now. See, the bus will come up and go for them. And then sometimes they won't be ready. . . .

The students in Woody's class who were fortunate enough to remain in school through the seventh grade had an additional barrier to cross. At the time, there were no high schools for black students who graduated from the eighth grade. So unless black students went over to a neighboring county to attend a school, such as Currituck's Snowden School, they didn't get to ninth or tenth grade. Many black families simply were unable to get their children to Snowden School. Woody offered a rather detailed description of Sawyer's Creek School. He suggested that even at its best, it could offer only a partial formal education. Most families simply did not have the money or wherewithal to ship their children fifteen miles east to receive the kind of education that whites could get conveniently at home in the northeastern Albemarle townships.

> Well, see, along then, if you had three rooms, the middle room was up two flights. It was first or second grade. And then you moved in another room (inaudible) coat. Then the other room was the kitchen sink. Yeah, then you start with teaching up to the seventh grade, yeah. And when you got to seventh grade, that's as far as you went, unless you went to Snowden to the high school. . . . Some people went there and some didn't.
>
>   No, now our school run out [of grades]. You see, you had to go over there and rent a room, and stay. See a lot of people they didn't want to send their children like that. Right. Unless they had some sister or brother live in town. See, then they would let them go over there, then they had to come home weekends. Carry wood over there. Things were tight.

Surprisingly, discipline did not mean spanking, per se, in Woody's narratives. Unlike his peers from the Erskin and Biggs families, Woody told of teachers using other methods to maintain order in the segregated school. Although his narratives were not without reflection on hitting students to gain compliance, it was not the only form of control he mentioned. This narrative is important for challenging the notion that black teachers used only spanking. It also adds to understanding teaching, learning, and discipline in the segregated school. It raises questions about why others did not mention other forms of discipline in the black school and why even Woody seems to accept "whipping" as something that was to be expected.

> No. Along then, see, if you do something in school your teacher didn't like, she would put you in the corner, you in one corner and whoever was with you in another corner, and you stand on one foot a whole hour. Every day for a week. (Laughter.) If it was a girl, she'd do the same thing.
>
> Yeah, and she'd hit you in the head with a ruler, and when they's in the woods got switches. Yeah, they'd send the oldest kid in the woods to get switches and tie you up. Then if you go home and tell your mama, or some of your sisters and brothers go home and tell your mama, you got a whipping, you got another one [at home]. You all supposed to (inaudible). But now it's different. If you whip a parent's child at school, they'd be out there with a gun and want to shoot you.
>
> Right. Yeah. If I go to your house and play with you, and you got a whipping, I would like to get one too. Yeah, I sure would.

Woody portrays a sort of social contract among adults that kept everyone in the loop and the "welcomed" obligation of spanking was shared by the "village" as part of "raising the child." He argues that today, parents, even those who request it by letter, are usually unprepared and unsatisfied when approached about spanking their child. Woody alludes to spanking at school as the pinnacle of historical school behavior, but his son and daughter-in-law seems to remember it otherwise.

Ross and Debra Winston

Ross Winston was the golden child of the Winston family as far as their family was concerned. Ross was mentioned quite often in the narratives of his father, partly because he was a survivor. Another unique thing about Ross is that he was one of the first black school administrators in northeastern Albemarle County. His wife, Debra, was skeptical at the beginning of my time with the family. She seemed to feel that I targeted her husband because he had been one of the pioneer black school administrators in northeastern Albemarle. Once I explained my "chain" sampling technique, Debra seemed to open up. It seemed to calm her that I selected their family because other families had mentioned them as people who would know about the early and late transition into school desegregation in northeastern Albemarle. Debra is a teacher in one of the neighboring counties and she seemed busy and tired each time I visited their home to talk. In the end, I felt that I had gained rapport with Ross and Debra, and the information they shared about their experiences of school desegregation both supported and countered that of their peers as well as members of the first generation, including Ross's father, Woody. Ross's perspective from the inside and outside of school policy making was crucial to understanding the full picture of school desegregation. Ultimately, Ross and I seemed to have much in common as insider and outsider, mainstream and homeboy, even though he experienced desegregated northeastern Albemarle schools a generation before I did.

Our first sentiments during discussion pertained to the school subsidy that northeastern Albemarle received for being a small school. The subsidy adds to northeastern Albemarle's overall per-pupil expenditures.

> SHERICK HUGHES: You know that there's a rural school subsidy that northeastern Albemarle gets, and I think northeastern Albemarle also gets a poor county subsidy [from the state of North Carolina].
>
> ROSS WINSTON: That's the small schools. There are small schools and (what's that term? It'll come to me in a minute), which Currituck County cannot participate in after this year because they have outgrown it. Their school population got so grown they can't get small schools.

Although northeastern Albemarle's overall per-pupil expenditure is similar to that of wealthier counties, it spends much of its funds on transportation to the three schools. Thus, northeastern Albemarle students and buildings fall into the tension of equity versus adequacy. Northeastern Albemarle would need a small school subsidy, and more, to improve the level of teacher effectiveness, culturally responsive teacher training, and increased student performance, whereby students reach their highest potential. Counties such as Orange, due to the types of families and children represented in the schools and due to the number of schools, can achieve more than northeastern Albemarle with a similar per-pupil expenditure. Although Ross agreed with this point off the record, his experiences as a student during segregation and as a parent and school administrator during integration offered the most compelling evidence for what northeastern Albemarle has not been able to accomplish, even with its comparably high per-pupil expenditures.

Fifty-two-year-old Ross, one of nine Winston children, identifies himself as a man "born and reared in northeastern Albemarle, and an African American." Ross and Debra are second-generation parents of two children who attended northeastern Albemarle schools. Ross says he tells people proudly, "I only went to one school, and I only had one principal. I went to one school and that was Marian Anderson High School, first grade through fifth." Ross didn't attend kindergarten, because "they didn't have kindergarten" when he began school in northeastern Albemarle. And Ross said with a smile that he had only one principal "in my entire life, Mr. Whitmore," during segregated schooling. Ross offered a narrative of school becoming boring to students and how the grades one to eleven student curriculum should be revisited. Ross said that another approach would be useful in the school experiences of the generation.

> You know, believe it or not, Sherick, I think you know with the information and stuff that kids are going through now, they might need to look at a one through eleven program. I'm serious, because kids get bored now and they're ready to move on. A lot of them now are taking college courses in high school, you know. So a lot of them are ready to leave. . . . Already sophomores [when they enter college]. A lot of people don't want to hear that, but I'm serious. They should look at shortening that twelve years.

Of course, not all students in northeastern Albemarle would be privy to the AP courses. In fact, black students in northeastern Albemarle and else-where in the state are disproportionately placed in the lower tracks, irrespec-tive of achievement. Perhaps Ross's position in school administration prevented him from considering the tracking part of the argument at that time.

When Ross and his classmates were in school, finishing high school was considered a good education for black folks. What he heard the older people saying was "this is a thing to get a good education," but that good education was simply a high school diploma.

> The primary thing is "finish high school." Everyone's goal was to get through high school, because most of our parents didn't finish high school. So that was their primary goal, was to get us through high school. Then after high school you know, if you could afford, or they could afford, you went to college. And the job market was good then because of the Vietnam War and the economy and everything was good, and you could get a good job. The job market was good then. You could get good jobs. At the Ford plants or [as] longshoremen or [in] communications. There were a lot of jobs out there when I finished high school.

These good jobs, however, were in Norfolk, as Ross's father mentioned. Black men of Ross's generation were unable to find such life-changing employment in northeastern Albemarle. This was partly due to northeastern Albemarle's reliance on agricultural work, and also the limitations of blacks for jobs in the other large county employer, the integrated schools. So that's what Ross was really saying about what a good education was supposed to get you, one of those good jobs—somewhere outside northeastern Albemarle. Other jobs were considered good back then, apparently, from Ross's narra-tives, as black people were moving away from farming and from work in northeastern Albemarle. Although Ross did not enter the military, he discussed it as a viable option for integrated, fair-paying employment for north-eastern Albemarle's blacks. Although the military had officially integrated during his father's generation, soldiers were taught to change their behavior, but not necessarily their attitudes. What Ross did not discuss was that black individuals such as Colin Powell have been able to advance on a case-by-case basis at the discretion of whites. Black soldiers as a group, regardless of performance, still face covert discrimination.

> Farming was a no-no. A farmer was a no-no. Don't work with his hands, farm, because my parents didn't say it, but I heard a lot of other parents say it. Their daddies had did that, and their daddy don't want them nowhere near that farm. But then there was a lot of people at that time, the military was strong too, these people, and especially blacks, because they were beginning to move up in the military. It was one of the most integrated places at that time. So the military was strong, and they were leaving and going to some of the bigger cities at that time. And also there was a thing about, you know, at that time, you know, there were a lot more blacks in this county than it is now.

Ross then discussed the employment and housing limitations in northeastern Albemarle as a cause for the depleting black population percentages. He argued that northeastern Albemarle blacks who aren't hired at one of the "good" jobs in Virginia, or offered one of the scarce "good" employment opportunities in northeastern Albemarle upon completing grade school are regulated to government housing—affordable housing in the neighboring county.

> Oh, man, yes. The black population of northeastern Albemarle has plunged, because we don't have public housing, so there's nowhere for people to stay, you know, so our poor people, and I hate to use that word, but our less fortunate people that need public housing, they go to the city.
> The only thing that we've got is EIC, you know a house, they'll probably get it for you, but as far as low-income or public housing, there is none of that in northeastern Albemarle. And a lot of people don't know it. That's why our income, the people that live in northeastern Albemarle's income is so high, because they don't have a lot of minimum wage jobs here and those people don't live in the county. They live in the city. . . . Okay! It's even more. Even more, because as I say, we don't have no place to put them.

Reverting to some of Ross's earlier memories, he talked during our first visit about a few of his experiences in school. He discussed both good and bad experiences that were poignant for him. Just as his father mentioned, he, like his younger siblings, were traumatized by the sudden death of their mother, who left behind nine children to experience segregation and desegregation with a single father.

> Well, my experience in school . . . I had a real good experience in school, up until I got to the fifth grade, and that's when I lost my mother, in the fifth grade.

I, you know, things wasn't the same then, but after I got over that, I still had a good experience in school.

Ross and I briefly discussed my observation that all the families thus far of the second generation came from huge families of seven, eight, nine, and eleven children, whereas members of the second generation had two or three children. On the one hand, Ross posited the advent of planned parenthood as one possibility for the decline in childbirth among blacks in northeastern Albemarle. On the other hand, he alluded to the need for more children for farm work. It was an interesting claim, since his father had discussed keeping the children in school and exposing them to field work only to show them that this was not work for them, that it was only those who chose to not complete a formal education.

> There ain't no way, you know. Our parents didn't have access to a lot of this birth control and stuff that the other community had access to. That's a good point. They wanted us to raise those kids so they could stay around here and work their farms. I'm serious. That's what they wanted.

Because Ross's grandfather was right there at the segregated school as the custodian, discipline was topic of much interest to him.

> He [Ross's grandfather] used to be a custodian in our school. He was a custodian at school from the time I was in the first grade until maybe the time I was in tenth grade.

Ross discussed discipline for black students who stayed out of farming as much as possible in order to attend and/or complete grade school. Ross offered a picture of discipline in school that was contrary to that of his peers from the second generation. He seemed not to romanticize the spankings and physical discipline. It was interesting to hear him say that, because I estimate that 98 percent of the people I had talked to previously said they wish that type of punishment was back in schools, and they think that's a big problem now, that we don't have that type of punishment any longer. Often it is connected to the biblical reference "spare the rod, spoil the child." And they feel that that was a large part of what black families lost during integration in northeastern Albemarle. Like his father, Ross argued that corporal punishment, with the interracial twist of desegregation and less culturally responsive teaching, would have ultimately brought more negative experiences for blacks. Unlike his father, however, he did not lament the loss of spanking as a form of maintaining order if the "races" could handle it without additional turmoil.

> I'm going to tell you what. I believe that we're over as far as punishment. I think the punishment in schools at that time was too severe for certain kids. And I've talked to a lot of people now that I went to school with that have problems, and they didn't have nothing to address those problems, no programs to address

those problems. And they just let the kids slide through school and you know a lot of those kids was problems in our society today because didn't get help with stuff when they were in school. I mean, if you went to school and you were, I don't know what term to use, if you had a known problem, hey, at that time they just slid you right on through school, you know. Because they didn't have programs to address those things with. They just passed you right on or whatever. But now it's different. Some of the disciplinary stuff was severe. I mean I've had teachers that would smack you. I'm serious. I remember this one teacher. The only thing that she would do was give you a backhand. She would backhand you. That's right.

It don't make no difference. You know, if you was writing something and it wasn't to suit the teacher, man, she would take a ruler and hit you across the knuckles, you know. It didn't make no difference. If there was anything that I would get, I wish I could have changed, I wish that that could have been addressed. But you didn't have anybody to go to, you know.

Now I would definitely differ with [other study participants], because some of the punishment that was given, and it all depended on if you was, you know, and a lot of people don't want to hear this, but there were the dark-skinned kids and there were the light-skinned kids. You know what I mean. And it all depends on what family you were from, or, you know, what connection you had. And the poorer you were, the worse you got treated. And I know that from experience. I know that from experience. It depended on if you went to this church, you know, the status of your family, or your family's status in the community, how you got treated in school. And that type of punishment that some of them give, you know, I would definitely disagree.

Ross continued to criticize some of the disciplinary efforts in his segregated Marian Anderson School, to my astonishment. He felt that if, for example, someone's mother or father had passed away, the school personnel seemed to feel that they had to keep spanking the child or "stay on them" to get them back "right," rather than try to offer something to help that child. From Ross's perspective on the subject, there was no sitting the student down and talking to a counselor.

Counselor? We didn't have no counselor. The counselor was the whip. The counselor was the whip. It wasn't the why you did something, it was what you did, and how you were going to be punished for it. Nobody looked at the problem that was causing you to do it, you know. They didn't know if you had problems at home, or they didn't look at none of that. There was no counseling at all in school.

Ross lamented the lack of a counselor and alludes to the fact that he himself could have used one in the segregated school as he dealt with the loss of his mother.

I can't speak for my wife, but I can say that a feel back, I feel like there was sort of a mourning here, because from '63 until '67, the time I got out of high school, I was still like in a mourning period, because I'm still trying to adjust to life without a mother, and I think my wife was in a similar situation. I mean, you know, her daddy got killed the same year my mother did. So we, there were a lot of other factors that we had to think about or trying to adjust to, and so really some of the challenges and some of the other stuff that might have been going on, I probably was concerned, but I still probably had other thoughts of moving on in life.

Ross offered narratives of both positive and negative experiences with the segregated school. One the one hand, he constructed a story that seemed to say that the segregated school was not all fun and games and filled with ethnic pride and virtue. On the other hand, Ross lauded the work of some of the Marian Anderson teachers in a way that reflected the positive, happy, harmonious stories of his peers. He said that sometimes teachers even drove students to ball games, because they never received an activity bus.

> And they didn't get no pay for it. They did it out of their pockets. I mean if there was a school activity or [inaudible] at another school, you know, people borrowed their parents' cars or whatever. And everybody packed them cars.

Ross also lamented the lack of a variety of sports choices in his school. He offered a view of football and other sports as good ways for young blacks to perform better in school and to pursue higher education.

> There's one thing that I do regret and I wished that we had had it, because I believe I would have been good at it. I regret that we didn't have a football team. That's one of my regrets. I believe that if I could have played football, had the opportunity to play football, I would have good at playing football.

And did Ross think that football might have led to him going somewhere else, such as college?

> Um hum. Yep. And you know a lot of the times, sports is very important to a child's education, because it helped that those extracurricular activities, you know, they are the rewards for your going to school and doing good. And I think at that time, the only sport that we had [was] basketball, and we might have had track. And then we had chorus, like glee club, the drama club, and stuff like that when I was in school. But as far as sports, the only two that we had when I was coming up, was basketball and track. And one of the most exciting days at school was May Day [an annual celebration of spring at the beginning of the month of May filled with outdoor educational activities and games set-up in the schoolyard].

Ross discussed other special things he believed the black schools did, schools such as Marian Anderson, Ivy Neck, and the Rosenwald schools in northeastern Albemarle. In Ross's account, the segregated black schools of northeastern Albemarle were similar in this way to those written about in

Caswell County (by Vanessa Siddle Walker) and Hyde County (by David Cecelski).

> Well, it was sort of like a meeting place for blacks. I guess it was something that the blacks controlled, you know what I mean, to a certain extent—their own PTA. It was just black-controlled, something that we controlled. You know what I mean? But when they integrated we lost that. And the black schools, we had all our black principals. And I remember Mr. Witherspoon would give, we used to call it Chapel Day on Friday. And he would call the whole school together on Friday, and each class would do a play on Friday, and you could talk black on black in school together. And you could tell a white [inaudible] for a black kid to get an education, you know, what blacks had to look out for. You could get that black one-on-one. Now you can't.

Where Ross's story took a turn was when he talked about assimilation. Unlike Siddle Walker and Cecelski, Ross adds a negative spin to what the black school offered in its curriculum. For Ross, it was a whitened curriculum, again challenging the simple story of the Afrocentric segregated school of the 1950s and 1960s. I wondered if courses such as history and social studies were taught any differently from Ross's recollection. Did the second generation, in their segregated school experience, get more of the complete story of black Americans?

> We didn't have no black history. We learned about subjects, I might deviate a little bit. We learned about the black what they want us to learn about. We learn about Harriet Tubman. We had teachers that would be innovative and try to give to us, but they still had a bridge that they couldn't cross, you know what I mean? We learned about the blacks that they wanted us to learn about. One of them was Booker T. Washington. You know, [and] Frederick Douglass. But you know, when I started reading about Booker T. Washington, now I look at him as another Clarence Thomas. I'm serious. Did you read about Booker T. Washington and his political views? I believe he would be another Clarence Thomas. But we learned about the ones that they wanted us to learn. I know a lot of the more popular schools around here was Tuskegee, Alabama. A lot of people went to Tuskegee. But then I got out and started doing some research on Tuskegee, you know, and I look at, hey, you know, people suffered down at that school. They had a lot of good people to go through there, but that Tuskegee experiment, and a lot of people suffered down there at that school. I mean, and that was the school that was picked for to educate the black leaders. That school was picked by the white community to for us to educate our kids, and at that time they taught them what they wanted to. Look at [inaudible], the state teachers college, if they wanted to be a teacher or something like that. But for you to get your degree in science or engineering, it was Tuskegee. That's where the blacks went to.

The Winston family pedagogy of struggle and hope added an additional level of complexity that seemed to illustrate more of the picture of school desegregation. Both generations shared narratives that lend themselves to pedagogy of hope storylines offering information to "grown on" from a past in segregated black schooling. Both generations shared a family story of educational struggle that has been and continues to be passed down to other family members. It is a story of living through the early crosshairs of school desegregation that ends in triumph and a look toward the future. Today, Winston family members of the later generation are perhaps the best examples of the successes of Winston family pedagogy and the educational resilience of their ancestors. Their family's pedagogy constructs another portion of the school desegregation story for its members, and anyone else willing to listen and learn from it.

This part of Winston family pedagogy is spoken to us most ardently by Ross who adds what he feels to be a teachable moment to our visit. He portrays the infiltration of a limiting key figures approach to addressing the contributions of certain black Americans in the school curriculum. Typically black key figures are those blacks known to and "approved" by a majority white school administration that also decides what parts of black heritage should be included in the intellectual repertoire of a valuable, culturally literate citizen. Ross suggests that part of the educational struggle and hope of his family involved supplementing the school curriculum to offer a more comprehensive version of black Americans that stems beyond a limiting key figures, cultural knowledge standard to a more holistic, critical knowledge approach where blacks are taught and regarded in schools as integral parts of the very sociocultural, economic, legal, and political fabric of this nation.

References

Hughes, K. (2003). *4th Sunday in the Dirty.* Charleston, SC: Imprint Books.

"I Prayed for the Children"
The Biggs Family and *Brown*

I PRAYED FOR THE CHILDREN
by Kent Hughes

I prayed for the children last night
I asked God to heal their minds
I asked that He give them joy
That only a child could define
I asked that He teach them wisdom
So only righteous . . . could they say
I prayed for the children last night
That they make it through the day

The Biggs Family

Larry and Rena Biggs

Praying for the children was woven into all of the elder Biggs family members' discussions of church and Bible study. Prayer certainly played a large part in how Biggs family grandparents ultimately gained and kept faith in the potential of formal and informal desegregated education. Larry Biggs discussed his take on school desegregation in northeastern Albemarle as a complex mixture of gains and losses for his family and the black community. Born October 11, 1928, Larry Biggs attended Ivy Neck School, one of the segregated schools for blacks in northeastern Albemarle in the early 1930s. The former school building is now home to the active membership of the Garden Light Church, which is located less than one mile from the Biggs home. Larry and Rena

Biggs were born in a time when more black families monitored, mentored, and sponsored each other and a time when white students passing by on their buses would not shy away from the "n" word. As Larry explained:

> Yeah. They used to spit at you. That's one thing. They pass you by and say "nigger, nigger, nigger, nigger." We came up on the rough side of the mountain. The blacks overcome so much.

His initial story of loss in desegregated schooling reflects a broken social bond among the adults responsible for the life of black schoolchildren. His narratives lament partly the loss of adults cooperating in rearing children (who may or may not have been blood relatives). Larry Biggs's notion of the black community sharing responsibility for the education of children is present in the narratives shared by previous black authors, such as Vanessa Siddle Walker. Biggs's tales of discipline and the relationship between the biblical "prayer and the rod," faith and discipline, closely mirror the accounts of Dora and Nolen Erskin. Larry argued:

> But see, that's the difference in then and now. See, everybody then raised everybody's children, and now nobody raises nobody's. Most of the time the children are raising themselves. See, actually what messed up was when they integrated schools. They took the rod out of the school. See, they were too, they didn't want any black teachers striking these, these white children. So they said, "Keep from showing racism." They said, "We won't let none of that happen." Because when I came up, just like it didn't matter, your age and everything, my daddy see me do something, he'd whip me and send me home and then I'd get another when I got home.
>
> Yes, sir. Yes, sir. Not only you weren't going to school in the lower grades. That was the same way when I went to up there to Sawyer's Creek School. See that house beside of it? That was my great aunt. But she'd sit on her back porch sunshiny days and watch them children over there at school just like I say a hawk watching. She'd see, and if she see any of them doing what they weren't supposed to, she'd tell you about it. Your parents would know it too, in a little while. She'd tell you. She'd tell you; mama would tell you. You didn't say you didn't do it. What they were saying, if they said an older person said you done things, they said what they telling stories on. You'd better not say anything. You'd better not say yeah. Because what an older person said, sometimes it wasn't true, but you could mistake somebody for someone else.
>
> Where we lost at was when they integrated and the time they took prayer and the rod out of the schools, that's where we lost because children have no respect now for their elders. They used to have prayers. Prayer was the first thing you did in the morning when you went into school before they were integrated. See, that was one of the main things. Settle yourselves together and have prayer and every morning, wasn't any warning, every morning. Since they took prayer and the rod out of the school everybody going wild because, see what actually messed up see when they put this law out that a child can divorce the parents.

Larry Biggs does not, however, bring to light the point that the same racialization he previously expressed as prevalent in the town could be problematic if the "prayer and the rod" were kept in the desegregated northeastern Albemarle schools. From his earlier accounts, it seems likely that the manner of prayer, shouting, and spiritual expressiveness of his black church would not be highly accepted by white school personnel. In addition, he wondered whether he would trust white teachers and principals to use the "rod" to spank fairly or to use lighter forms of discipline for black students. We already learned from Gean Whitehall, a white teacher, that even she felt her desegregated northeastern Albemarle high school "dropped the ball" when it came to disciplining white and black students equitably. The ambivalence of many whites during school desegregation perhaps made it difficult for the Biggs family to make this connection, even as they recounted the white hatred and fear tactics used against them. Some of the second-generation Biggs family were among the premandatory desegregation students, as Larry's brothers opted to let their children attend the white northeastern Albemarle schools during Freedom of Choice:

> When they started to say that you had to go, they accepted it. [Some in my family] went down to before they made it permanent you had to go, Lawrence's [Larry's brother] Leala, she started, and they burned a cross, and the cross burned in Lawrence's yard.
> Yeah, they burned a cross in his yard. Then Sister, Roger, and Bennie, they went. I believe they were kind of half-afraid of Gregry [another of Larry's brothers] because Gregry told them somebody was talking about burning a cross and he said, "Yeah," said, 'You burn a cross there, I'm going to shoot you." He even told the sheriff that. They were burning crosses. I don't know, I reckon they would go down the road to the first stop and walk and stick that cross and after he would light it a car would come along and go on.

Unlike his brothers, Larry waited for mandatory desegregation before his children attended school with whites. He and Rena claimed to have a productive relationship with the northeastern Albemarle schools. Their youngest child, Mack, was the only one to attend the integrated Northeastern Albemarle High School, and perhaps their positive relationship had much to do with the young age that most of their children experienced school desegregation. Larry explained:

> I didn't ever have any problem. Seemed like my children didn't ever get in trouble. Seemed like everybody, seemed like they liked my children. I don't know why. . . . We had a good relationship [with NE Albemarle's integrated schools] because when I go out there, I didn't have to go out there, but only one time because all the teachers when they'd meet me and some of them now that are there say, "You have a nice bunch of children." Says my children didn't ever give them, after Mack didn't, he was the only one that gave them any problem. But

he was a mischievous little boy. Of course he was the baby. I didn't have any problem with the school system. I thought they did a tremendous job.

Larry also admitted that he remembers his children interacting mostly with black teachers: "I don't think it was any different because most of my children, their teachers were black everywhere." He quickly connected his children's experience of having more black teachers for sponsorship and mentoring with his grandchildren's loss in the third decade of desegregated schooling in northeastern Albemarle. Similar to the narratives of the former black teachers narratives in Chapter 3 of this book, Larry Biggs said he is distraught with what he feels is a conspiracy to rid the school of most of its black teachers, and to keep only enough to be "in compliance."

> Not now. No, see that's what happened. Since all my children graduated and everything, see, those teachers that were there then see they retired, and they wanted to retire, see they replace it with a white teacher. . . . If a black person goes to a school to try to get hired, he's overqualified or it's no opening for that particular class that you're . . . trying for. That's one thing I can't understand why they have this overqualified.

Larry also offered criticism of blacks that have been elected by the predominantly white school personnel. Few blacks have become school board members or county commissioners in northeastern Albemarle over the history of the county. Larry argued that those who have seem somehow co-opted, "a little bit, yes," as Larry put it. In his opinion, elected black officials who have a responsibility to the schools neglect the needs of black students and black families:

> They don't want that. See, that's the reason why it's hard to find a black person to run for any political office in this day and time because it seemed like all blacks will not, I say, back them up. They'll stick you out there, but then once you get out there, yeah, I'm going to back you up, but times kind of get a little tight, I'm going to back up.
> They're not trying to push [the black man] out because I think, I say this, I myself, because he's a little bit—yes. If you get somebody that's going to stand up, right up for real rights, they try hard as they can. Just like, I think it's next month, election, see, now you've got on the school board, you've got two blacks running for school board [two black male candidates on the ballot for the election of school board members].

Larry returned to his family's loss and the black community's loss of direct lines of communication. He blamed school officials for pushing out those who would stand up for his rights. He also found the schools at fault for severing the ties of caretakers, beyond the biological parents of a child, to the school. This narrative again spoke of the loss of intergenerational relationships and finds desegregated schooling at the helm:

Yes, sir. Head folk, yeah. That's where the problem is at. . . . One thing in the school system I don't know what it is, afraid or what, but they can't get our black teachers to talk. If something they know is—is going on wrong, you just can't get them to talk. They say everything is all right, which they know it's ridiculous because I haven't been out to the schools much since they got this going now that just like my grandson, if he does something and they suspend him from school, I go out there and try to find out what it's about [but] because you're not his parents, it doesn't concern you.

Yeah. It doesn't concern you. You've got to be the guardian or the parent before they won't [will] even talk to you.

They [blacks with legitimized authority in schools] will not cooperate. See, they're just like a crab in a bucket. You take a crab, once you get all the way out but one leg, and they catch that and another one will reach out and catch that one leg and pull him right back in there, not going to let him do it. See, that's the way it is. They don't, they're afraid to help a black person to get ahead. See, what they don't know. See, no, I'm not going to help him. If they—two of us working together can get somewhere, then after I get where I'm at, then I can help you. See, that's what they will not fail to do.

Consequently, for the first-generation black family members, like Larry and Rena, going "out there" to the school became something bad. It meant that there was a problem, so in their narratives they seemed to pride themselves on not "having to go out there." Larry discussed going to school for only one of his many children, Mack, because he, like his father before him, was "mischievous" in the integrated school. Neither Biggs parent apparently stood up to go to the school initially, and both were reluctant to "go out there," a direct contrast to the intergenerational responsibility in the life stories Larry relayed from his segregated school years:

I said he was a little mischievous. He kept, I reckon, talking or doing something in school. Teacher kept sending him out to try to quiet him down and all that, so I tried to get my wife to go, but she wouldn't ever go. So one day I decided I would stay home from work and go out there and see what the problem was. So I went out there and took him right along with me. Went in the principal's office and sat down, and the principal was telling me about what he was doing and all that. So I told the principal, I said, "Now you do what you have to do here," but I said, "If that doesn't settle the problem, you send him home to me." From that, that was the end of that.

Rena Biggs interjected here with comments about desegregated schooling and hope:

You mean anything that I hope for. I hope my children do like I did. I mean, I hope people can do better than I did. The way I came up, it was hard. I mean, well hard, my mama and daddy, I mean my mama wasn't married to my daddy. My mama had to take care of everything. So I hope it would be better now than it was when I was coming up. I had it hard. Ought to be better.

Although the Biggs family limited their interactions at their children's schools, Mack and his siblings undoubtedly benefited from the pedagogy of education struggles mentioned above as well as pedagogy of education hope at home. Mack was a focus of their hope, and went on to graduate with honors from a four-year local HBCU, Elizabeth City State University, as one of the top three students of his class. Larry Biggs explained with a gleam in his eye and said proudly:

> He [Mack] graduated from there in with three of them with the highest honor you can get. It was him and a friend, one of his classmates from Deerfield, New York, and a white lady. I don't know where she was from, but he tutored the white lady, and she beat him one point. He's now something like a troubleshooter for the space shuttle.

The Biggs family narrative about Mack provides hope for present and future Biggs children and adults. It illustrates well that such narratives represent pedagogy—the narratives become educative tools for black families, such as the Biggs and Erskin families. This was the first time that I really began to understand family pedagogy to involve educative stories of hope. Larry's concluding statements about a trip that Mack prepared for his family to visit his work further elucidates this point:

> I've been up there five or six years ago, but he didn't, he was working. He didn't have the time to take me around much. But I think 2001 myself, Ellen, no Carla, Ellen, Ana, Mary, and we call her Sweets, Jenny, we all went up back and spent a week. He took that week off, and he carried us around, and he took us in where he worked. We even got a chance to ride in the space shuttle that John Glenn trained in. Everybody up there that I run in contact with up there was just loved him because when he went on the job showing us around, it was a few people working. He had to go in there and do a little work to show somebody how to do something before he left. It's amazing. He's got what you call, like on your radio, he go out, and he come back, he's always got a message. . . . He keeps checking, somebody's always calling him about something about the on the shuttle.

Rena participated fully during my third and final visit at the first-generation Biggs home. She was hospitable and vibrant, and was helpful in setting the mood for the early morning visit. "Do you want to cut the television down?" she asked. "Yes, that [turning down the volume of the television] would help me," I replied. Their story was again told through the narratives of struggle and hope, through experiences with one of their many children, the "golden boy" Mack. Larry and Rena glowed with pride as they chose to tell more of their educational story through events of Mack's life, displaying his work ethic, and their parenting, and his appreciation of their parenting.

> RB: He was a bad little kid.

LB: I reckon like myself. See, he wasn't anything but a boy. Along this time of the year, people pick corn. He would go in the field, made him a little cart, get the field and he gathered corn and go around and peddle it. He walked the road, and he'd see peoples' grass. Say want me to cut your grass.

RB: It'd be up before he got back home. He'd give us some money. Bring us some money back.

LB: Make his own money.

RB: Gin' [he had given] us some money too.

LB: He'd find him a job.

RB: Yeah, he would.

LB: I've seen that. He'd find him a job.

RB: Find him a job, but it was something

LB: School was out that's what he'd do. He'd find him a job, and he'd go to work.

RB: Uh huh. I didn't have but, didn't but one graduate from northeastern Albemarle High School. That was Mack. I had grandchildren to do it, though. She graduated there. I heard her say that it wasn't much different. I mean, they didn't pick on her or nothing. Mack said the same thing. He said the same thing. He graduated with honors.

At the Biggs home, I began to understand how messages of struggle were constructed as family pedagogy to provide hope. Hope through stories of struggle, a message of "see what I used to have to do, but see where I am now," from Biggs parents to children. In another dialogue between Rena and Larry, the story of trial and hope, of education struggle, has a bittersweet ending—and ending that seems to say that where they are now is better that what they had to endure to get there.

LB: I just would tell them, I says, "Just go ahead and try to be the best you can be." I told them, "I see things are not going to be like it was when I was coming, because you don't get. . . ." I said, "Try to get a high school education if nothing else," I said, "because I didn't get it." I see where I failed by being hard-headed, I say hard-headed because I had a chance.

RB: I didn't have a chance. I stayed and keep my mama's children. That's why I didn't go to school.

RB: [Women took care of their] Mama's children for them to go to work. . . .

SH: Did y'all used to tell your children, "Look, we had to do this."

RB: Yeah, I told them. "Y'all have got to keep on going and going," I said, "because y'all don't have to stay and keep any children," I said, "because I didn't ever keep any of mine home keeping children." I worked and kept them too.

LB: My children got started going to school and everything like that. Lot of this farm work you used to have to do, see, it was safety because they had the machinery and, see, before when I was growing up like cotton, corn, soybeans, stuff like that, that was done by hand.

RB: I picked cotton.

LB: Picked cotton. See, my children didn't ever have to keep them out of school picking cotton because I didn't farm. So there wasn't any price to pay.

RB: All doing all right.

LB: I made it. I had four children and worked for thirty, to mill for thirty-two dollars a week, fed the family and bought a piece of car [a used car regularly in need of repair or a lemon].

The Biggs narratives included a timeless message as well. The first and second generations of Erskins also offered portrayals of interactions that involved repeated words and phrases that were clung to from early desegregation to today, all to help the children through school. They were messages that did not specifically speak to faith or discipline, or the triumphs of one particular family member, such as Mack. The messages were like heuristics, little rules of thumb for the family to heed while remaining steadfast in educational progress. Another of Larry and Rena's dialogues further explains:

RB: The same thing worked. Didn't have to tell them nothing else. Didn't have to tell them anything else. Didn't tell them anything.

LB: Well, I told mine and they were in school, I told mine the girls and boys both, I told them. I said, "Go to school and try to get all the education you have." I said, "If you get grown and decide to marry," I said, "if you get married and the marriage don't work out, you don't have to look for nobody to take, to survive. You can get out and get your own, not depending on anybody." So I worked and wasn't making much money then.

Well, like I taught my children, don't care what a person say about, just don't retaliate back, you know. Just go on. They can call you anything as long as they don't put their hands on you. Just be cool because a lot of time do this and do that but they just want you to get in trouble. I tell mine, I said, "Just be cool." Don't give everything somebody tell you. Study hard and try to make it." I told them, I says, "Anything I can do, I'll try to do my best to do my best." I provide for my family. I used to walk from this place right here to Newby's Corner to go to work.

Faith appears to work two ways in the Biggs family narratives. On the one hand, there was prayer to stay healthy physically and mentally as well as to obtain equitable opportunities to reach one's highest potential. On the other hand, faith was a primary source for judging one's life outcomes as moral. For the Biggs family, Mack's work with the space shuttle is highly moral. Faith is strong in the Biggs family and the children apparently began with Sunday school at New Sawyer's Creek Missionary Baptist Church, where their father is a lifelong member.

> LB: Oh yeah. It worked. Some of them, not all of them I guess, when the government started passing these here grants. Well, I didn't have any hand in it but they fixed it up some kind of way. By the help of the Lord they all made it. . . . As long as the Lord is still on our side we'll make it.
>
> RB: I just kept faith, honey. I just kept on going.
>
> SH: Faith is what helped keep y'all going through.
>
> RB: It helped me.
>
> LB: Lord gives you health and strength, you'll make it. That's all I say. Because see, well, when I first started working out going help a man pull weeds out of peas or chop corn and stuff like that.
>
> RB: I did, too. I would have a baby and baby two weeks and go on back to work. Back in the field chopping corn, setting out cabbage, picking cotton. I've done all of that. As soon as I have a baby, every other year, but I still went.
>   They would die [women today]. I went back to work two weeks, that's right. We hardly had any doctor. I mean, you had a doctor, but they would tell me, they wouldn't tell you anything. I reckon they knew too that you had to go on to work or something. When I was here, I didn't ever hardly go back to the doctors. I went back to the doctor when I was pregnant again. Having another baby was when I went back. They never tell you anything like that. They kept on going working, working and having babies. That's what I did. All my life. I mean, until I got up here. Then my baby's thirty-eight.
>   I did my children the same way when I was . . . when they were smaller. I took them. I don't do it now. I don't go . . . but I did. I used to take my children to Sunday school.
>
> LB: Sunday school and worship, too. See, and it's like the Bible said, train a child in the way he goes when he is gone, when he is old.

From his early narratives, I sensed that Larry enjoyed school for the time he attended. Like most of the first-generation participants, however, he did not complete his formal education at a time when it was thought that "If you get a high school education you had good education." I had previously learned of the sense of responsibility that black northeastern Albemarle youths of their generation felt to help their families survive. The duty of helping the family to remain clothed and fed and to maintain food and shelter seemed to strongly influence decisions about formal educational. As Larry explained:

> See, the whole time I went up there to that school we would ride the bus from home to Hastings Corner, walk to school from there, from school back to Hastings Corner. I just went from the eighth to part of the term in the eleventh grade. Then I dropped out. . . . Well, see, the only thing, my daddy was a farmer.

I presumed that, like some of his peers from the Winston and Erskin families, Larry had little choice but to work and leave school so his family would survive a winter season. But it was because Larry was presented with a different opportunity, albeit a limited one in relation to his white counterparts at the time:

> Yeah. When I was going to high school, he looked, see he owned this farm here. He tended this farm; so my daddy owned it. See the reason I stopped, the crops got ready see he planted a lot of cotton and the cotton that you had to pick cotton. He didn't go to school on the rainy days, if it didn't rain, you did go to school. So after cotton had to gather corn. I gathered corn, and I just missed so many days and so my daddy did tell me, said, "Well, I'll tell you. Now if you want to keep on in school, I'll do all I can to send you, but if you don't go to school, you're going to have to work."
>
> So that's what I chose. I chose work. I stopped then and went to the farm, and after he got his farm laid then I went out and got me another job until . . . and I go to work on that job and make it plain to the man that I'm just going to work so long. For a few years I would work with my daddy two days a week and I'd go and work with the other job three days or reverse it. One week I might work three days with the man and two days with my daddy. . . .

Larry experienced the struggle, the notion that a black segregated education could get you somewhere else, but not really get you "somewhere." "Oh yeah," Larry later added. "When I first started working thirty cents or three dollars a day is all you'd make. Then every year . . . as the years go by the wages start going up." Larry seemed to understand the education–employment tension and the limits of education and work opportunities for black men upon leaving school at the time. Larry linked this tension to his choice to quit school. He went into some detail explaining this connection:

> See it was, about to say, there wasn't plenty of work but there was a lot of farm work. There were potatoes; there was cotton; there were beans. Things like that that you didn't have to have any skills for. Well, I reckon there weren't and that was one reason why I quit school. See, along when I was going to school, they weren't teaching any skills. There weren't any skills. Only thing you would get was that reading, writing was the first thing, spelling, going the first thing you would do you had to learn your ABCs, to say them backwards and forwards just like—then your multiplication tables and count from one to a hundred, and then multiplication one through twelve. You had to know all that before you start reading.

See, and I couldn't, wasn't any trade learning, just English, history, geography, stuff like that. Then . . . and all those folks right there, but see this day and time if that's all you've got, you're in trouble.

That mill work. Mill work and most were helpers. That's the only thing black folks were, helpers. Only way a black man got up in that way in my day and time he go and work with a white man and the white man thought enough of you to show you a skill. You worked hard and he liked it, he'll do all he could to see that you got a fair job done or pretty fair work. Then there wasn't anything but sitting here in this part of the county farming was the only thing. You had to go to Elizabeth City to get millwork. See, that's why two-thirds, that's what I've said, two-thirds of the people in northeastern Albemarle County now are working out of the state of North Carolina because nothing there [in NE Albemarle and Elizabeth City].

In the last visit, Larry again spoke about leaving school and his reasons for doing so. This final discussion about his educational struggle continued the thread of the problem of employable skills. Perhaps it was not until he reflected upon the pedagogy of education hope and struggle he shared with his own children that he saw the hurriedness of his own youth. If this was a new connection for him, it certainly became a revelation for me. For it was because of Larry Biggs's final statements about why he left school that I felt embarrassed about using the academic term "field work" to describe my research. My "pencil" work could not compare with the experience of black farm children of the 1930s and 1940s, who were doing real field work out in the fields. Their field was a place of backbreaking, finger-bleeding, hellish labor, and the children doing that work should have been in school like their white counterparts.

But I have always been a person that don't believe in begging, but worked out there, I say, after my daddy told me that I had to work, I said, "Well, if that's what I choose, so there's no need of getting mad because you've got to do it."

Well, I told them [his children] everything I could to keep them in there. I didn't want them, had to be out here demanding money like a lot of people because *if I had known then like I know now, I'd been like you walking around with a pencil instead of out here using the equipment* [emphasis added]. But I just wanted to get grown fast. Well, I just got tired of being out of school and being late. See, because I didn't ever miss any grades, but just had studies.

Then, like I said last night, see, there weren't any skills or anything to compete with today. When I was growing up. Those skills are gone until I got into high school, skill was welding or bricklaying. Didn't even have any carpentry class. Black schools didn't have any shops or anything. English, arithmetic, reading, spelling, writing, and stuff like that. That was then. Black folks back there used to make cheese out of goat's milk and all that stuff like that. See that's what we—me come up on.

Larry Biggs spoke as a man who was clearly reflective and reflexive about his educational life. He knew that schooling for a vocation like bricklaying rather than education through a vocation could lead a black person to employable skills without necessarily offering that person the knowledge for structural mobility to achieve educational aspirations that could take his family to places it has never been in America. Both the curriculum of traditional liberal arts schooling and that of traditional trade schooling were important for blacks today from Larry's assessment. At the same time, I felt that the type of field work that I was doing was important to him, but lacking in direct applicability to helping the daily educational struggles of people at home. I agree with him. And the time I spent with his offspring would allow me to trace how much of his early family pedagogy transferred to the educational life experiences of the next generation of Biggs family members.

Willis and Virginia Biggs

The first thing Willis Biggs recalled about integration was some racial taunting and slurs from white-flight students who were being bused from northeastern Albemarle to one of the area's all-white "academies." It is a story he has told before, but this time he appeared to search for more detail, for more meaning at this stage in his life as an adult, as a parent. The second thing he recalled, which he seemed to link with white busing, was Klan activity in northeastern Albemarle. He shook his head from in disgust and disappointment. Willis spoke of many northeastern Albemarle whites as living an existence he found to be unethical, ethnically insensitive, and "downright ignorant" at the time.

> Speaking of the bus, I always know for years, and I tell it once in awhile now, riding the school bus, and I think I was probably in the eighth or ninth grade, because everybody in northeastern Albemarle rode together. You know how the school did. They'd drop you off here, and then they'd go and drop off at one school and then they'd drop off at the other school. And you know where the stop light is going to my mama's house? Belfast Road, and there used to be a place called [Powhiteboys Store.] And that area right there was a pickup for [Albemarle area] Academy kids [to attend] when it was all white.
>
> That was like a stop for them. There would be like six or eight of them, where their parents would put them there, and the bus would come through and pick them up, you know, the Albemarle Academy bus. And you know, when our bus came to the end, they would either stick their finger up or say "niggers" or something like that. And we'd put the window down and say, "You white crackers!" I'll never forget that. (Laughter.) And you know, they would say it to us and we would say back to them. There would be a few whites on the bus, of course, because we had integrated, but it was just those mainstays, because it was Albemarle Academy then. It's called Albemarle School now, where black and white go now, but like I told them, it will always be Albemarle Academy to me. That's one thing I'll never forget. They used to say, "Niggers!" and we used to say, "You white crackers!" You know, just back and forth. And that was one of the main things. That was a pickup spot right there. There and then they did one down at northeastern Albemarle by the school.

Yeah, like they would make two stops in northeastern Albemarle. There wouldn't be many of them after we integrated. But it was those mainstays, like you say, "My child is not going to school with black people." Um hum.

They actually walked around in white sheets, too. Oh, yes. Northeastern Albemarle was one of the biggest counties [for Klan activity].

Willis discussed the importance of extracurricular activities such as athletics to drive a certain positive response from many whites. Such whites used extracurricular factors, such as black students' athletic abilities, as a guide to the student's value at the school which, in turn, steered the inequitable distribution of harsh treatment and/or privileges (albeit limited). Willis also spoke of how he believed that other black students suffered at school if they did not have a "good" family name, as the Biggs family did, with whites. Overall, he said his experience left him relatively unscathed personally, but that blacks lost much as a group:

I'm kind of different because I was into athletics, so I was looking to go to college on an athletic scholarship. You know, that was a way, you know, of course we couldn't afford to get to send me outright with money, so I had to go the other route, which I did get some help, and ended up going to college. But a lot of my friends, you know, they didn't get a chance to do that.

No, because as far as sports now, they just interacted. Of course, they went with their friends, but they would always try to pick the best black guys to go on their team. Now I do remember that. It might not be but one, but they would always say, "I've got so-and-so." As a matter of fact, in basketball I would always be the one black guy they would want. "I've got Willis!"

Because most of the time everybody, whoever, like we used to do, like pick a captain as they say, and he will pick all blacks, and he will pick all whites, but you would always come to that point where they would get one black, and nobody would get any whites, but the white guys would always try to get the one or two black guys like that. And it was funny how they knew that they needed some help.

But as far as interacting and playing and stuff, the young age wasn't bad, you know, and then because as we got older, it wasn't that bad either, because you had already grew up with them throughout so it started out as say riding the bus, because everybody rode the same bus—you know, middle school and high school, you know, everybody rode the same bus, so it was the older ones that always had things to say, and when they kind of graduated or moved on or whatever, then things got a little better as time, you know, just like anything. You know, time sort of heals all.

What Willis did not discuss until later, and what his father did not mention in our lengthy conversations, is that the Biggs children were held back so they did not have to desegregate until required. While being held back, Willis would not have been exposed to the harshest racism in school as whites had an extra year to digest the idea of what was happening. Willis told the story in some detail:

Right. Primary school was all white. Yes, it was the elementary school, as they say. And I think, if I remember correctly, it was actually third grade when integration came. I don't know what year it was, but we waited until it was mandatory. The next year was mandatory. The first year wasn't mandatory. You know, you could go if you wanted to. And Daddy and them, I think, kind of held us back until it was mandatory.

SH: So your dad held you back, and then for the fourth grade . . .

WB: Right. That's when we integrated. They changed the name to Northeastern Albemarle Middle School, or elementary, or whatever you want to call it for the Granville Primary was first through third, or kindergarten through third. And the fourth, fifth, and sixth, seventh, and eighth were the middle school. It was fourth through eighth is what it was back then. Then of course ninth through twelfth was the high school.

    Um. Well, it was sort of like, you know, it was new because it was something we hadn't came into effect before, you know we had dealt with white people in going to the store or working, and you know, stuff like that before, but actually mingling with the children every day was a different experience. It was something that we weren't used to, of course, but it wasn't as bad as everybody thought, you know. That's why I think Mother and Daddy held us back that year because they weren't sure what to expect, and so they were a little skeptical about [us] going to school with the white kids, and how they would perceive us as well as how we looked to them, so, but overall I think it did pretty good, you know. There wasn't that many incidents, I don't think.

Like Candice Erskin Brown, Willis remembered school as not being filled with attacks of racialization against him early in school desegregation. Both were relatively young when they experienced the early transition into desegregation. This point is important, as it means that their white counterparts would also be very young, and less likely to harbor years of deeply rooted racist practices at school. Willis seemed to understand the impact of his youth on his experience of integration. He recounted feelings of anger at racial slurs. He mentioned before that these comments were most often from the older children at the school, and he mentioned the slurs as nothing new, shocking, or debilitating. He offered a narrative that concurs with this interpretation:

I can't remember, of course I was younger. I think more bad things happened—well, I'm not going to say "bad," I'm going to say more incidents happened more on the high-school level, where the kids were older.

    We got along, because I guess being that young, you could deal with it. Kids saw you as kids, not as black and white, I'll put it that way. Because we got along pretty good with kids our own age. It was the older ones that would pick on you or say things about you, but the ones that were nine and ten just like we were, you know, they were just regular kids.

    You know, "Little niggers." You know the same things. "Go back to where you came from." You know, and those type of slurs. "You don't belong here." You know, stuff like that. It wasn't a lot of cussing, it was just those hard words.

That "nigger" word was like cussing to you, but it just made you that much madder because you knew you weren't that, but that's what they've always called you, you know.

They would say something, but it was more like there wasn't a whole lot the bus drivers could do. They could "turn you in" as they say, but you'd get suspended from the bus or whatever, but, and then too, you know it was like you wasn't supposed to tell. So if somebody said something, you still weren't supposed to tell on him, you know what I mean? Unless another older kid heard it, and then he would jump in it., and then there you go, you might have a fight or something.

It wasn't that bad. It really wasn't when I was coming along, you know. The early years weren't that bad for me.

The complexity and ambivalence associated with school desegregation were clearly illustrated in Willis Biggs's latter comments. On the one hand, he recalled life as a student where "the early years weren't that bad," and where policies were fair. On the other hand, Willis was able to weave in his dissatisfaction with the desegregated schools. Like the Erskins and black former administrators who participated in this study, Willis lamented the loss of black teachers, the ability of the black family to influence school policy, and the intergenerational closure among teachers, students, and schools. Willis said he does not foresee a change coming soon:

I'll tell you what, on that, with the policies, they wouldn't have been for me or anybody I don't think, or any black. They were strict on their policies, especially towards us, you know. It wouldn't have been no [inaudible]. Whatever we said wouldn't have even mattered. Because the decision was already made, but yet we're going to talk to you anyway. It's like we're not going to change our mind, but yet we'll listen to what you have to say. So, I believe we didn't have any way of changing their minds, especially about racial issues. The decisions were made before you get there.

Nothing like that I experienced, even with friends. Normally, when we were coming along, if they said it, the parents or the community found them responsible for what they said they would do. So it was kind of hard for them to go back on their word. If they publicly said it, then they had to go through with what they said. And I was never affiliated with anything like them going back and changing something. That never happened, you know, that I can remember. Northeastern Albemarle was pretty good when it came to their policies and actions. If they said everybody is suspended because of smoking or whatever, then everybody was. It was that a white was not suspended, or a black suspended because a white wasn't. If everybody was caught smoking then everybody was suspended. So they were okay in that aspect.

I think to me I was more comfortable with the teachers when they were all black, of course. The administration, you know, everything was all black, so you felt like they cared about you, instead of seeing this white lady here, just going on and looking at you as a number or chair or whatever. But you felt comfortable, and you saw these ladies other than school, too. You know, the teachers, you know, you would see them at church or at the store or something like that.

You know, you knew them other than that's Miss Richards, that's the teacher.
You know, you would see them other places, but these white teachers you didn't
see them other than at school, because you didn't. . . .

Probably in northeastern Albemarle I would think that they could have
kept, I don't know if they retired, but a few more black teachers. You know, it
was mostly white teachers when I was coming up. You know, even still. You
know, I think we didn't see that many black teachers after that. I know we
didn't. But they're not going to change. Right. Their mind's already made up.

Although the messages of black teacher shortages and loss of autonomy
and closure in schools were prevalent in the previous narratives, Willis offered
a different interpretation of integrated school resources. Only the former black
schoolteacher and counselor Harriet Talis discussed the lack of extra amenities
upon entering the desegregated school. Willis told about black students who
still received old books, even in the desegregated school, and about the great
new resources blacks were supposed to receive:

The resources, because I remember my book be old, and they had new books.
(Laughter.) I mean, you know, they keep passing them down year to year. And
when they changed they'd always give you the old book and their books were
almost new. . . .

Yes, you still got the older book. I didn't matter. Unless the whole grade
book was new. You know, like, say you were in the fifth grade and the fifth grade
got new books, then everybody got new books. But if that book was used from
year to year to year, you'd get the old book and they would get the newer book.
I ran into that many times. Yeah, we'd get the old books unless everybody got a
new book. Um.

Right. They [counselors] didn't. They didn't encourage us to go to college.
They didn't. And they didn't really help me get in schools. Like I said, our relationship wasn't bad, it was pretty even keeled.

"We gained less crowded schools," Willis added. Immediately following
that statement, Willis expressed a loss that seemed to disappoint him most,
the loss of religion in schools. As he noted earlier, Marian Anderson had a
gospel choir and the school had assemblies every Friday portraying the community's black cultural art and music. Like his father, he offered a narrative to
explain his experience of losing faith-based activities once schools integrated.
For both of them, the loss of devotion and prayer in schools signaled a decline
in morals, which they believe is largely the problem with current black students' and other students' performance:

When we integrated I think we lost. I think it was the beginning of prayer getting thrown out of schools, because the white people are a lot of liberals, and
they say "Don't push this on us," and "Don't do this," whereas we believe in
praying before, and the Pledge of Allegiance, singing songs, and all this good
thing. You know, because of devotion. You know, we had devotions every morning, and stuff like that. And we lost those type things. And that was the beginning of the end of prayer in schools. It really was.

That changed a lot of morals. That hurt a lot of morals in schools. The children too, because if you don't hear it all the time, you won't . . .

They said, "We don't need that." You know they were the ones initiated getting it out of the school system in the first place.

Willis's competitive efforts in sports also seemed to spill over into the desegregated grade-school classroom. To this point, no other participant had discussed feeling the competition with whites that they had not previously felt with their black peers. Willis's narrative on this subject paints a picture of black white competition as being helpful for him. He did not seem to connect this competition as working against other families that he felt suffered in the northeastern Albemarle integrated system much more than his own. Willis also did not see the more collegial, highly expectant learning atmosphere of the black school as something that was lost at the hands of competition—a competition that whites at the top of the hierarchy wanted in order to weed out black students, in a sense to prove a point. Willis spoke at length about his experiences with competition in the desegregated school without making its other, negative connection to oppression:

I guess integration brought about an opportunity that maybe we wouldn't have had to, say, go to college, because you start to seeing how these other kids were thinking about college, and so forth, because I know myself, I wouldn't have went to college if maybe it did stay all black 'till I was twelfth grade. I'm pretty sure I wouldn't have. Playing ball or not, I still probably wouldn't have went to college, because you know we didn't see college as a thing I guess that we could achieve. You know, because I was in school like most guys, just to get out. I didn't, I mean, I gave an effort, but I didn't put forth the effort I probably should have.

But you see those white kids over there, and you're looking at a [test score of] 72 and a [white kid has a] 92 and . . . that make you want to get a little [better], so it did push you a little bit to try to do, you know, so you wouldn't feel inferior, you know, or as we say, dumb.

Like I said, one of the biggest changes was, you know, like we were talking earlier about being competitive. When you see little Johnny's paper. He got 92, and you got yours and it's 72, then they'll look at you like you're not so smart, as they called it. Then you would try your best from then on. You know, it would bring out this thing in you where, "I can't let him outdo me!" "I can't let him think I'm dumb." "I can't let the teacher think that I'm less than average. You know, I need to be a little better." So it brought out—it made me study more. It made me try to listen better in class. So that was the biggest thing, I think, for being integrated. It helped us understand that competition aspect. Even though you looked at it with them, but it was still within yourself, because you knew you had it in you anyway, it's just that they brought it out of you a little quicker 'cause, you know, it didn't matter whether my friends made 92 or not. You know what I mean? That was great for them. But if little Johnny made 92, he can't beat me! You know.

Toward the end of our discussion of the early transition, Willis claimed that some black families were left behind. He had just spoken about competition and how he felt that competition helped his grades. Some black families apparently did not benefit from feelings of competition. Willis explained how the black family name was crucial to a child's school experience. This meant that the name of a black family deemed by white school personnel as a "good" black family went a long way toward how an individual black student was treated. Willis elaborated:

> I'm sure it would depend on who the kid was, and, like you say, if the parents would come out and question the suspension or try to you know try to find out what's going on, that black kid probably would get longer time. I mean, that happens all the time.
>
> Well, I think so. Um hum. One thing I found out through the years, white people in general associate families. Now if, just like myself, knowing me and then knowing my daughter, if she had children and they go to northeastern Albemarle County, they would associate those children with me and my family and would say, "That's a good family," not know if the kid's good or not. You know.
>
> You know, if the kid's bad, you know, "He's not their child. He's from another set." It's like they associate good with good and bad with bad, so they're going to keep thinking if that father gave them trouble, they'll think the son will give them trouble, is what I'm trying to say.
>
> And the son might not even give them trouble, and they say, "He was bad, and now there's his son," and the boy may not have said a bad word to them. You know, they associate like that. You know twenty years ago, on down the line, they associate you by families, I think. If you were a good family, then they think everybody's good in the family. If you were a bad family, or one kid's bad, then everybody's bad, and that's not the case, but they really categorize us in that manner.

In his final comments about the struggles that came from school desegregation, Willis offered a message about agency and structure. Like Candice Erskin Brown, Willis seemed to understand that there is a power structure in schools and the society engulfing them that can be more culturally responsive to black students in the latter years of integration. His narratives on this point, however, relayed an equal feeling for the impetus of young blacks to be responsible and to set high goals for their educational lives. For Willis, students are also accountable for being irresponsible by failing to use a changing integrated climate to their advantage.

> I think that the perception of the [white people] . . . People can see black kids as something less than what their [white] kids are, I'll put it that way, and you have to strive and get them to see that they're just as good, can do far better than what they are trying to reach to. They limit themselves. They would just take what's there in front of them instead of reaching a little higher to try to gain a goal that, you know, they just don't set goals. I guess that's a better way of say-

ing it. They need to set some goals and set them high. I see kids all the time coming in and out of that recreation center, you know, just whatever. You know, like "Did you go to school today?" No, sir. They'll just come out and say, "No, sir, I did not go." Well, what're you doing over here today? You know, you're not supposed to come over here when you don't go to school. You know, and stuff like that. You know, it's just amazing. I'm talking twelve-, thirteen-, or fourteen-year-old kids just don't care. And that's not good.

When I realized that I did have a talent, such as playing basketball, I could get in. I've always worried about, you know, my daddy did the best he could with us. And I always didn't want to put another burden on them for paying for my school, so when I realized that I was good enough to play college basketball, it dawned on me then that I could get a quality education and could do something that I enjoyed doing. So that's when I realized that, "Hey, go for it."

Right, instead of just . . . because I knew, you know, I knew a 6'1" guy that played center all his life would never make the NBA. I knew I had to use my talent, what I had to gain me an education. Then I could provide for my family, or even if I didn't get married, I could still provide for myself, and come back and not just hang out on the street, or just be another statistic.

Stay in school. You need to get as much education as possible. Of course they don't want you to do anything anyway. I mean you know basically, you know. Like with [his daughter] Kady, she went on and got her master's and is doing real well. But you've always go to strive for that goal. And education is a key. An educated person can go a long way. You know, a lot of people, you know, way before us, went through the struggle to get us to where we are, and we have to take advantage of it just like that.

Willis and Virginia Biggs' Pedagogy of Hope

"There's hope in education," Willis declared as soon as we began our third visit. Even so, he recalled many of the white teachers having little hope in black students as he entered the desegregated school. Early in our conversation, Willis responded, "They [white teachers] didn't have hope so you had to get it from home." The internal dilemmas and ambiguity of how desegregated schools played out were evident in his narratives. For soon after Willis recalled that he had to get hope from home, he sighed:

> I just, like Mother and Daddy, I just wish they had pushed me a little more, made me realize my potential a little earlier, because, like I say, I wasn't in trouble, it was just that coming along then, you did enough so you wouldn't get left behind. And as black males, you know, you were a little tougher anyway, because they didn't think you were supposed to be an A/B student, you know? And it was kind of rare, because black guys just did 70 work, you know, just enough to pass.

One powerful way that Willis got hope in education was from the few remaining black teachers after northeastern Albemarle officially desegregated its schools. "You had to get it [highest potential from education rather than

training] from a black teacher," he noted. He went on to discuss the importance of Mrs. Lois Whitmore in his life and in his obtaining hope in education.

> Mrs. Whitmore . . . I had her in the seventh and eighth grade, 'cause then, you
> only had one teacher who taught you everything, you know, and one day I think
> I was acting up bad, and she said, "I'm going to call your daddy," and so forth,
> "and straighten you up." And then she told me one day, "Willis, you're a good
> student. You've got a good attitude, but you like to play too much. You don't
> take things seriously." This was seventh grade. I'll never forget it. She said, "You
> like playing ball. You're a good ball player, but you've got to realize that other
> people are watching you." Which meant other kids, and faculty, and everybody
> was watching. And it never dawned on me that, you know, I'm being a clown,
> and I thought it was funny, but other people were looking at it like, "That guy,
> there's something wrong with him or something." And she made me realize
> right then that without a good education people are going to perceive you as a
> dummy. If you don't have even a high-school education, they're going to say,
> "He never finished school, so he can't do anything." She made me realize right
> then that I needed a good, solid foundation to get started, so I buckled down,
> and went on from there. And I ended up going to college. And that's always
> been in the back of my mind. I never thought about college, but I always had
> that glimmer of hope that I would go, and then, like I said, by the time, I was a
> senior, it dawned on me that, hey, I can go . . . I can really do this. But she was
> a feisty old lady.
>   They [the few black teachers] would always come up and say, "Are you
> doing all right?" You know. And, "Keep up the good work," if they found out
> you did something good, and stuff like that. But it wasn't many.

The second component of hope in education that Willis offered was
related to what I call "timeless messages." This is a category to recognize
words and phrases that a family repeats to its children and at family gatherings
with the students' wellness in mind. Willis Biggs, like both generations of the
Erskin family, conveyed the messages that he heard as a child and which he felt
were useful for maintaining hope and confidence in his youth. Although
northeastern Albemarle schools had moved to a different time in desegregation, Willis seemed to believe in these words as being transferable to the experiences of his two children. I later understood that he was relaying these
timeless messages to me so that I could carry them on; to either use them for
myself or for my children. It also seems that in relaying these messages, he
added to his own level of comfort about his actions and his parents' actions in
providing tools to motivate the students in the family. As Willis said:

> Well, it just made me realize that I wasn't less than they were. You know I was
> just as good and equal. I was not less as a person. I could learn just as well as they
> could, you know. I could do whatever I wanted to do, don't let anybody tell you
> any different. You know, it was always that reassurance that they gave me that
> you can do, you can do. No matter what they say, you can do. And Daddy always
> said, "Don't give up on yourself. No matter what anybody tells you, just don't

give up on yourself." You know, that confidence factor that they was behind me, and you know, feeling that they listened to what I had to say.

Yeah, like they might say something, you know, like somebody mentioned something to bother me, and Dad would say, "I'm going out to the school," or something like that, and I would say, "Nah, that all right." I said they didn't hit me or anything. I said words are just words. Everybody's saying it and everybody's doing, 'cause, you know, once in awhile, you know, everybody get flared up, and so, you know, to keep him from going out to the school, which I say he didn't have to go out there for me. You know, just to keep peace, I'll put it that way, so he wouldn't have to do anything that might embarrass himself or cause us kids, we didn't want our parents coming to school now. Back then I didn't anyway. You didn't want them to come out to the school, because you didn't know if they were coming to get you, or somebody else. But Daddy would get me just as good if I was in the wrong. But they backed us. I'll give them that.

Just get all you can get. You know, just get the best education you possibly can. Just don't go through the motions. You know, learn and grow. Because just like me and my job, because Daddy worked for the city for almost thirty years, and he'll tell me right now, that "Stay right there. The money ain't great, but you know the benefits are," and stuff like that. To our kids, do the best you can. You know what I mean, with what you've got. Just make the most of it.

Then I strived for 85 and above, because that was a B, as they say. Because they graded on the 7 point. It was 10. A is 100 to 93 and then 92 to 85 is a B. So anything other than an 85, 84 was a C, but 84 was a good number, you know, but you still strived for that 85. You wanted that B. And as long as you were in the B range, you know, I know you settle for certain things, but if I got an 84 or an 83, then I had to settle for it. But I was striving for that 85, that B. I have them [his children] to strive for the A now. See, like I say, you live and you learn. And now with our kids, we've always said, "Do the very best you can. Don't just settle for . . . [waitress interruption]. But we always try to get them to do the best that they can. "Try for that A, even if you don't get it. Still try for it."

The Biggs family, in Willis' portrayal, was a sort of poster family for whites to place on a pedestal during integration. Although he graduated two-and-a-half decades ago, his family would have fit the white model of what a black family of students should be at that time. The Biggs children were good athletes and students who did not cause much trouble. For whites, the black athlete, the "superspade," was important for bringing pride to a school's athletic program, similar to today. The superspade was a black athlete with exceptional talent beyond most athletes of any ethnicity. The practice of whites in selecting one or a few superspades to dig teams out of the muck of defeat into victory certainly contributed to the stereotypes of black athletic prowess. Of course, whites were happy with black students who would most often not retaliate in situations where they were called "nigger" or treated as second-class students. Willis explained in depth the position of his family within the desegregated schools as they portrayed the type of black people that "should" be at the school. It is important to note that blacks who were not superspades, and who became aggressive in school upon hearing the "n" word, were deemed troublemakers and pointed to by whites in power as the reason why desegregation was useless. The dynamic apparently worked so well for Willis's family that he did not even recognize the racial disparities in discipline, when even white teachers Gean Whitehall and Barbara Needham did. Willis argued:

> I thought it was pretty good. You know, our family was well known, because we were all in sports, even my sisters, and you know I think I respected the system, you know. It was just hard sometimes in the attitude—let me see how I can say this in a good way. Some of their discipline procedures, I'll put it that way, they might be a little bad as I was coming up, and then as Kady was going to school, you know, it was like a twenty-year difference and their procedures changed, which, of course time changes a lot of things. I mean, procedures about discipline throughout the years.
>
> The suspensions and stuff like that, you know, I think they're a little quicker nowadays than they were when I was in school on suspensions, because they do long term suspensions now, where a kid will get kicked out of school for a year, and can't come back for a whole year, which is good now. But when I was coming to school, you might go home for two days, and you're right back. And that's for fighting, you know. But I think the Biggs [family] had good relationships with northeastern Albemarle schools.
>
> I never had to go out there for Kady. I mean, she wasn't a bad girl or anything. The only time I had to go out there was when she received an award or something. Or she played in a game or something like that. So I never had to experience where I went out there in a bad kind of way, you know. It's always been a recognition type thing when she was in school. That's a hard question how they perceived me. I mean I guess in that manner they treated me the same.
>
> Right. And that may have helped because there were so many of us, and you know nobody really gave the northeastern Albemarle County schools much trouble. You know, my sisters didn't, and I didn't, and even Mack and Marshall didn't. Like you say, I think you know we had that label of a good athletic family, and of course being as long as you are doing for them, they like you. I mean, you know.

Willis and Virginia also found hope in their human agency (belief in self to operate and even manipulate a given structured social space) as a black parent couple. This human agency (Giddens, 1979) was highlighted by Willis and Virginia, particularly in their ability to teach their children to code-switch. Code-switching is a term used by Hecht, Collier, and Ribeau (1993) and others to describe black persons who can easily traverse the borders separating mainstream English and black English vernacular or Ebonics. For their family, teaching their children to code-switch provided hope that their children would reach their highest potential in America. As I did, prior to this dissertation, Willis and Virginia did not add to the equation that there are two crucial points in black American life. First, although their child may code-switch, there are trade-offs to consider and internal dilemmas as one crosses the language border. Second, although their children may have the ability to switch language codes when necessary, that does not offer them the ability to escape the white power structure within which they are bound. This white power structure of northeastern Albemarle, for example, still fails to hire black teachers and principals who are qualified, regardless of their ability to speak "the queen's English." Virginia Biggs discussed this point:

> And when to speak what kind of language. So I tell the kids, "Pretend you have a plastic spoon, you have a stainless steel spoon, and you have the best sterling silver spoon. Okay? When you're out in the hallway, and when you're on the basketball court, and when you're around your friends, you can use that plastic spoon all you want, because it's like a picnic. You can use it all you want. But when you come to my classroom, I expect you to use that stainless steel spoon, one that you use every day. You know, good language, no slang and all that. But if I give you a speech, and you have to come up in front of the class to deliver that speech, I expect you to pull out that sterling silver spoon—the best language you have. So you need to know when to use the different languages.
>
> And you don't have to lose it [black English vernacular]. Nobody's saying, "Never use that."
>
> I have to tell my daughter [it's okay to code-switch] because she said, "You don't talk like that at home." I said, "You can expect me talk at home like I do in school."

Just as Willis' mother and father spoke of their family's educational prowess through one child, Mack, Willis spoke of it through two golden children. For Willis, his use of timeless messages ensures motivation for hope in education. And his older daughter, who has received a master's degree, and his young son are examples of how those work, thereby leading to more hope in education. Of course, Willis and Virginia also find hope in their agency to influence their children's versatility with the English language. In teaching their children how to speak for different audiences, they find hope that their children will reach the top of the educational-economic hierarchy. The stories of Kady (Katrina) and Lee have become part of the families' intergenerational narratives of what can be, of what a Biggs can become, in light of educative narratives of hope and struggle.

> She went to Mississippi State, and then she got her master's at Howard University. Oh, man. What you talking about [I'm so proud of her]?
>
> Like with Kady, what I told her is, because see at first she wasn't thinking about going on, just coming out and do four years and get a degree in social work. But she had what you call that natural gift of just learning, just picking up things, and just grasping, so she was an A student, A/B, whatever you want to call it. So she applied and got in. And I just kept telling her, "Get all the education that you can, because that's something they can't take away from you no matter what."
>
> I said, "You go out here and get in corporate America, and think about 'Well, maybe I should have went.'" I said, "You've got to do it now while you've got your mind on school." And so I just said, "Just get it all now. Just get all the

education you can." You know, like Lee now, we want him, even though he's only four, we tell him—you know, he goes to preschool . . . preschool as they call it. And it's integrated . . . and they get along real well. And you know, he's adjusting, and he's learning, and like I said, kids don't see black and white, at that age. That's my little man, and that's good. And we just hope that he'll grow and learn as much as he can. I just hope things will get better. You know, with time, and I think it will, by the time he gets in middle school or something like that, we'll probably see another turn. . . . He loves it. He loves it.

Because she [Kady] had the opportunity to go to Carolina State and Duke, too. And of course she didn't want to leave home, but like I was telling her at the time, you know, you have to grow them wings and go on out on your own and take chances. And see, like your little brother, we're going to try to get him to realize that, you know, the sky's the limit.

In the following exchange, Willis seemed to use his experiences with his first golden child to inform his pedagogy for her little brother.

SH: You're going to get him to think about it early.

WB: Right. Get him to think about it early. . . . Not just wait until you get into high school, in the eleventh or twelfth grade, and start thinking about college, you know, think about it in the eighth or ninth grade. . . . Get your ducks in a row early. . . . Exactly. I know I didn't think about college probably until January or February of the year I was to graduate. I hadn't even thought about it.

The final component of hope in education found in Willis and Virginia's narratives was faith. Again, faith seemed to operate in two ways in relation to the Biggs family's education during desegregation. Faith was there when times got rough in schools, when being called a "nigger" was difficult to stomach, and yet the need to complete school remained strong. Faith was also there to remind the Biggs children that an education for blacks in America could afford them a moral life. These messages of faith suggest that the dual function of religious faith for forging hope in education was clearly transgenerational in the Biggs family. Willis also offered a brief window into understanding white policymakers and their reasons for approaching the faith-based black community to serve their own political needs, rather than advancing black families:

We lived in church. Daddy was always, Mother and Daddy have always been a big part of the church, and they made us, see I said "made," us go. I mean, you know, of course we went, and they made sure it was a big part of our lives. And Sunday school. Yeah, we had to get up and go to Sunday school.

Oh, yeah. When I was in school, you needed faith in the Lord, because, as they say, some of these things that were happening, you would lose your religion over. [Laughter.] You know, because of the way you were treated, you know, but like we've always believed in a strong faith in the Lord, trusting in Him that He would guide us through, no matter what people said or what people did, that He had a plan for us. And that's what we believed, that he had this plan mapped out for us—hey, you're going to go to college, you're going to succeed, you're going to come out, you're going to get married, you're going to have a family. You're going to be able to tell your children, "Continue what we've started." You know, just keep on and branch out, and just go. But faith in the Lord has brought us a long, long way. And that is the backbone.

That really is, because you know, we've always been interested in it since this high, whether you want to go or not, they will take you. And once you got there, just like your whole attitude changed. So I know as I've gotten older, I'm going to church more now than I did when I was younger because nobody has to make me. I want to go. I want to learn and listen and understand.

And now we're bringing up Lil' Bruh [Willis and Virginia's son, Lee] in the same manner, you know some Sundays, "Dad, I don't want to go!" But he goes, and once he gets there, he has a little bounce to his head [inaudible], and that's the foundation. And if you've got that, and then when you're in the [inaudible] and things start to get a little tough, and your classes start getting a little hard, you just fall back and say, "Lord, I just need some help. Just help me." He'll bring you through. You know, you got a B or an A, and "Thank you, Lord. Thank you." I mean religion plays a big role in any black family. That's why it's amazing when you see a lot of us thinking that they are on their own.

Yes. They [whites] will [come to our church]. The only time they come is when they want something.

Through his schooling, adulthood, marriage, and parenthood, Willis followed most of family pedagogy of his parents and grandparents. It is a family pedagogy steeped in religious faith and the connection of spirituality, prayer, teaching, and learning. The family prides itself on its diverse abilities and internal teachings. On the one hand it values the need to learn how to navigate and do well in schooling by the traditional white middle class standards. On the other hand, it relies upon a supplemental family curriculum that engages Christianity and a balance of vocation and liberal educational tools to live closer to the way they feel God would have them to in our society—to do best with the family pedagogy God has afforded them in the place and time of the birth of each Biggs generation.

References

Berg, S. (1975). "What's behind the N.C. 'earnings gap.'" *The News and Observer,* November 2, pp. 3, 8, Section IV.

Giddens, A. (1979). *Central Problems in Social Theory: Action, Structure, and Contradiction in Social Analysis.* Berkeley: University of California Press.

Hecht, M.L., Collier, M.J., & Ribeau, S.A. (1993). *African American Communication.* Newbury Park, CA: Sage.

Hughes, K. (2003). *4th Sunday in the Dirty.* Charleston, SC: Imprint Books.

FIGURE 1: Black Desegregated Cafeteria Workers

FIGURE 2: Black Desegregated Students at Church

FIGURE 3: Black School Bus Driver

FIGURE 4: Rural Working Class Black Grandparents with Grandchild

FIGURE 5: Rural Working Class Black Youth

FIGURE 6: Segregated Black Class

5 The Erskin and Winston "Life's Play" in *Brown*'s Theater

LIFE'S PLAY
by Kent Hughes

I'm known for being in control of my direction
Taking the lead part in the play of my life
Never getting emotional, I'm exceptional
With a mind as sharp as a knife
Always challenging the storms with protection
Knowing the clouds can't rain me down
I love me so I show me affection
I'm programmed to when no one's around
My strength comes from so many places
My cries are buried deep inside
My faith battles the monsters of my many faces
And hope reaches out with arms open wide
I hold myself responsible for my happiness
Anticipating and appreciating each day
I will search for peace nothing more nothing less
And let GOD be the critic of my play

Part I: The Erskin Family

Dora and Nolen Erskin

My second visit to the home of Dora and Nolen Erskin home was on a brisk fall day on October 23, 2002. At this point, the family stories were becoming more like a play to me and each person had a script and role with pedagogical dialogues, internal monologues, and soliloquies all performed in a post-*Brown* educational theater of hope. During my second visit to the Erskin home, we talked more about their relationships with northeastern Albemarle's desegregated schools. Dora was to be home all day that day, so we set a time to talk near 11:00 A.M. Memories waxed and waned, but the negative images and feelings of the time were clear and poignant. Dora first discussed an incident involving a daughter, one of her eleven children, and a "white boy," which intensified the girl's fear for her safety at school during the early transition into 1970s desegregation.

> I don't remember anything that happened in my family with children [during desegregation] . . . but I had one, she carried a knife to school in her pocket every day. . . . There was a boy [white] had ran into her and knocked the books out of her hand on the floor, and then that's when they scuffled and fought and called one another names and this and that. From then on she carried a knife to school in her pocket.

Of course, the incident begged reporting, but there was no acknowledgment from the school, not even to Dora and Nolen. "No. No. No! Kept it quiet," Dora explained. "The teacher didn't even contact me about it." Dora continued the story later that day:

> Now he [the white boy] thought that was going to be a big thing, but nobody paid it any mind; so they went on like they ought to. He thought somebody else was going to come along and do something to somebody else. Like he was trying to start something. . . .
> I don't remember exact words. But I told her I said, "What did you do?" She said, "Mother, he ran into me and knocked my books out of my arms and I told him pick them up. He told me he wasn't going to pick them up. 'You pick them up.'" So that's when they went to hitting and pushing and tussling, wrestling, you know. . . . That's when I found out she had a knife. I didn't know she was carrying a knife until that happened. Maybe she told me, "If I could've gotten to my knife I could've cut him or something." I said, "What kind of knife?" I said, "What kind of knife?" She said, "Mother, I carry a knife in my pocket every day." I said, "Show it to me." She looked in her pocket and showed it to me. It was open. Sure did. She wasn't taking anything off them [white students]. I said, I told her, "Don't do it. You don't have to take anything off of them. Don't stand back like you're scared."

Nolen expressed the mood of the times to help me understand how this sort of incident could be left unresolved. It was his longest reply to any of my questions. Dora explained what she said to her children during the 1970s and 1980s to help them deal with their white peers:

> I'll tell you the truth, what I told mine. I might have been wrong. But I told them, "Don't pick any fights with anybody. If anybody hits you, you hit them

back; you fight them back." That's exactly what I told them. "Don't bother anybody until they bother you. Stick up for yourself. Don't take anything."

Nolen soon added that the problem with school desegregation as seen by whites was "They don't want blacks on top." Nolen's statement was undoubtedly fueled by situations with his daughters: one was assaulted by a white boy, and another was refused the opportunity to skip a grade because she was black. Only one of their daughters graduated from Marian Anderson. Perhaps, if the other daughters had attended Marian Anderson, such atrocities would not have gone unanswered. Dora believed the all-black atmosphere served her family better locally, but she seemed to have less faith in the ultimate power of the state to deny the educational rights of her children. I asked Dora, "If Marian Anderson had wanted your child to get to another grade, do you feel like they would've worked with you a little bit better and that your child would've gone on and moved from one grade on, skipped to the other?" Her reply was simply "No." When further questioned, "Because of the state?" Dora abruptly lamented, "Right."

When asked about what some of the things were that they thought their children lost due to integration, they couldn't note any losses, only gains. As the tape was about to be turned off for the second day's visit, Dora began a new narrative, relating pain of the past to violence of the present—a narrative offering insight into her messages for her daughters to not "take anything" from whites during school desegregation as the climate had shifted from memories of her youth in the 1930s.

Part of Dora's reflection on education struggles was introspective. She suggested things she could have done better to help her children through integrated schooling. Dora posited that at least a portion of the issue was the lack of recourse for school offenses against her children, which was distressing to her and a burden she had to bear. Indeed, her narrative on this topic relayed regret and a shared responsibility of the parent and the school to buffer black students as they went through a desegregated northeastern Albemarle school. As Dora said:

> Maybe if we had done more, maybe, but we just didn't get involved like we should've gotten involved. I wouldn't have had to have parent–teachers meeting. I didn't attend that like I should. I didn't know what was going on. . . . Like I say, I didn't attend, I should've gotten involved more.

To the question, "You think you would've felt more comfortable if it had been a black school?" Dora replied, "I think I would."

Fortunately, education struggles endured by the first generation of this family were tempered by educational hopes—hopes based on experiences of perceived positive changes in their family's quality of life and of teaching them to others. Toward the end of the second day with the Erskin grandparents, they began to discuss more gains than losses from northeastern Albemarle's school desegregation. This shift is important because I was pressing them to relay negative experiences. Dora would not be denied her opportunity to discuss her understanding of how her children gained from desegregated schooling. She offered her beliefs about advantages of desegregated education for her family, even though I had not planned to ask about them until the third visit. Dora's shared experience of gains led to an initial understanding of her family's relationship between education and hope. Essentially, her initial comments spoke to the capabilities of black children and their families to learn by default some of the white–middle-class rules and norms of a hidden curriculum that guides survival and success in northeastern Albemarle public grade schools. As Dora put it:

> You know what? My children, all of them graduated now, but I think they got better educated, and they got better jobs. . . . I ought not to, I shouldn't say it, but seemed like they didn't learn as much at an all-black school as they did to the white school, but they didn't, might not tried as hard. I don't know. . . . All of them graduated and every one of them that graduated got nice jobs, working alongside those that went to college. I don't know if that would've happened if they would've stayed in the black schools.

The third visit with the Erskins had hope as the focal point of the questions. It was important to discern how education hopes worked to temper black education struggles, at least, and to overpower them at best. Some larger education struggles that were part of a hidden curriculum did, in fact, seem invisible to Dora. Consequently, the struggles of which she was aware were mitigated by experiences that conveyed messages to maintain hope in education despite those struggles then, now, and to come. Almost immediately, education hopes and faith were linked to counterbalance existing school struggles for the Erskin family. Dora remarked:

> I prayed a lot because, we asked the good Lord to help us. If it wasn't for him, I don't know where we would be. He was my hope. . . . If it wasn't for the Lord, we wouldn't. He had a lot to do with it. He was the one that kept us together. Yes, that's something, that's something that's really, really important to find a church home. That's something that I really look forward to every Sunday is going to church.

Nolen confirmed: "We wouldn't have made it if it hadn't been for the Lord."

For the Erskin family, religious faith maintained a belief that their children would complete the twelfth grade, still largely the pinnacle of education at the time in northeastern Albemarle, when fewer high school graduates were pressed to obtain higher education. Religious faith also worked for the Erskin family on a second level through schooling. For finishing that pinnacle of formal schooling, Dora and Nolen believed, was linked to their children being able to live a life closer to that of a good Christian. The old biblical adage of "honor thy mother and father" was alive and well in the Erskin home, as well as the allusion to the rod of discipline, if children did not "mind" at home and at school. Stories from the third visit illustrate this connection. Devastated by the mere recounting of the house fire story, it seemed imperative to ask Dora and Nolen, "How did y'all help them keep hope and staying in school?" To this, Dora responded:

> Well, honey, we talked a lot, and prayed a lot and try to make them understand the best way because they were small. Keep them out of trouble. We haven't had one that's ever been in prison, never pulled time, never been locked up in jail. . . .
>
> I didn't have to get up every Monday morning and have to get one out of jail. I didn't have to do that. I didn't hear talk of fighting when they came home. They came home Friday night, Saturday night. They didn't ever come home the next morning. I think I've done pretty good in raising them. . . .

Between the two responses above, one of their sons, Aaron, walked in silently, nodded at us and then headed straight upstairs. "Yeah, stays here with us," Dora said proudly, "I didn't have but three boys, Nolen Jr. and Aaron and Clarence." So the Erskin children were and still are being raised to link education and schooling with religious faith, at least subconsciously. After this moment, I asked Dora if their children were raised to mind in school just as they minded at home. Dora commented:

> They minded [they weren't hard headed]. They listened to me. The things they didn't know they would come to me and ask things that they didn't know that they wanted to know. I told them the best way I know how. I didn't have to beat and shout and talk all the time to them for them to listen at me. They listened.
>
> They all graduated from high school. I didn't have any of them go to college but we weren't able to send them to college. I was just glad to get him through high school. I had eleven head of children to raise. . . .

The dual-purpose message of religious faith leading to determination was one that Dora felt was timeless in the home education of those that she raised:

> I don't think I'd change anything different because I have said because what I've said then is paying off now. They minded me. They listen to me. Now they've grown, they still listen when I talk to them. I try to raise them like I was raised, done the best I could. . . . Well, we didn't, we didn't change any of it. Well, you know. Right. Right. Right. I mean, I am not bragging because they were mine, but I had some good children. They weren't hard headed. They listened when I spoke to them—they listened. . . .

"I raised eleven of my own and two grandchildren—had all of them in the house. I think I did pretty well," Dora offered proudly toward the end of my visit with her family. She was not so pretentious as to leave out the contributions of her husband of over sixty years, however. In her shared reflection, she seemed to rely upon two men, her husband and her God. It was understood that Dora didn't need to be pushed for answers, but that taking what she said for what it was worth and not pushing her opened her up to relay more of her family's educational experiences with whites.

With Dora's strong personality and Nolen's reserve in discussion of formal education, it might seem that his parental services were a mere backdrop for her demands, but it was not so. And, as evidenced by who spoke to me the most, it seemed that the Erskin grandparent with the most formal education was designated by the couple to give the most advice pertaining to formal education. Still, in her final comments to me, Dora passionately commended her husband and his importance in having the children prepared for facing the often harsh realities of the newly desegregated school. As Dora explained:

> It was very important [to have her husband]. Very important because wasn't any need in my leaving him with a whole house full of children. What would I have done with a whole house full of children? I couldn't have made it if it wasn't for him. . . . He got out to work some cold days, snowy days that he didn't want to work but he had to. My husband was smart [hard working]. He wasn't lazy. He fed his children. We ate. We didn't starve. We might not have what we wanted, be we had enough to keep us living.

Candice Erskin Brown

Candice Erskin Brown, one of the youngest Erskin children "next to the baby," attended all three of the then newly desegregated northeastern Albemarle primary, middle, and high schools. Candice started school as a seven-year-old in the first grade. Unlike others who came before her, such as older students, parents, and school personnel, Candice remembered the early seventies as a somewhat pleasant time for her in school. Her narratives of her youth excluded the turmoil and violence faced by older blacks at the time. Her memories about early childhood and whites also suggest that her experiences were limited in terms of strife from white teachers, parents, and administrators throughout the county and state who clung to the idea of "separation of the races." Candice graduated from a northeastern Albemarle Middle school, formerly Marian Anderson, and Sawyer's Creek School (the same school attended by her parents). At fourteen, she tagged along with her sisters to work at the beach in housekeeping to earn money for her school clothes. Candice graduated from northeastern Albemarle High School in 1981 and first considered careers such as art and cosmetology before earning an associate's degree in business from the College of the Albemarle (COA).

It struck me that Dora Erskin said, "I didn't have any of them go to college." Community colleges, such as COA, were perhaps not presented to parents as "real" colleges with the same legitimacy as traditional four-year colleges and universities. With the ability to type eighty-eight words per minute, Candice landed her first career job at a law office before moving on to work for the Superior Court, while holding two part-time grocery store positions. Candice recalled the following experiences of struggle during her middle- and high-school years:

> There were not many blacks in that group that fell into that curriculum. You were teased if you were in the high track, if you dressed better, seemed that teachers liked you better. Mom used to bring us clothes from white families, for our school clothes. Mrs. Talis [Harriet Talis] always dressed nice and was a role model for us. She taught the girls how to sweep . . . to try to prepare us for life as a mom.

These experiences seemed to influence how she prepares her own boys for the desegregated northeastern Albemarle schools. It was during this first visit that Candice also shared messages that repeated her mother's lessons for her children, grandchildren, and me. As Candice explained:

> I preach, if you get it up here [pointing to her head], you'll always have It. I always tell them to prove people wrong. Black people are in jail. I teach them to speak correctly. They used to get teased for talking like white children.
> I noticed they had been teased, then they used slang. I tell them, No. Never drag to talk that way. I tell them to talk that way every day at home, and at school, because if you do it every day you won't ever lose it. . . . You just don't know how strict I am with homework. The middle child, it's almost impossible for him. They have an agenda, and I said, don't show any fear. I'll put that belt out for them.

Although Candice offered messages that reflected the transgenerational nature of the Erskin narratives on school struggles, she was more proactive in her relationship with the schools. Like her parents, Candice experienced race-related struggles in northeastern Albemarle schools. Unlike them, she discussed making her presence known in the school. For Candice, the struggles in desegregated northeastern Albemarle schools are accompanied by immediate, hands-on action at the school to lessen the impact of the struggle on her children. She recounted experiences with white teachers in a manner reflecting a sense that if she didn't show her face at the school enough, her boys would endure more pain:

> Education is very important to me. I am trying to prove them wrong. With the Lord, I can. I show up to the school unannounced. They look shocked. I asked the teacher for a time and day, and then I show up unexpected. I learned that because some of the black teachers and black assistants helped me. Black teacher assistants are so helpful, they watch. The same black teacher assistant sat on the

porch to help my [elementary school-aged] son get his lesson, when he was having problems understanding it. She was the black teacher in his class. And the white teachers don't have patience. One white teacher was known for having trouble with black males. I had my son removed.

Even with Candice's narratives about school involvement, vigilance, and persistence in her children's education, she was still plagued with struggle and disappointment that she attributed to her son's race, and the inability of white teachers and administrators to afford her family the same treatment as most whites. Candice began to weep as she shared her experiences with her child being held back in second grade, even though he passed the state's gateway End-Of-Grade (EOG) test, with "flying colors." It was a recent struggle and still rather painful to her. Her discontent brought tears to my eyes as I witnessed her family's struggle. She recounted:

> He passed the EOGs, they had a meeting, so we kept him back. I trusted her. [pause] He's doing really well now. The black teacher assistant who worked with him on the porch, we talked. She said, "I can't believe you let him be held back, he doesn't need to be held back, he was doing so well!" I felt like I was a failure. He not only passed, but did it well. I trusted her [the white teacher]! I think I would have let him go on. . . . She [the white teacher] already had her mind made up for him to stay back. And she had convinced the principal.

The only people at the meeting were the teacher, principal, and Candice. Apparently, the black assistant teacher who had worked so much with the child was not part of the decision. Candice suspected, "The principal had her mind made up. She was definitely on the teacher's side." Tears again came to Candice's eyes as she said, "The Title I, black teacher was upset that he was held back. She had given him checks and 100s on everything. They should have involved the black Title I teacher, and maybe the teacher before," she cried. This was not the only incident where Candice felt "devalued, deskilled, and infantilized," as a single black mother of children in northeastern Albemarle's schools (see Bloom, 2001). Her experiences with the high school also reflected her perception of the struggle to attain power in her children's schooling:

> I went to the high school. They mail a schedule. My child had passed. The young guidance counselor talked down to me. She looked down on my finger. She asked me, "Where is LaSean?" She talks down to me. We always used to accept the curriculum they have him on, but not any more. "Oh he's on the right track now," she said. Some of the things were his fault, some were not. We're on the third guidance counselor. We should have had him tested. We agreed some slipped through the cracks. They don't make me feel comfortable. . . . They don't care, or try to make me feel welcome. . . . I don't think I'd have to worry about them passing if the school was black, like Marian Anderson.

Candice's narratives about race-related school struggles are particularly compelling because she identifies herself as "color blind," and she prides herself on attempting to bridge racial gaps when she was in high school in the late 1970s to early 1980s. Her stories of racism became more compelling for me upon listening to her diverge from her parents' view of how to relate to white people. During the first visit, Candice convinced me that her narratives about race were more balanced than the other participants' because of her personal mission and vision:

My parents always said, "The white people, they don't care about you." I have this block in my mind that makes me always try to prove them wrong about that. I don't pay attention to color until they start acting nasty. I can't tell you if I was called a name. My boys say, "You don't know if they are white" when they question me about someone from a story I tell them. One white boy spent the night with my boys, and a white man at northeastern Albemarle Rural Shopping Center called the boy a name, he called him a "nigger lover." I hug him like he's one of my own. The thing I remember my daddy talking to older white men and saying 'yeah sa' to men his age or younger. That bothered me. He [seemed] afraid of the white people, but my mom [did] not. I'm more like her in that I stand up to them, but I am more [humble] and friendly like him when they aren't being nasty. . . .

My mom only came to school if there was a problem, she would go then. One of my sisters couldn't learn her lesson because she needed glasses, so she went in to take care of that. If my mother had dropped in at school . . . she never asked if I had a project, I would have tried harder. No positive feedback. I am the opposite [of her].

What Candice did in her narratives, however, was appreciate the messages shared by her mother and father as they shaped her parenting, teaching her what to do and what to rethink. She admired their sacrifice and persistence and she seemed in her early portrayals to be thankful that her parents are part of her children's education today. Candice also seemed to agree with her parents that black teachers are the most beneficial for their family. Whereas Dora admitted she felt that her children learned more at the white school, perhaps there is the missing link in her idea of the role of black teachers in the white integrated school. There is a sense in both Candice and Dora's narratives that they want the school-aged children in their family to "get it while they can," while the children's worlds can be less complicated, albeit with continuous struggle, in the buffering life of K–12 schooling. As Candice said:

My daddy always talked about how he had to work. My mother taught my dad. He could only read his name. My [mother] says to my boys, "Why don't you go ahead and get it? You can learn. Grandma don't want you to be left back. Getting that education, it will help you not to accept a 'less than' job."

They probably would have made her [mother] feel uncomfortable [if Dora had been as proactive when Candice was a student]. I mean it wouldn't have been . . . no, it wouldn't have worked out. [Laughter.] They probably would have called the sheriff or something. Oh, gracious. Um, um, um. I feel like we as blacks can identify with other blacks, so we need more black teachers. It needs to be put a way they understand. . . . Yeah, that would have made the parents feel more comfortable, and the children. You're surrounded by people who you haven't been around before.

Candice called for what Delpit (1995) and others describe as "culturally responsive teaching," consistent tutoring, and high expectations. In several of her narratives, she discussed gains and losses of such teaching:

Probably tutoring [is a gain]. When I was in school there was no tutoring for the people who needed it. Children just gave up and dropped out. And tutoring probably would have helped a whole lot. I think we gained when they integrated. They wanted the best for the whites, so we were included. Now that's a good thing. But we lost, I would have to say, if they had maybe black staff that could sort of relate to the black child, it would have helped a lot. Where the white teacher, she couldn't relate to a black child who could not understand what she was taking about, you know . . . so she was sort of left behind.

It seems hard for them [black children] to be given the credit they deserve. With all his [elementary son who was retained] weekly papers, checks, pluses, no Xs. But when the report card arrived it would be up to Cs, you know, and it should be As . . . And when I go to conferences, "He's right on schedule." That's all she says. "He's at the level he should be." But the report card says different also.

I really consider my little boy. Because they can do it. They are capable of doing it. That's one of the things I always say. "If you couldn't learn, I wouldn't be so hard on you, but there's nothing wrong with you, you can do it. You're the best. Now get out of there." That's my story. "Get on out of there." I don't want to stay in there a year longer than I have to. You can ask them. They hear it all the time.

Despite the sadness and injustice, Candice's narrative of struggle was inspiring, from having to return to school after experiencing a tragic house fire in which she lost two sisters and a niece and was hospitalized herself, to being "tricked" into agreeing to have her youngest child repeat second grade. As a student and now as a parent experiencing such struggles in the desegregated northeastern Albemarle schools, how she maintains her dignity and stays the course with her lofty beliefs about the importance of education can only be linked to one thing: hope. Candice's hope in education was included in the narratives concerning her high school peer group, employment opportunities, and timeless messages of motivation passed down from her parents. Her most in-depth narratives of hope in education, however, were steeped with faith, school assimilation, and discipline.

Peers

The subject of peers was not something originally conceived in my research as venues of hope for black students and families during desegregation. It was not until Candice Erskin responded without pause that her hope was linked to her school peers that I considered it. Her peer group not only shared school experiences, but also church membership and aspirations beyond grade school, such as becoming mothers and going to college. Candice and her peer group of four all went on to attend the College of the Albemarle:

> Friends. We started together and we wanted to finish together, I guess. Like I said the other day, I was real close to my classmates. We went to church together, most of us. And Monday to Friday we'd see each other again, so I guess starting with them and wanting to finish with them kept me going. . . . I would have to say one key to [hope] was my peers.

Yet, even though everyone in her peer group started college, Candice was the only one of the group to finish. The other areas of educational hope discussed provided a fuller view of how Candice kept enough hope in education to temper the struggles she endured.

Employment Opportunities

Another construction of hope in Candice's narrative was the idea that education would lead to a "good" job. At fourteen, she had worked (before work permits) as a housekeeper in the nearby Outer Banks of North Carolina. Soon afterward, she discerned that cleaning cottages and hotel/motel rooms was not good employment. Coupled with experiences "at the beach," her later venture into the world of grocery store bakeries evolved into the narrative below:

> In my mind, this education would get me a good job. And by good job, I'm meaning not having to work all the time [long hours for a white family's farm or store for minimal pay and little to no benefits package]; when I went to college, I was working at a grocery store in the bakery. And graduating from college would get me a job better than what I had. A full-time job. And I've always said from day one, I wanted a job where I could retire [with benefits].

Unfortunately, a full-time job in northeastern Albemarle is often not enough to support a family of four. The nature of a "good" job in northeastern Albemarle means more than full-time wages. The latest U.S. Census suggests that about two-thirds of northeastern Albemarle households work at least one full-time and one part-time job. This information suggests that both parents work two jobs, leaving limited time for the type of parental involvement in formal education that can be a major asset parents, children, and schools. Thus, the ability of a single parent such as Candice to pursue all of the necessary venues to compensate for what her children miss in the integrated school presents quite a crisis. Her hope of retiring from that full-time, "good" job near northeastern Albemarle will most likely mean partial retirement, as her needs and those of her children persist.

Timeless Message

Candice suggested that she understands the dilemma above, "preaching" education and yet, upon achieving a college degree, having little time for anything but work. Still, she has hope in education, and in timeless messages that will help her children see that even though she works much of the time, their lives could be worse without it. Even so, she has noted that children see and understand such quandaries, and that a college degree won't necessarily get you what you want:

> I'm not going to change it. Uh-uh (no). I'm going to stick to what I say. Probably when she [mother] said to go ahead and get it, "Do your homework. Go ahead and do it." And that's what she tells them now. "Go ahead and get it, or you're going to worry your mother. Go ahead and do it." She'll say, "You all are not dumb. You can learn." You know, she says the same thing I say, "Go ahead and do it."
>
> I am an optimist. I tell all three of them, I've told all three of them from first grade on up, "I send you to school to learn." They've heard it so many times. "You are not there to talk back. You do what the teacher says." Sometimes they'll come home: "She doesn't like me!" It seems like I'm always on the teacher's side. So they know not to come to me with "she doesn't like me" stuff. "She just picks on me!" Now, she's got twenty students, why is she going to pick on this child? So, they don't even try it any more, because they know if it sounds wherever, I'm going up there and you're going to repeat what you said. They know. It's like one of the teachers said, "If you believe everything your child tells you, I'm going to believe everything your child tells me." So I don't believe what they come home and say the teacher said. And I hope she won't believe when they go back and say, "My mama said . . ." "My mama said you make me sick." You know.
>
> Isn't that something? And I don't know why, you know. I'm usually not that kind of person, but I said the same thing to my oldest son. "You're doing it [inaudible]. You're doing exactly what people want you to do. Prove them wrong. Prove them wrong. Go ahead and do good. Go to college. You know, get a good job. Prove them wrong." I'm always told I'm a strong believer in that . . . there've been [good] kids, men, reared in homes where there are single parents.

Readiness/Preparation/Assimilation

A fourth component contributing to Candice's narratives of hope involve school readiness, preparation, and assimilation. It is a narrative that is indicative of integrated schooling. Her hopes seem to be tied to the belief that if her boys are articulate and well read that they will escape much of the trials of discrimination in their schooling. Candice offers a message of resiliency to her boys, to "prove them [whites] wrong." It was her interpretation that what she may have taught them in Marian Anderson would be perceived as "wrong" to many whites. Particularly white school personnel, administrators, and (most likely) her children's future employers would need to be proven wrong, especially if her children remain in northeastern Albemarle, a town with no minority-owned businesses (2000 U.S. Census Online). As Candice said:

Sometimes we read together. Sometimes I hear, "I don't have any!" and they know what's coming next. "Get a book and read." I think maybe if we were white I don't think I would be preaching so hard. But in my head: "Black male, black male. The jails, the jails are full." You know. These three, I'm trying to do my part to keep them out.

If I had a choice, every single black female, you know, you're rearing a family alone. You're trying to be mother and you're trying to be daddy, you have to be both. If they were as much like me, you know really, we're known for not being readers. Let's read, let's get educated. Let's prove these people wrong who has us as being dumb. Let's prove them wrong. Like I tell my boys, "Let's prove them wrong." They're building more prisons. You know. You don't want them filled with us. Let's do better. I just want them [other single black mothers] to try to raise these children and not give them so much freedom. Keep them in church. Teach them how to pray, you know. Turn these radios off with this rap music or whatever. And there's not always a father figure in your household. But we can do the best we can, you know. If you take them to church, there's a role model at church.

Still you've got to have time for the kids. The children are not prejudiced. They can see where your time is. Take them to the library. A person who reads has a vocabulary different from a person who doesn't. You know.

When these black males go to apply for jobs, Raheem against James, you know, white males against black males, who going to get the position? You know. Let's get rid of these names. These made-up names. They bother me. And one of my real good friends, a real good friend from my knee, had a baby child, and we had to write down some things for her that she would open after the baby was born. And everybody, I don't know what they wrote, but I kept writing. I had a whole page, and the thing was the child's name, she kept saying what she was going to name the child. The father's name was James. She spelled the baby's name backwards. The baby's name is Semaj. On my letter is what I said, "Remember that this name has to go with this child to his grave. You know, think about it before you use this name." But she didn't. She didn't pay any attention to what I said. The baby has the name of Semaj. "James" spelled backwards. They don't care. They don't care. This man 50 years old with the name Semaj. And people wonder what his mother was thinking about. But names are very important.

I think the teacher already knows. Checking that list before school starts and know how many black students they have. Oh, me. [Laughter.]

Her message of readiness and preparation is also one of assimilation. In an ideal situation, her boys could have names that were African, or African American traditional, without any negative consequences. Candice's narrative of naming and control over the naming of black children as providing hope is evidently based upon her experiences and vicarious experiences with others. Somehow her construction of educational hope often relies upon things *we* can control, such as names. Yet, this point also denies the fact that "first" names such as Megan were also different initially, but they became more readily accepted in predominantly white schools as appropriate or normal. Although the degree to which the Erskin-Brown children assimilate, and their names are within Candice's control, her narratives still were replete with negative accounts of racialization through reflections upon incidents in her children's schools. The final two elements of Candice's narratives of hope offer additional insight into her will to persist in favor of education. They are narratives of faith and discipline, narratives of hope that are closely linked in the Erskin family with the biblical "spare the rod, spoil the child." Although the Erskins see hope in faith and the rod, the idea of the rod in their construction does not always mean spanking, yet the threat of a "beating" remains. Candice discussed her faith this way:

> I felt as if I had to help myself. I had to do my part, and then the Lord would do the rest, so my faith in Him strengthened me to go on and care for my boys. Like tests. You know I always say, "Nobody has to know you are praying when you take that test. You know the Lord will help you." That's what I always tell them. And one of my friends, she will say that they would pray before they would leave from home. We're always rushing and we don't have a chance to do that, you know, but I do tell them that. "Just whisper a prayer. He will help you. Believe me." You know. And then they'll come home and say, "Mom, I did pray, and I made 100." And while they're praying, I'm probably doing the same thing. You know. "Lord, please support my boys." You know. Sometimes I may call them by name. Sometimes I don't.
>
> But I am self-assured in my friends that I pray that my children [inaudible]. That's one thing I tell them, too. We all need each other. I tell them, "We all need each other." I tell them that all the time, "We all need each other." Don't go through this world thinking you're not going to need anybody, because you will, and you do. I'm training them, I'm really training them [her sons]. With my faith. I'm trying to prove everybody wrong who said I couldn't do it.

Concerning "spare the rod, spoil the child," Candice offered more insight into her values of discipline:

> I'm trying to do more now to prepare them to be fathers to their children. You don't have to always fuss. Like my mother always told me, "You don't have to always spank. Talk to them." She said, "Talk to them some." That's what she said. And she was a believer that you could spank meanness into a child. She always taught us, which I have always gone by, when they get twelve years old, she always said, "If you haven't done it in twelve years, if you haven't changed that child in twelve years, don't even try it. Don't try to go spank them."
>
> Exactly. If you haven't done it from one up to twelve, don't try after twelve. But still I will. I get my belt and talk to them. But I know what she was talking

about. She said if you're going to haul off and hit a sixteen-year-old, he's going to take a bat and knock you in the head. Don't try to get him then. You're going to have to get these children when they're younger. Everything they do is not cute. You know, and she's just a person who doesn't talk much, but when she says things, she says that you can love your children, but have your children so that somebody else can love them. She's always said that. Make them mind. You've got to make your children mind. A lot of times I go to church and I say, "Mother, why do you always have to spank my children?" Because they are your babes, you know. 'I have the hardest-headed children I've ever seen in my life." You know, because I'm always talking to somebody. Pow! You know. Pow! And they don't know I'm watching them. But they should know how to act, you know.

And I understood that. You see a lot of children and grownups can't even talk. "Food, Ma, food!" When I was young, you better if company drove up, you better go in and tell your mama and you go on out the back door. You know you weren't allowed to stay in the house. Sometimes you see people who can't even talk for the children. My children know to get somewhere and play. Grownups are talking. I'll say that in a minute. "Grownups are talking. Nobody's talking to you." Make them mind, you should love your children, but always have them so somebody else will love them. Who wants to love a bad child? Somebody who's talking back to you. I strongly believe in that spanking. I'm not joking. I strongly believe in that. My belt, and they know it. I look up at that sixteen-year-old and I say, "You're next." He knows I don't mean it, but he knows, "I'll get you, too." That's what I say. But I won't. He knows I won't. But I'll correct him. I'm a strong believer that you can't show your fear. You can't show any fear. They'll know your weaknesses. I think a single mom with boys always has to be stronger than a single mom with girls. I'm trying to make a man out of these boys.

Candice's constructions of faith and discipline clearly reflected messages that were passed down to her from her parents. Those messages led to understanding of right and wrong, and that wrong led to consequences of emotional and sometimes physical pain. Narratives of discipline seem to relate to Candice's ideas about preparation and assimilation for the integrated school as well. The stories also add that there are others that affect the life of the child, both white and black. Like her mother, Candice wields the power of motherhood to keep children in line at home, in preparation for school and life beyond school. Her narratives were also indicative of a transgenerational message of looking to a power and energy higher than oneself for inspiration when times become tough at school. Faith provides hope, hope that a higher power is in control and will help one who continues to struggle. Surely the narratives of prayer and discipline within the black community are not new to education research, but the distinct ways in which Candice Erskin and her family constructed those narratives as vehicles for hope is unique.

Part II: The Winston Family

Woody Winston's Pedagogy of Struggle and Hope

A grandfather and long-time widower, Woody Winston plays a significant role in the theater that is the aftermath of *Brown*. In his family life, Woody, like Candice, plays the role that requires enough endurance to battle external stigmas, public ridicule, and the internal struggles of black single-parenthood. This role intersects with his role as a conduit for connecting home life to the sometimes turbulent, always challenging part of northeastern Albemarle's desegregated school community. Woody's narratives concerned approaches to remedy perceived turmoil and discipline in northeastern Albemarle schools. He alluded to the notion that there is a problem in longing for things such as spanking and "the rod" in the school, while understanding that race relations are still problematic, at best. He was the first of his generation to speak about and recognize this disciplinary dilemma. While his peers lamented only the loss of spanking in the desegregated school as the "problem with kids today," Woody also argued initially that the existing racialization would cause even more problems in situations where a white teacher hit a white child or vice versa. He also took the issue a step further in his narrative as he noted a problem with teachers even attempting to break up "interracial" conflicts at school, such as fights. He seemed to believe that with the racial dynamics in northeastern Albemarle schools, violence would beget violence in situations where "interracial" fights or corporal punishment were at play. In the end, however, he returned to the "problem of kids today" argument offered by his peers.

> But you know what ruined the children nowadays?
> I'm going to tell you why. All right. You the teacher, right? I'm a white teacher, and you the black teacher. The old white teacher want to hire you be nature. . . . They be fighting each other. And they don't want to mess with them neither. I've seen a colored girl tearing a white girl up and people walking right by. Because they know if they jump in, all them school children would jump on him. Understand?
> When they start to integrate the school, see, they done it themselves. They didn't hire me to whip their children, but it'd be all right for them to whup ours. . . . That's right. See, a lot of people don't understand that. But that's so. They don't want how you whupping their children.
> That's right. That's the reason you can't whup them. That's the reason they're so mean. But if they start a fight, there's nothing in the world to do but let them fight. Because if you try to part them, ones going to get you, and make you hit them. You understand? And then you've done lost your job.
> See, when they integrated the schools, there isn't but one thing I could say, they weren't going to hire the black teacher whipping on white kids. You understand? And that's why the kids are so bad now. But I reckon they had to do it to

integrate them. You get me now. Yeah, they weren't going to hire the black teachers whipping their kids. That's the reason they can't hire them. And that's the reason children are so bad.

Woody, like the Biggs family, did not force his children to attend schools with whites prior to mandatory desegregation. His children remained in Marian Anderson during the Freedom of Choice period and therefore were not subjected to some of the early backlash from retaliatory whites. As we learned in Chapter 2, his brother-in-law and sister experienced cross burnings at the hands of angry whites who were unwilling to allow blacks the freedom to choose schools without another arduous fight. Woody labeled such reactionary white racists as some of the "mean ones." He noted that some of the cross-burning whites are alive and well today. I learned later from his son, Ross Winston, that some of the cross-burning whites serve on influential education and commerce boards in the area today.

> Well, I'll tell you. When they first integrated the schools, all right, my kids, they didn't want to go. And I didn't force to send them. But the kids that did go, even down to my brother in law went, you know they burned a cross in every one, all the people's yards?
>
> Because then my brother-in-law worked with me. I was supposed to pick him up. He was right there. I said, "What you doin'?" He said, "They burned a cross in my yard this morning." They didn't burn one in mine because my kids didn't go.
>
> Yes, sir. There's some mean white folks around here, living here right now. I can tell you that right now.
>
> Yeah. They're living. Oh, yeah. Burning a cross in the yard. The one that started going to these high schools.

Given this struggle to obtain an adequate education for blacks in northeastern Albemarle with cross burnings and the like, it was imperative to learn how parents handled the conversation about the event with their children. What did parents, single parents like Woody, tell black kids about those incidents of early school desegregation in northeastern Albemarle? Woody's response, or at least his reconstruction of his conversation with his children, was simple. Fortunately, Woody disallowed his children to exercise their so-called Freedom of Choice to attend the schools. From his narratives, I found a construction that, if actually played out, could have left the already motherless Winston children without a father as well, at least a father that was not incarcerated.

> Well, I didn't tell them nothing. If they want to go, that was up to them, you know. But they didn't want to go right then. Then, see, I had three or four went at the time, see. And you know if they don't want to go they'll start fighting with one another. You understand?

But I'll tell you, long at the time when they were burning those crosses, if I had caught one burning a cross in my yard, he would have got some shots in him.

He would at that. If I had caught him, you know. But you see, you couldn't catch them. They would do it while you're in the house.

Although Woody was perhaps exaggerating about what he would have done to white cross-burners, I believed this part of his story because it was one of the times where he became most serious during our talks. To begin our second visit and continue our discussion of school desegregation, Woody offered what seemed for him to be a troubling story. It is the all-too-familiar story in northeastern Albemarle about an "interracial" dating couple being divided by family and school. The Whitmores, Gean Whitehall, and others participating in this research noted that one of the residuals of school deseg-regation was increased black–white or "interracial" teen dating. The narrative of black–white teen dating for the Winston family was quite disturbing, as a young white female and a Winston son, Frank, began a high-school love affair during the first year of mandatory school desegregation. The school skipped the middle man by not talking with Woody Winston about the situation. By Woody's account, the local county school superintendent suggested the removal of both students—the white female to a neighboring county school, and Frank Winston to Job Corps in Seattle. Frank ended up staying in Seattle for the rest of his life.

Frank was in school. And I'm going to tell you, Frank was in school, and this white girl and the end of the road was crazy about him. And everybody knowed it but me. See, I was the last one. The way I find out, I was in the barber shop, all right. And one of the girl's uncles, he wanted to do something to Frank.

Yeah. But her daddy, he kind of slacked back, and then the superintendent . . . well, yeah, because after that happened he told somebody it would be best for him not to go there because they might do something to him. And then Frank went in the Job Corps.

Yeah. See everybody knowed that but me. I was the last one knowed it. That the girl was so crazy about Frank. And she even wrote him letters. Yeah, she certainly did. And the girl's still living. . . . Yeah, she lives right down the road. This man out here's daughter.

He didn't have no driver's license. He didn't get no driver's license. But she was coming along in her daddy's car and pick him up. See, at night. I didn't know it, you know. All the people knowed the girl was crazy about him, they sure did. You know, he got kind of scared, and he went in the Job Corps.

See, nobody said nothing to me about it. . . . Right. Yeah, the people were talking about it in the barber shop. I said, "I didn't know nothing about it." Yeah, they said this old Chanler Suggs, he wanted to kill him [Frank], you know, because he was going with his cousin's daughter. But after a while he got all right. He [Chanler Suggs] calmed down [and stayed back on his side of] the lane. . . . because he knew I wasn't going to take none of his stuff. But anyhow, the girl's still living. She married a white guy, I think she married a white guy, or a colored guy one.

Although Woody explained that the interracial incident happened in 1965 or 1966, his memory must have waned. He seemed sure that they met at school. He was also sure that his children were not part of the Freedom of Choice group, which is corroborated in the stories of previous participants who did not mention his children as part of that group. Thus, it seems that Frank was involved with the white female in the 1969–1970 school year, which would have made the young couple approximately seventeen years old at the time. The 1969–1970 school year marked the first term of mandatory desegregation for northeastern Albemarle schools. A former student of those early transitional times and now a teacher, Barbara Needham remembered such school struggles with vivid detail and she corroborated Woody's story in Chapter 2. Even from Barbara's apparently more privileged white perspective, she described 1967–1970 as a difficult time for northeastern Albemarle schools. And clearly, from Woody Winston's voice and body language, it was a terrible moment in his family's educational history. It had been less than six years since his wife passed away and the children all had roles to fulfill. While Woody worked in Virginia to make ends meet, the oldest children were responsible for cooking and cleaning, while the youngest attended school, all while trying to deal with the loss of their mother and their older brother to the Job Corps in Seattle. Ross Winston later revealed that he remembered less about desegregation turmoil in the early years as he was still lamenting the loss of his mother.

> WOODY WINSTON: Well, all I could do was go to work, and I had another lady here help me tend to them, you know, while I worked. So I worked in [inaudible] and they were going to school. And my cousin, she helped [inaudible phrase]. Their mother, she passed in '63. Carl was three years old when his mother died. He wasn't even going to school. It was a few years [inaudible] started.
>
> Yeah, yeah, right. I teach that they had to work. People would take you for granted, they would go pick up stumps out of the field for them you know, pick up white potatoes, truck corn, all that stuff.

Woody wouldn't allow any white man to come in and say, "Hey, your daddy said you could work," as he recalled from his youth, even though the wages of extra workers could have helped.

> No, no. It wasn't like that. No, there weren't no white man going to school to get them, now. I saw to that. Now probably they'd be home some day during the day when they would come asking, "Boy, do you want to make some money?" To help do a little stuff like that. But it wasn't no going out to the school doing it, no.

I became interested in what Woody felt was his relationship with the school as a black single father. What did Woody feel his relationship was with the school, or did he feel that he had a relationship at all? I understood that he worked often, but I wondered if he felt that school personnel were ever responsive to his "need to know" as a parent. Could he talk back to them, and if he did after the incident with Frank, did they listen to what he had to say? He proudly offered a narrative, similar to his peers in the Biggs and Erskin families, that said, "I didn't have to go out there." That part of the first-generation mentality rang clear in his narratives, even though he stated earlier that he would have liked to have known about Frank's experiences with the white student long before he heard about it from the school superintendent.

> They didn't ever have to come to me about the children. You know, I tried to hire them to mind, you know, when they were going to school. I didn't have no trouble. You see my daddy, he was counselor out there, too.
>
> Oh yeah, they didn't have to come to me from northeastern Albemarle when my children were going there. 'Cause they knew at that school when they do something wrong, I was going to punish them myself, you understand?
>
> They could have told the superintendent [regarding Frank's situation] or whatever, could have come and told me. You understand? But they didn't do it. Where I got mine from was through the grapevine. Yeah.

Woody undoubtedly lost a direct line of communication with the change from black segregation to desegregation in his community's public schools. Yet, toward the end of our second visit, as with all of the other participants, Woody spoke about what he felt the Winston family gained with desegregation. Similar to the families who spoke before and after him, Woody offered a narrative, albeit brief, in which gains from school desegregation seemed to compensate for losses.

> Well, I can't say right now that they lost anything, because my kids did pretty good in school. You know what I'm saying? Yeah, they did pretty good in school. All of them got pretty good jobs and they can go for themselves. Understand?

As with the Biggs and Erskin families, Woody and I talked extensively about his feelings concerning the "goodness" and necessity of formal schooling. With all the negative actions and occurrences documented from that time, such as Frank Winston being forced to leave town, how in the world could a black single-parent widower like Woody keep hope in education, especially when he didn't even complete grade school? Further answers seemed to lie in his ability to substitute as best he could, either by himself or with help, in the roles that a second parent plays.

> Oh yeah, right. See, I always had somebody here to help me fix for them, you know. Feed them so that when they come from school their supper would be

done. And then I had somebody help them get their breakfast before they go to school. See, that the main thing. You can't go to school hungry and expect to learn. You have to have some food.

I had to buy for them, too. And see, one or two of the boys were big enough to cook for them. Jim Carlton and Rodney would cook for them, see, for the rest of them were small. And they's a time when one of them was old enough to get his driver's license, I would get the driver's license for them.

Well, you see, I had food there for them. Yeah, cause you can't learn nothing if your hungry. You can't even work hungry. You know what, I used to buy so much food. . . . Carl was a little boy. He used to come and tell me, he said, "Daddy, you're some kind of good to us. All this food you buy for us."

I had asked all the families more specific questions about hope, but this topic seemed particularly crucial in this case. How did Woody keep and convey hope that education would lead to good things for his family with all of the negative experiences he had to deal with? The components of educational hope in his narratives were congruent to those offered by his peers.

Family Resiliency

Woody discussed how black families, including his own, exhibited resilience at the time with what little education many of his generation had. But it was not the resilience of birthright or genetics; it was the resilience of using the faculties and opportunities available to better your quality of life. He commended his own children's ability to cope and bounce back by using their available tools when he stated, "Yeah, all the time for they not have no mother. You understand?" Woody further described how black families—including my own—made it with what they had, without monolithic, once-per-decade feats, but with persistence, agency, cooperation, and frequent strategic moves toward the type of small day-to-day social victories that can lead to positive, permanent social changes.

Well, I'll tell you, some people made it in a different way. You understand. Some worked on the farm, some didn't. See, that have a lot to do with it. You understand?. . . . Yeah, see, if your daddy hadn't worked down that [inaudible] he would never have been like he was today. See? He came down there, left the farm, and came down there with us. See, and all of us pulled together because we're from North Carolina, and looked after one another. Now, you take a boy up there today, he farmed, he wasn't doing nothing. He asked me one day if he could come down there, and I said come one down there with us. He came. He stayed down there and retired. . . . Right. So your daddy would never have did nothing but working with those sawyer and stuff on the farm. No, he couldn't.

Right. I helped many people. I worked people on my job who couldn't even buy nothing to eat when 12:00 come. I would come up there in my car and buy them something to eat . . . Unh unh. The colored. So I helped many people. Thank the Lord I could do it. You understand. Yeah, I helped a lot of people. . . . You see, if you want to do something you can do it. Don't let nobody fool you.

Part of Woody's narrative of resiliency as something that was part of a group effort involved a story of him helping my father. It became imperative for me to ask if my father had repaid the favor. "Oh, yeah, yeah, [he] would pay me," he said. I had a feeling that his family's participation in this work had much to do with my family's previous relationship with his. With this revelation, I began to challenge my previous ideas regarding self-efficacy and resiliency. These concepts began to signify more important qualities of humanity to me that were more interwoven and complex than I had ever fathomed at that point. At this moment, my previous understanding of how northeastern Albemarle's black families found hope in their experiences of schooling began to feel too linear to me and in fact my initial ideas now seemed somewhat shortsighted and immature. The individual in this tightly knit community is so closely bound with others that can bring further barriers to efforts to resist, or to practice one's agency, that the notion of individual resiliency and self-efficacy breaks down as linear and builds up as more of a complex web of interactions bringing educational hopes to the surface.

Family Faith

The Winston children were no strangers to the church and faith was closely linked to the hopes Woody had for his children in education. Before Mrs. Josephine Winston passed away, she was instrumental in teaching the faith to her children and reinforcing faith as a family practice. The children learned literacy and interaction skills in Sunday school, representing one link to faith. Woody also saw himself as presenting pedagogy of hope to link faith and education in order to ensure the survival of the next generation of school-age Winston family members—to ensure that irrespective of the struggles of desegregated schooling, Winston children would most likely be "all right."

> Well, at the time, I just trusted in God, I reckon, because you know, I guess things would go on all right. Because our children didn't have no house. On account of Sunday school and stuff you know, so they could learn and mingle with the people. And so that's what happened. Just trust in God, and we'll be all right. I know I had to do my part, because they didn't have nobody else to look out for them but me.
>
> You see, their mother growed up teaching them stuff, you know. And she used to carry them to church, because she was a church woman. And then after I, you know, I would take them to Sunday school. And a lot of time I would wait for them, or carry them up there and go pick them back up.

What other things did Woody say or do to help his kids have hope in education's possibilities? His next narratives led to what I call a "glimpse of the struggle," as maintaining hope. Woody not only talked to his children about working in the fields, but he took them there to experience it in adolescence. My own father used to come home and say, "Boy, unless you want to pick up and do beans, you better get it somewhere else." The Winston kids glimpsed that struggle firsthand. By "glimpse the struggle," I mean that the narratives suggest the child was invited to see how one's quality of life could be worse without an education, so that hoping for the fruits of an education would strengthen and sustain them.

> Well, see, long then, in the summertime, they would go in the field and work, but after it got kind of large, I would carry them down there so they could make some money, you know, then by the school close, they go to school.
>
> Right. Right. See, I carried some of them down there who weren't no more than fourteen or fifteen, but they were large to their age. And the work was kind of scarce. And I worked them. I sure did.

The final two elements of the Winston pedagogy of educational hope involve high expectations and, again, the timeless message. Woody's narrative of high expectations are relayed through the anecdote of one golden child, his granddaughter affectionately called Sonja Babe. Sonja Babe is the youngest child of his eldest son. By Woody's account, Sonja Babe was not expected, in northeastern Albemarle's desegregated schools, to be as successful as she became. He suggested that high expectations, along with family support for Sonja's persistence, offered an example of what positive life quality changes that struggle tempered by hope can render for his family. Her story is potent for Woody's hope narratives as Sonja Babe was the first to serve the ILA union, not as a laborer, but as an executive, office type, an attorney—a clear upward move in quality of life due to education, in the narratives of Woody and the other participants.

> Well, I'll tell you. Now, when Jimmy's daughter finished school, she told her daddy that she was going to make the honor roll. . . . When you finished the school and there was something you got to be head of [valedictorian 1990 or '91]. And she was, and the teachers said she would never do it. But she did. I forgot what it was. Carl could tell you exactly what it was. But anyhow she made the history on it [one of the first blacks to do so in desegregated school], because Jimmy bought her a brand-new car. It stayed down here two weeks before she finished school. After she finished, he gave it to her. Now she's a lawyer. . . . Yeah, she's a lawyer for the longshoremen there in Norfolk. . . . Yeah, that's the baby girl. . . . We call her Sonja Babe. . . . Yeah, she's a lawyer now for the longshoremen down. . . . Yeah, yeah. She would never make it. But she made it. It's something when you finish high school. And they make you over something there. Anyhow she made it. And when she made it, her daddy bought her a brand-new car. It stayed down here two weeks before she got it.

Timeless Message

Some folks say that as the times change, we must change the way we talk to school kids. Did Woody Winston change the way that he talked to them? No.

As with the Erskin and Biggs family members from the first generation, the notion of a timeless message to keep hope in education was part of Woody's communicative repertoire. He presented the message as if he were teaching me, as if I were a third-generation member of the Winston clan.

> Well, I stuck to the same message until they got on their own. Now they know me, they don't give me no lip for right today. For I'll tell them, "You forgot where you come from." You understand? Don't ever forget where you come from. I tell all kids, "Don't ever forget where you come from."
>
> Well, they always said, "Daddy said this," and "Daddy said that." And that could stick with me. Yeah, they did. Then I tell them, "Do the thing right, and then you won't have to take no stuff." Don't let nobody run over the top of you, when you're grown. You know right from wrong.
>
> Always, you know, do the thing that's right. You understand? Then when things come to push and shove you won't have to take no . . . you know . . . Right. You can tell them. Always be right.
>
> Well, I did all I could to educate them. Some of them went to college and some didn't. And some went in the Army and came back and went to college and finished. I got three schoolteachers out of the bunch. The rest of them from the high school. But all of them did all right. After they went through high school, they went in the Army. I had one daughter and she finished school. She went to school for a schoolteacher. And she's teaching school now. . . . She's in Virginia.

At this point in my work, both the Erskin and Winston families offered messages alluding to me as a vehicle for their pedagogy of struggle and hope. I was becoming even more cognizant of my role as a potential vehicle by the time I met Woody. Woody's son, Ross, and daughter-in-law, Debra, offered additional information about struggle and hope for the second generation. Their story also allows me to be a vehicle for their narratives and future black generations in northeastern Albemarle.

Ross and Debra Winston

The earliest period of school desegregation discussed by Ross, as with his peers, was the Freedom of Choice period, although his peers did not name it as such. The first wave of narratives in northeastern Albemarle involving black janitorial staff and white educational staff members during this period were among those incidences that Ross could remember. Ross's uncle, he was the "Lucas" of the story. Everybody kept saying, "I remember one of the first ones was Lucas." Nobody could remember his last name, but of course Ross did. At this point I began to cherish Ross's ability to remember details from the past so well. Everybody had mentioned Laura Biggs and Walter Leir and "Lucas somebody." Ross finally discussed the now-deceased Charlotte Baines as the first one to go to the white northeastern Albemarle high school during the Freedom of Choice period. This confirmed the story told by other families and school personnel who spoke of this time.

> I can tell you exactly who it was. This first one was Charlotte Baines. There was Charlotte Baines. There was Lucas Skinner. There was Linda Biggs. There was Aaron Barnes. There was Walter Leir. And those are the ones that I can remember. Some of the first ones that went over there . . . But Charlotte Baines was the first one to go . . . She was the very first one to go over there . . . Yeah, she's passed away. But she was the first one to go over there. But anyway . . .

The rest of the first to integrate the black school are still alive. Ross said that Lucas is "down in Georgia. He's a minister down in Columbus, Georgia. He has about a thousand-member church down there." The minister of such a large congregation, however, was once the victim of a cross burning. Just as his father recalled, Ross discussed the cross burnings by reactionary whites in the yards of the northeastern Albemarle four who desegregated the school—who merely exercised the so-called Freedom of Choice. Ross's one-story red-brick home sits across a road from the now abandoned two-story green house that was once the site of a cross burning.

> I remember the house right across the road there, you know, where they came and burned crosses in their yard. . . . Yeah, they burned a cross. . . . That was Lucas. Um hum. He lived right across the road, in that green house right across the road. They . . . Uh hum. They burned a cross in his yard. They burned one in Walter Leir's yard. You know Walter Leir? . . . They burned one in their yard. They burned one in Laura Biggs' yard, and I'm trying to think of which other one. I do know that they burned one in those three yards. I bet nobody done told you that, did they?

Ross was correct. Other than his father, who did not remember all of the names of those who had crosses burned in their yards, I had heard of only one cross burning. They told me about one of them. I didn't know that this group of whites had gone on a tirade, although one cross burning is enough. As noted in the story of white teacher Barbara Needham, the Klan burned a cross in her father's yard to scare him into joining, so we at least have an idea about the culprits. Ross claims to know who did the burning and that they are alive and prominent citizens today.

> And I know the people that did it. Because lady [inaudible] people told me. I was at the telephone company and I had friends, and they told me exactly who the people were that did it. That's right. The people that did it now they'll ride around and look at me [inaudible] but I know where they came from. . . . I know exactly the people that did it.
>   Um hum. It was in the newspaper. As a matter of fact they had a picture of that cross over there. My granddaddy went out and threw a bucket of water on it. And they had a picture of that in the paper.

Ross also claimed that blacks in his peer group were phased little by the cross burnings of whites.

> Oh man, at that time we were young and crazy and we didn't care. We just thought they was crazy. They didn't scare us. We weren't afraid. We just thought it was crazy. I just thought they was crazy.

Like his peers and forefathers from the first generation of the previous three families, Ross offered a story about a school bus of white students taunting blacks. His story added that whites threw objects at the black students, whereas the others only relayed stories of racial slurs.

> And it seems like I remember the kid standing out waiting for the school bus. And I remember the white school bus was drive by and kids would throw paper and stuff at us.

So the whites would throw paper at Ross and his peers. Ross would not say how they retaliated or what they said to the white students in return. He offered a second critique of the administration and showed his dismay with the administrators' failing to provide Marian Anderson with its own activity bus. The bus likely would have served as a source of pride, as well as accomplishment.

> No. Just roll down the window and throw a piece of paper, and you know, we didn't pay it no mind. I looked at them like we knew that we were being belittled, but we didn't let it bother us, because they had problems, you know what I mean? And it's something I never quite understood. I remember from the time, and this is something I might be criticizing the administration at the Marian Anderson school. I remember from the time I was in the fifth grade until I graduated, and people would tell you this right now if you talked to them, we had big fund raisers and we raised money for an activity bus from the time I was in about the fourth or fifth grade until I graduated. And we never saw that bus. We never saw that bus, and nobody knows where the money went. (Laughter.) If you talk to people that was in school at that time, they would tell you the same thing. We did see a bus in 1968, but the high school didn't have a bus, I mean the Northeastern Albemarle High School didn't have a bus, and we didn't have a bus. But in 1968, both schools got new activity buses. So we don't know whether they took the money and bought theirs, or whether the county bought them, but I think the county bought those buses.

A final instance from the early transition into school desegregation relayed by Ross was a story first told to me by Margie Hines. It was the story of a black student walking from the white high school to meet his aunt at the newly desegregated Granville Elementary school. It was the last time he made that trek, as a group of racist white students struck him with an object thrown from a moving vehicle, an object that hit the student in the head and later ended his life.

And oh! There's another incident. I think his name was Roy Denson. He was a student out at Northeastern Albemarle High School. And I can't remember, I don't think . . . that had to be the year or so after I graduated, which was after they consolidated. And it had to be back in '71 or '72. His aunt worked at Granville Primary School. And I remember he was walking from Granville Primary School to the high school, to meet his aunt to go home with her. And some white kids at the high school rode by and threw a bottle and it really messed up the boy, and nothing was ever done about it. But you know, years later I know exactly the people that did it. And one of them is a professor [inaudible] right now. That's right.

Ross felt that the whites to this day have no remorse for killing the young black pedestrian.

Oh no, no, no. They don't feel bad about doing it. They were just glad they could do it and get away. You know what I mean? The only fear they had was getting caught. But they knowed they had about everybody on their side in their families and they wasn't going to get investigated. And the people know. The cops probably know who did it.

Certainly in northeastern Albemarle as in other places, the later years of desegregation would bring less overt racist incidents. In fact, Ross mentioned that he witnessed that change by the time his kids were going through northeastern Albemarle schools. He discussed the use of school counselors, something he lamented as absent even in the segregated Marian Anderson School. He also refuted the connection that other blacks in this study made between the decline of black students and the lack of corporal punishment in schools. Ross claimed that he wouldn't want white or black teachers and school personnel to have the privilege of spanking his children, an opinion like his father's, but removed from statements on the topic offered by the other Black participants.

Oh yes, yes. When my kids went, it was a lot better. It was a lot better, because they had like a school psychologist. They had like special programs. In school, when I was in school, what did they call it when they had somebody that was slow performer, what did they call that? I forgot what they even did [for] them. But there was a program, but that wasn't until my later years in school that they started doing that. I pray for those slow kids now. It was like institutionalize them, you know. But getting back to this punishment thing, you know when people say they wish they had it in school now. . . .

Man, some of these people that's in school, I look at their lifestyle, and I wouldn't want them touching my kid. You know what I mean. . . . No, no way. When I look at them, and I know what their lifestyle is and the things that they do, I wouldn't want them disciplining my kids. And I think the situations is that what's happening is, it's a responsibility that the parents today have, but they don't want to do. They want somebody else to do it for them. Spanking their child, they don't spank the kids at home, but then they feel like someone at school should have the privilege to spank them. And some of these people, I wouldn't want them touching my children. And they've got this thing now, you know, at that time it was black on black, you know. But now you've got you don't know what the person's racial thinking is, or I think a lot of people say things without even trying to you know address or even think about what they are saying, when they say they want people to discipline their kids. They wish it was like it was when they were in school.

Like his father, Ross said was that the makeup of the school personnel is not all black any more in northeastern Albemarle, so he would have to deal with some other race issues too as a former administrator.

> It's just totally different. . . . Then you see you've got that thing about even with the punishment now, you know, a lot of black kids fall through a loophole of being more severely punished or privilege taken away. . . . That's even here today, you know.

Even with Ross's arguments for the current northeastern Albemarle school system, knowing that his kids were going through the system, and that it was different from what Ross experienced at Marian Anderson, he and his wife felt a special duty, as black parents, to educate their children about certain things, to help prepare them in ways that they may not have been compelled to as white parents. Similar to Shujaa, Ross offered the notion that black students are schooled and not educated, but he used the term "trained." He seemed also to be in the middle as a former school administrator who tried to make some changes, and as a parent who felt that he could use his agency to educate his children at home to counterbalance the training they received at school.

> Number one, we had to let them realize, you know, although they were being educated. I don't like to use that word, "educated." I like to use the word "trained." Yeah, I like to use the word "trained," because education to me comes within there. And I think we're sending our kids to be trained, not educated. We should educate our kids ourselves. I think they're being trained. But anyway, you see, that's our fault.
>
> I like to use the scenario, you take a dog and he jumps through a loop. Is that a trained dog, or is that an educated dog? . . . I would say it's a trained dog. But I would say that's a trained dog. But a dog that takes a bone and goes digs a hole and buries it in the ground for later, that's an educated dog. That's just instinct. . . .
>
> Another example that I use: A lot of people holler about the Greeks and the Greeks. If they would dig back and really read their history, it was the Egyptians, you know what I mean. It was with the Egyptians that all this knowledge and stuff really came from. And you know, there is the story told, and I read some books about how it was taken away or stolen by the Greeks. But a lot of people, you know they, and that's why I have a problem with some of the Greek letter organizations, because I don't think some of them really did the research that really needs to be done some of these organizations. I don't . . . I mean, I

like the organization, but I still think some of them have been leading us astray for a long time.

So what was the number-one thing that Ross claimed he and his wife felt they had to tell their kids?

> Never forget that you are black. Never forget that you are black, and I don't care you know how much in school they pretend that you're friends and you're this and you're that, when it comes down to the end, and it comes down to you versus them, it's going to be them. It's going to be them. And I try to tell them you know, I don't give a damn who it is, because there's a lot of black folks I don't like. I just tried to tell them to treat people like they want to be treated. And that in order to get respect you've got to give it. And you know, don't tell me nobody will like you or not, as long as they respect you for what you are.

It is a convoluted message at first glimpse. Upon further examination, it seems that Ross's message to me and to his family is: "Remember that you are still black in northeastern Albemarle; even though things have changed, not everything has changed." His notion that whites are still in power and that they will use that power in northeastern Albemarle to deny blacks an education but to train them and still offer them inadequate employment holds true to his previous narratives. Ross believed that this message has worked for his family, overall.

> Well, you know there were a lot of bumps down the road, but hey, you know, there's nothing wrong with having bumps. You can make all the mistakes in the world, but as long as you learn from your mistakes and move on. . . . And people tell us, "Hey, man, it's good to make mistakes. " They're wrong. You know you learn from your mistake. That's the best way. But I differ with that. To me I always believe you learn from other people's mistakes, but a lot of us choose not to do that.

Debra and Ross first discussed a loss of disciplinary control at school, but they discussed that loss in different terms than most. For them, it was a loss of control not of spanking, but of the verbal and motivational tools used to keep black children in line.

> DW: Maybe the discipline with the children. You know, when the schools were integrated, the black kids, they did lose something. Well, I guess maybe it was a part of culture in a way. You could not longer discipline, as black on black. You could no longer talk, like okay, you're out in a white world. You had to address the schools on a whole.

> RW: In the schools, they'd pull you over and say, "Look, you can't compete against these white kids. You'll have to be twice as good." [inaudible sentence]

> DW: You couldn't do that once they integrated.

Second, the couple discussed a loss of control over whom black children sought in school for dating relationships. The dialogue on this loss revealed the first rift in the couple's construction of losses during desegregation. Debra's concerns seemed to reside closer to those of Harriet Talis, Gean Whitehall, and the National White People's Party when she alluded to the mandate of desegregated schools as a leading cause of "miscegenation," commonly defined as "interbreeding of 'races' especially of Whites and non-Whites." Ross, whose deceased brother had been virtually exiled to Seattle for dating a white female classmate, seemed to disagree with his wife on this topic. Ross spoke briefly but assertively in reply to Debra about black–white teen dating and the degree to which such dating should be viewed as symptomatic of just another disadvantage brought upon us by the *Brown* decision. First, Debra explained:

> And then too, I think that's why we have so many mixed. The younger schools, I don't think, pays as much attention as the older ones. Like the young ones now, you know it doesn't matter with kids where they're dating black, whether you're black, white, or anything. You know, it was a big deal when I was in school, but you know now, it's just the way it is. And I think when they integrated, that was an advantage or it could have been a disadvantage for some people. You know, it mixed the dating. And I think that's why we have so much now of miscegenation. That's one of the reasons. One of the things that came out of integration.

Ross responded adamantly:

> That's always been done, but it's always "miscegenation" [to blame]. [Black–white teen dating] has always been done. But it was [almost] always done [outside of the range of the public eye].

A third loss for the black community constructed by Ross and Debra was the education that traversed the borders of school and church. Blacks brought information from school into church, as many teachers were church members. They also brought information from church to the school, issues of moral and virtue, maintaining faith as motivation during the struggle of desegregated schooling. Debra and Ross in dialogue added comments about blacks who were co-opted by whites in power, who consciously or subconsciously hurt efforts of moving blacks beyond "training" to gaining an education in north-eastern Albemarle:

> DW: I know many years ago the black churches played a huge part in, you know, helping blacks to overcome some of the obstacles and mistreatment, especially in the '60s. The black churches was a very important, you know, meeting place and place, you know, you could get information.

> RW: It was like a refuge, that we knowed that we could go and discuss things. And still and yet what about somebody leaves the church and goes back and tells

a white man. We'd say, "Well, we know we'll be back out into the community as soon as we leave the church." . . . Even when we had those meetings at the church, there were some things that couldn't say because we saw Uncle Tom, that would go back and tell people everything that we said. And so that made it a group [inaudible]. You know what I mean?

Apparently, White families did not lose as much closure in at least two of the five northeastern Albemarle area schools. From experiences conveyed by Ross and Debra, we are provided a picture of the typical white family in the area as having multiple allies within the school system. Sometimes those whites are old family friends, and other times they are actually family. In both situations, the white child has more of the intergenerational closure at the integrated school that mirrors what blacks once had in segregated black schools such as Marian Anderson. Ross explained:

And you know for some, it's always a family that's, you know, got more people working in the school system than anybody else. It's always one family that's going to try to dominate anything that one of them get involved in, they going to try to dominate the whole thing. And off the record I'll give you their name, but on the record I won't give you their name. I just want you to check that out. And when that family, the first one that came here, and they weren't even qualified for the position that they had. But they got it because of the family name. And now sisters, cousins, nieces, I mean everything, the whole family is in there.

Ross and Debra Winston also presented narratives that illustrated a link in their lives between hope and education. Given the lengthy discussion of struggles, including Ross's losing his mother during desegregation, hope also must have been present, as Paulo Freire reminds us. Accompanying their narratives, which involved a myriad of losses of things they felt were missing in their education due to desegregation, they offered concrete messages of hope in education. They maintained the idea that education can and does in fact lead to positive changes in the quality of life for their generation, the one before, and the ones to come. Within their narratives lie components of hope that also surfaced in the stories of the Erskin, and Winston families: (a) high expectations, (b) agency, and (c) authentic white allies.

Although Ross admitted that he did just enough to get by and get out of school, he had higher expectations for his children. His narrative suggests that he felt racism existed in the desegregated northeastern Albemarle schools, but that the climate was certainly much better for his children. It was not until this point toward the end of my final visit with Ross that I learned that he had been signed up for Freedom of Choice, but chose to pass on the opportunity. And who could blame him? As Ross explained:

Number one, to be honest with you, when I was growing up, I knew I wasn't going to go to college. I didn't prepare myself to go to college. I wanted to be getting out of school, get my high school diploma, and then to join the work force, but I knew I had that high school diploma, if I decided later on to go back to school. . . . Right. That was my goal to get out of there, because when I was in school, I was a big kid, you know. I had my mustache, I had my beard, you know. And my goal, like a lot of my friends, was to get out of there. It was just to get out of there. Because we saw the integration coming, what they call the consolidation of the school the next year, and we wanted to make sure that we were going to be around for that. So that was our goal. I had signed up one time to go to Northeastern Albemarle High School, you know when they had that freedom of choice.

Yeah, I signed up. But then I thought about that thing, and I said, "Nah, that's not for me." Because Lucas, my uncle, he done go over there and some of my friends, and Laura Biggs, she was over there, and all them. And I think the last day, I went and said, "No, I don't want to go over there."

Ross felt that he would be giving up too much, and since it was his last year in school, and he felt that he would "rather have been, and you know, now I can say, I was the last graduating class in Marian Anderson High School." Knowing his children would not face such a fixed choice at such a turbulent time, he and his wife raised the bar for school performance to a level they felt their children could reasonably reach with their capacities to learn. They constructed an experience of pushing their children to learn the most they could, without pressuring them to meet white standards of school success. Ross spoke about these issues with passion:

And if you be going out in the work force. But we've all got our sights set on you know, my child made the A honor roll, or this and that, and I see the bumper stickers on the cars. And you know that's fine, but where the drop comes when you put your child up there, "My child is going to do this," and your child makes a B or something a subject, then that could affect your child, because they feel, hey, I disappointed Mom or Dad. So really he's working to satisfy his parents, you know what I mean? So I would say so much emphasis might not should be put on that, just as long as you know that your child is doing . . . you don't have to push your child [too excessively], but as long as you know that your child is doing their best.

Another component of hope in education stemmed from Ross and Debra's narratives of participation in their children's education. In active participation at the school, the couple finds hope that their visibility will lead to coveted educational outcomes. In their construction, what was coveted was a moral, taxpaying position in society, using the education made available to them and their family. Ross said:

I think we've all been so vocal if we had a problem with all the people to take care of it. If we had a problem, we would make sure we voiced our opinion, and forget about it.

I wondered just what helped or hurt their relationship with the school. The trust their families had that participation would help warranted further questions about the home–school relationship. What did they remember about what that relationship was like when they were going through school? And then the transition when they were helping their kids go through the race-conscious northeastern Albemarle schools? Ross recounted this experience:

> Well, really, I can't think of no negative. . . . I mean there are some negative, but you now, nothing that was, that would really stand out. When we had problems, maybe you can think of them with our kids going to school. Because I mean, they were so minor, when we did have a problem, you know we just got on top of it and got it addressed.

All of the first generation of blacks and some of the second have said one thing proudly, "I never had to go out there for my kids." Some of the younger folks will say, "I like popping in the school and seeing what is going on with my kids." Going to school doesn't necessarily have a negative connotation to them. Why would Ross and Debra differ in their view of "going out there" to the school? Where does this hope originate? Ross answered:

> You know my daddy had to work all the time. So really, we better not mess up so he had to take a day off from work to come out to the school for us. Because you know like, our mother had to teach, and if we messed up in school were punished right in school. You know we had no corporal punishment, but I guess it was called corporal punishment. But that was taken care of right in the school when we were there. I never had my kids get in fights or anything. You know what your family did when you got into fights in school.

Even with a working father, a deceased mother, and impending decisions about his Freedom of Choice, Ross seemed to find educational hope in agency. The structure was not always kind to Ross, yet he and Debra maintained that the individual can achieve in harsh learning environments. I asked them how. Debra said:

> But you know what? Like I said, we were still able to learn, if you wanted to. If you want to learn, you can always learn. Because like I just mentioned, I was out of high school over twenty years, graduated from the last class, and I was able to go to school, after being home over twenty years and graduate with honors. And you know, out of those classes with kids that were like nineteen or twenty years old that were just not even working to their potential, didn't even care, you know. But I guess I was old, too, so that made a difference.

To further understand this hope at work, I asked an additional question: "Do you all think that there are still some black families that suffer today because of racist school decisions that were made in the past?" I heard a range of answers to this inquiry. Some families mentioned their feeling that certain black families were targeted from negative things, like the Biggs family for being student-athletes. I learned from the Biggs and Erskin families of a shared feeling regarding white school personnel who unfairly treated individual black students according to their family's public name recognition and reputation.

If your black family "had a good name," you were fine, whereas individual white students tended not to be held responsible for an entire family's misgivings. If you were a student from a "general" family and had no name, so to speak, with the school, then you may have harsher punishment and you may be more of a target to be viewed as a usual suspect for questioning about negative occurrences at school. Some argued that such white treatment put some black families behind other families. For example, some lighter-skinned, more European-looking black families have sent more kids to universities, while others are still struggling in their attempts to do so. Ross, like Debra agreed that this phenomenon existed to some degree, but they also hold on to human agency (exertion of individual will) as hope for education, even though agency is not always enough:

> We all came up poor and hard, and we were looked down upon, you know, and look at him. I still say it's going to, if that really happens to a family or happens to a child, and he realizes that it has happened to him, and he wants to do something, in my opinion, it's going to make him stronger. If he really wants to do that, because he's going to break that barrier to show, you know, that all of you all tried to hold me down. So really, I don't see where that would really hold a kid back if they had access to all the information and everything that anybody else had, I don't see how that would hold them back. Now if they was denied access to let's say, like, to use the computer, and they couldn't, or everybody else had books and they didn't. So if they were denied access, because of that reason, yes, I would see it, but as long as they weren't denied access to information was available to them just like it was to everybody else if that child was determined, really in my camp, speaking for myself, that would make me stronger, to go ahead and go on. And I don't think anybody should use that as an excuse that somebody else held them back, you know what I mean?

Many of the families have said that this perception is not as direct as "you black kids can't go into the lab," but if you did something without permission, and without a stellar, white-approved black family name, you faced more severe consequences—negative differences in disciplinary actions, such as suspensions versus demerits for committing identical insubordination offences. It was sort of an indirect racialized discrimination, and it was harder on some black families than others. Yet in the end, following in the footsteps of each black person who talked to me, one additional glimmer of hope emerged from the Winston family pedagogy that spoke to the promise of authentic white allies in their desegregated school community.

ROSS WINSTON: . . . I always had the [white] people that was fair in life. . . . Two of the darkest days in history, that I'll always remember when I was in school, was number one, was the day that President Kennedy got shot. I remember how that echoed around the black community, because he was considered a friend of the black community. I remember that day. Of course, the other dark day in history for most black people was the day Rev. Dr. Martin Luther King, Jr. was assassinated.

References

Bloom, L. R. (2001). "I'm poor, I'm single, I'm a mom, and I deserve respect": Advocating in schools as and with mothers in poverty. *Educational Studies.* 32(3), 300–316.

Cecelski, D. (1996). *Along Freedom Road*. Chapel Hill: University of North Carolina Press.

Delpit, L. (1995). The Silenced Dialogue: Power and Pedagogy in Educating Other People's Children. In *Other People's Children: Cultural Conflict in the Classroom*. New York: The New Press.

Giddens, A. (1979). *Central Problems in Social Theory: Action, Structure and Contradiction in Social Analysis*. Berkeley and Los Angeles: University of California Press.

Hughes, K. (2003). *4th Sunday in the Dirty*. Charleston, SC: Imprint Books.

Siddle Walker, V. (1996) *Their Highest Potential: An African American School Community in the Segregated South*. Chapel Hill: University of North Carolina Press.

U.S. Census. (2000). *Profile of General Demographic Characteristics: 2000. Geographic Area: NE Albemarle County, North Carolina*. Online. http://censtats.census.gov/data/NC/05037029.pdf

"Blemished Visions"
Pedagogy and Policy
in a "New" South

BLEMISHED VISIONS
by Kent Hughes

Humanity moving in migratory
Searching for a place to belong
Blemished visions of dreams gone sour
Trusting words of a primitive song
Heavy-handed mouths speak politically correct
Premeditated conversation in the light . . . while . . .
Bombs are being dropped on the cream of the crops
As the illustrious loosen tongues at night
The leaders stepped up to the place
The uninformed has the ball in their hand
The underprivileged watches as leaders play gods
While the oppressed are treated less than human
Hate mongers are kept top secret
The devils are turning us gray
Reprehensible feeling doused in fear
They're going to kill us all someday
The blind mimic the sound that leads them
The strong thrashes ideas at the weak
The ignorant being tortured by the ghost of hope
Blemished visions in dreams as they sleep

Synthesis

How hope was constructed and how it served the Biggs, Erskin, and Winston families through desegregated schooling is a complex story of blemished visions and dreaming toward a better quality of life. Indeed, the story of educational hope for these families is complicated. It changed my original ideas of hope as a mix of distinct variables, which had emerged from literature reviews and remnants of postpositivist ideology—variables of resiliency (goal-seeking individual persistence through struggle), future orientation (reflection of individual goals for evidence of things unseen), and enlightened self-interest (reflection of belief in self and others; actions that reflect self and other obligations). My initial hunch about the educational hope of black northeastern Albemarle families experiencing segregated and desegregated schooling was, simply, linear. I now find that the wealth of education research alluding to resiliency, future orientation, and enlightened self-interest to exist as linear variables that merely skim the surface of understanding how hope works in the educational lives of three northeastern Albemarle black families. In northeastern Albemarle, hope is a ghost and yet a concrete foundation upon which to stand and fight; a road upon which to migrate to something better, but yet to be experienced or seen by most.

Perhaps each time a theoretical topic, like resiliency, was introduced it became reified. The in-depth study of the "thing" focused analyses upon "thingness" and stripped it from the context of actual, lived experience. In such research, hope is a variable that is explained by treating black students and their families as variables. No doubt educational hope among black families in northeastern Albemarle involves resiliency, future orientation, and enlightened self-interest—but not in any formulaic, deterministic sense. Hope is so much more than such linear information portrays. When considering the previous literature (e.g., Lee, 1985; Scott-Jones, 1987; Bempechat, J. 1991; Luster and McAdoo, 1991; Jencks and Phillips, 1998) on hope-related constructs and black student achievement, a deceiving linear model emerges (see Figure 7).

Figure 7: The Deceiving Model of the High-Achieving Black Child

This model represents the merging of resiliency, future orientation, and enlightened self-interest in an area conceptualized as hope. It also emphasizes the influence of the mother as teacher, her effect on the student, and her proclivity toward hope in education and high achievement. A black student seems to obtain a strong sense of hope for school success from his or her ability to recognize and build upon a strong mothering influence. Strength in this area appears to motivate a black child to rise above obstacles of social injustice time and time again in route to success in school. This model, however, is deceiving in many ways. First, hope does not evolve in this simplistic way for the black families in this book. Second, the model reduces the black family to essentially the mother without extended family, which was so important here. Many of the high-performing black children in this book, like those of the Winston family, construct hope through intergenerational family pedagogy. The deceiving model also ignores the intricate relationship of hope, struggle, and pedagogy in black families after the *Brown* decision.

My research findings can be understood as more representative of the "relational" worldview rather than the linear one (Cross, 1998, p. 145). The relational view offered me more tools to interpret the family constructions holistically, while discouraging me from adopting wholesale beliefs that the "problem resides in one person" or family (Cross, 1998, p. 146). With the relational view, I came to understand family resilience, future orientation, and enlightened self-interest as multiplicative; as "holistic and complex interrelationships that . . . allow a family to not only survive but also to grow strong" (Cross, 1998, p. 151). In the end, the results of my study suggest that much of the reviewed education research has oversimplified the dynamics of all three of the central concepts of my work with black families—pedagogy, struggle, and hope.

Pedagogy

Pedagogy in this study is complex and multiple and relational rather than linear and formulaic. It is present in narratives of hope, struggle, and in narration itself. Experiences of struggle and hope are conveyed pedagogically through a particular narration reflecting intent, and cultural specificity. Narratives of struggle cannot sustain black families continuing formal education without narratives of hope, and so a pedagogical move is again made by the black families to provide sustainability to the struggle for adequate educational opportunities in northeastern Albemarle.

The multiplicity of pedagogy in this study was displayed and portrayed under at least four conditions. First, there was intergenerational pedagogy in family and community, a condition I called "teaching the children." Second, as the families themselves learned or relearned the pedagogy through relaying it, there was a condition of pedagogy, or what I called "teaching themselves." Third, the stories shared with me by the families and the decisions they made about what information to take across the borders of insider/outsider and mainstream/homeboy were conditions of pedagogy, or what I called "teaching me." The final condition of pedagogy in this study stems from my analysis and the components of their pedagogical narratives that I feel obligated to share with others, or what I called "teaching them."

The stories were educative in themselves. The narratives recounted perennial lessons in the families. Three generations could recount, for example, that "Grandma always said, 'Work twice as hard as whites, watch, and pray.'" This pedagogy was illustrated by the families from their portrayals of segregated and desegregated northeastern Albemarle schooling. It was pedagogy of survival, where struggle and hope were conveyed through transgenerational stories and constructions of family experiences. In his *Pedagogy of Hope,* Paulo Freire (1996) paired hope for better social conditions with an active struggle to attain them. Freire tied this knowledge specifically to education. Education narratives of the three families centered in this book were, as Freire foreshadows, always situated somewhere between the pedagogy of struggle and of hope.

Pedagogy of Struggle

For the families of this historical ethnography, struggle was not merely the instrument that produced improved educational conditions. Participation in struggle was the improvement itself. Hope was not separate from action, and action in the mid-to-late twentieth century for black Americans constantly required struggle. Hope is what sustained their actions, their struggle for a better quality of life through education. Each generation of the four families constructed struggles and hopes of desegregated schooling that are crucial to understanding change, both what changed for better and for worse, and what still needs to be changed. Struggle was also educative in that desegregation taught the lessons of a need to be critical of racialization and the superiority complexes therein.

The citizens of northeastern Albemarle shared with me the power of struggling through a "hidden transcript" to rebuke the actions of the school "behind direct observation by power holders" (Scott, 1990, p. 4). In light of their use of the hidden transcript, I must acknowledge that the families must have made certain choices about what narratives to share with me. Their oral histories then were tempered by decisions about what to take across insider/outsider borders, similar to the generations before them (Scott, 1990, p. 4). What would black citizens truly say to the school administration in person? Scott cautions us to not judge the truth of what was said in this manner, "power relations are not, alas, so straightforward that we can call what is said in power-laden contexts false and what is said offstage true. Nor can we simplistically describe the former as a realm of necessity and the latter as a realm of freedom" (1990, p. 5).

These families could also use the power of performance. Nate Shaw (cited in Scott, 1990, p. 34) discussed the theater of power and how it can, by artful practice, become an actual political resource of subordinates. Scott (1990) further explains, "what may look from above like the extraction of a required performance can easily look from below like the artful manipulation of deference and flattery to achieve its own ends" (p. 34). Conversely, having power means not having to perform as much, "not *having* to act or, more accurately, the capacity to be more negligent and casual about any single performance" (Scott, p. 29). The black families of northeastern Albemarle are clearly capable in the way of pedagogical performance, and the dynamics of their ability to balance educational struggles and hopes is promising.

All of the families portrayed pedagogy of struggle through narratives concerning the collective struggle for intergenerational closure, and the prevalence of ambivalent, contradictory whites influencing education. Narratives concerning intergenerational closure revealed experiences of a series of losses with school desegregation, all connected with the loss of black school administrators, mentors, and sponsors. Similar to the predominantly white group of Iowa mothers on welfare portrayed by Bloom (2001), the Biggs, Winston, and Erskin families shared feelings of being "devalued, deskilled, and infantilized" by school personnel in numerous meetings and situations.

The family pedagogies were also replete with narratives of backhanded help from ambivalent, contradictory whites who didn't seem to care "how close they got, as long as they didn't get too high." The Dora Erskins of the world to those whites were "needy" blacks, the hired help who could cook for them, have their hands in the biscuits, and serve as nannies, but who were not to be on their PTAs. We learned from a former school board member that northeastern Albemarle used an organizational strategy Eisenberg (1984) calls "strategic ambiguity" (Eisenberg, 1984, p. 230). Strategic ambiguity promotes the façade of unified diversity in three essential ways that pertain to school desegregation in northeastern Albemarle: (1) it is essential to organizing because it allows for multiple interpretations to exist among people who contend that they are attending to the same message; (2) it is essential for organizational goals that "need" to be expressed ambiguously to allow organizations the freedom to alter operations which have become maladaptive over time; and (3) it is essential for facilitating relational development through the emergence of a restricted code to which only certain individuals are privy (Eisenberg, 1984, pp. 230–233). Strategic ambiguity can be a detriment or a blessing for school personnel. For example, it was a blessing during the September 11 horror of 2001, when I was a teacher's aide at an elementary school. It was crucial for our staff to strategically limit the information we gave to the children (many of whom had family in New York and Washington,

D.C.) to decrease false stories and unnecessary emotional strain. However, strategic ambiguity was a curse for black school personnel during the aftermath of *Brown* in northeastrn Albemarle.

When equally and exceptionally qualified black applicants attempted to become teachers and administrators the strategically ambiguous code of the day was "they're not ready yet." When darker brown-skinned teachers sought to help in the desegregation of the formerly all-white high school, few black families knew that being "good to look at" was a key criterion, thereby leading to lighter-skinned, more European-American-looking teachers filling the early school desegregation positions. Black librarians were among the first to desegregate school personnel because they had the least contact with the children, but white administrators could argue "see, we have blacks" and thus the progressive mystique was fueled by strategic ambiguity.

Sadly, along with the loss of most black school personnel, the family narratives conveyed a loss of voice via (a) increased racialized, one-sided school decision making, (b) less welcoming school environments for black parents, (c) less community control over student discipline, and (d) some black community collaboration. With little black representation, and only narrow and white support after northeastern Albemarle schools desegregated, the black families had to endure education through other means—means I interpret to be indicative of pedagogy of hope.

Pedagogy of Hope

Let me use my research findings to propose a counterconceptualization of hope. The Biggs, Winston, and Erskin families constructed hope with narratives that portrayed a more complex relationship than I initially understood. For these families, educational hope seemed to settle at the intersection of future orientation and enlightened self-interest—an intersection indicative of faith. These faith narratives of educational hope were both secular and religious in nature. Now, faith can be understood here as involving "prayer, positive thinking, or other practices families learn to do to bring about a positive outcome or to bring positive spiritual intervention" (Cross, 1998, p. 153). The pedagogy of hope for participating families represented learned positive practices meant to counter struggle—primarily struggle associated with northeastern Albemarle schools, and secondarily struggle associated with negative actions from within the family and community.

The pedagogy of hope narratives here are indicative of faith in several ways.

Initially, I interpreted religious faith as the only faith represented in the narratives. Faith in religion as "the substance of things hoped for, the evidence of things not seen" (Hebrews 11:1). Participating families with religious faith were shown to have a pedagogy of hope through narratives involving the ideas that (1) one should pray for black children to complete twelfth grade and perform at their peak and (2) high school completion would allow those children to live closer to the ideals (crime-free, thankful, humble, and pious lifestyle) of the Missionary Baptist Church Christianity practiced by all of the families.

Although religious faith was prevalent in the narratives, it was only one of several portrayals of faith. Families also recounted a faith that federal mandates would render positive consequences for black families in the desegregated northeastern Albemarle schools. They spoke of a faith that desegregated schools brought, a gain of learning resources and useful skills taught for blacks to achieve in a white-dominated county. There emerged a faith in timeless messages used intergenerationally to achieve and exceed educational goals of the family. Further narration mentioned a faith that other blacks who achieved community goals can be vehicles for publicizing the need for more positive educational consequences. Each of the participants, to my surprise, discussed a family faith in a few authentic white allies who worked directly to help local black students or who worked in some higher administrative function for the area (e.g., Gean Whitehall), the state (former Governor Jim Hunt), or the nation (e.g., John F. Kennedy). Finally, there were narratives in all participating families of faith in assimilation—a faith that through "standard" language, dress, and/or behavior, their children would reach their highest potential with northeastern Albemarle teachers, schools, and society.

Pedagogy of hope narratives in my findings are not separate from struggle, but they are embedded in struggle in stories of family resiliency. The struggle of northeastern Albemarle schools, with all its damage to the families, created an environment where stories of survival were developed, sharpened, and actually played out to be pragmatic (Cross, 1998, p. 151). Just like the narratives of faith, those of resiliency serve the family pedagogy of hope by implanting "beliefs and practices that go with them across generations to provide a great deal of the energy needed to face adversity" (Cross, 1998, p. 155) with northeastern Albemarle schools again and again. The stories of resiliency I found were narratives of positive temperament, personality attributes, and family triumphs, as well as stories to explain how and when to seek useful social support systems, such as people from church who can help a family through difficult times.

It is important to remember that in these narratives, hope is constructed in the process of struggle for civil rights inside and outside of schools. It is equally crucial for interpreting the results of this study to understand storytelling as an artful teaching resource, indeed as pedagogy "for communication of identity, values, and life skills . . . for who our people are and what they stand for, providing role models and subtle expectations" (Cross, 1998, p. 153). The home was a key place to accomplish this pedagogy. bell hooks (1992) helps us to understand the importance of home, but even home as noted in the Winston family story was not always a safe space, as racism and classism and the fear of "niggers getting too high" invade. hooks writes, "No

home is altogether safe from the effects of low wages, and no home can pre-
vent the burning of crosses on the front yard." Paula Groves-Price and Jean
Patterson (personal communication, AERA, April 14, 2004) further explain
that unlike "white and middle class notions of home . . . for many black families home is [also] the place to nurture many of the skills and knowledge to
survive the brutal realities of racism in the outside world" (p. 5). Even television, was noticeably important for the families of this study, as an escape and
as a way to learn vicariously some of the hidden rules and norms of the white
middle class (e.g., humor, wit, language registers, etc.), which would be
needed at school and at work (Guttman & McLoyd, 2000).

Struggle, Hope, and Pedagogy

Thus, the relationship between hope, struggle, and pedagogy from the families' narratives is not a simply linear, or even circular. As the pedagogy of the
families here exudes hope and struggle, perhaps the best pictorial description
is yet to be found. Freire's (1996) work helps to explain the difficulty of illus-
trating this relationship:

> the attempt to do without hope, in the struggle to improve the world, as if that
> struggle could be reduced to calculated acts alone, or a purely scientific
> approach, is a frivolous illusion. . . . Without a minimum of hope, we cannot so
> much as start the struggle. But without the struggle, hope . . . dissipates, loses its
> bearing, and turns into hopelessness. (Freire, 1996, pp. 8–9)

Bourdieu's work offers further insight into pedagogy as defined in this
book. Pedagogy for Bourdieu operates to produce a particular class of conditions that he calls "habitus"—a product of history that, in turn, produces individual and collective practices and ultimately more history. In relation to this
theory, habitus helps to further explain the reproduction of variegated capital-
ist opportunities, hopes, and struggles for northeastern Albemarle's black families. Bourdieu (1990) later discussed the obtaining of cultural capital for the
subjugated (or the mastering of the communicative behavior of the dominant
class) as a means to balance the scale of social and economic benefits. We find
these concepts concerning pedagogy playing out in the lives of the black
northeastern Albemarle family narratives.

Even more than Siddle Walker's work, this study offers complex understandings of the segregated school, and multiple portrayals of the transition to
desegregated schools. Pedagogy in the narratives of the black families featured
in this book can be ultimately understood as being situated somewhere
between education struggles and education hopes. I must add to the comments recalled by retired black teacher Eva Watson, who quoted the former
superintendent in the area when he announced: "If we're going to desegregate, we might as well give them something good to look at." This statement
meant that teachers like Eva, with darker brown skin and less typical Euro-

pean facial features, wouldn't be among the first hired to work in the formerly all-white schools. Thus the darker-skinned family members of this book had an additional fight within the large framework of hope and struggle. Dark or light, all the black family stories can also be discussed in terms of the theoretical debates concerning agency and structure through the dynamic of assimilation and maintenance of separation.

Assimilation and Separation

Assimilation was also offered as part of the pedagogy for all of the families, but assimilation was consistently challenged with stories of sustained separation of certain cultural markers. Arguably the most lucid account of the settlement of blacks as involving both assimilation and separation in the twentieth century was posited by W. E. B. DuBois. DuBois (1903) explained in *The Souls of Black Folk* that the United States citizens of African descent suffered this cognitive dissonance of identities—one African and one American, each contextually tugging, defining, and redefining the black self. DuBois wrote, "I would not Africanize America, for America has too much to teach the world and Africa. I would not bleach my Negro soul in a flood of White Americanism, for I know that Negro blood has a message for the world" (p. 17).

Perhaps the dynamics of assimilation and separation are most present in the family narratives through the use of language for education hope purposes. Hecht, Collier, and Ribeau (1993) discuss code-switching as something that black families such as the Biggs family described as useful for driving hope. The second generation of Biggs constructed a narrative of hope through learning how to speak differently at home than at school in order to assimilate, while maintaining separate, "Black English" at home. Candice Erskin Brown's approach differed in that she wanted her children to speak mainstream English at home and at school. Along with this assimilation tactic however, she sought to remind her three school-aged sons of their blackness, and pressed the need for them to "prove people wrong" about black males. James Hines (son of former cafeteria worker, Margie Hines), was one of the black fathers of the pilot study who wanted his boys to speak black English at home and at school in order to maintain what he felt was authenticity or "keeping it real." Again, the work of Pierre Bourdieu (1977; Bourdieu & Passenon, 1990) also offers pertinent material to explain how the tension between language assimilation and separation actually works as cultural capital for the Erskin and Biggs families, as well as the others in predominantly white spaces such as desegregated schools. In particular, Bourdieu's education theory concerning pedagogic action, along with his widely cited notion of habitus, pertain to this concept.

Policy Implications from Narratives

At the 2002 "Resegregation of Southern Schools" conference, Professor Jack Boger, a former attorney for the NAACP Legal Defense Fund, alluded to education policy in North Carolina as currently facing "The Perfect Storm." Just as the *Andrea Gail* sailed into three powerful natural phenomena (a cold front from the north, warm air up the jet stream from the south, and a hurricane from the east), education in North Carolina faces decreased funding for school finance, resegregation within and between schools, and the high-stakes testing accountability movement.

It does indeed appear that we are enduring the perfect storm in the schools of northeastern Albemarle. We are also witnessing the expansion of massive national vessels in this educational sea of shortsighted standards, from Goals 2000 propelled further by liberals, to a more conservative ship named No Child Left Behind. Both liberals and conservatives endorse top-down federal initiatives holding states accountable for producing a national standard of educational excellence through high-stakes testing. States such as Texas and North Carolina are often lauded for their educational accountability systems and student test-score achievement gains. The news, however, is not all good for such states. Ladd (2001) explains that both Texas and North Carolina suffer from high rates of exclusion of minorities, increasing minority drop out rates, and questionable teaching/testing practices. In this storm, black families and their teachers are often tested prematurely and then ridiculed for being ill-prepared. Seldom are they given more resources to meet standard goals, which usually require some development and implementation of necessary changes to have, literally, no child left behind.

The often-cited psychometrician Robert Linn (2000) concurs that "assessment systems that are useful monitors lose much of their dependability and credibility for that purpose when high stakes are added to them. The unintended negative effects of high-stakes accountability uses often outweigh intended positive effects." In this storm, rural northeastern Albemarle schools must consider education policy problems stemming from their previous inability to negotiate home, school, and standardized test identities. This inability to negotiate identities in desegregated schools has built an unequivocal and frequent distrust, and a perception of a hidden transcript of racial discrimination among black members of the school community.

As a brokering vehicle for these multiple identities, I must also consider what I can bring to the surface here with my education and my capacities. This portion of the book helps me to fulfill my obligation to share a complex school story. As I convey the trials and triumphs of my participants, I am driven by the motives to help undo any negative influences that school desegregation had on the region I call home. I discovered that through policy implications, I can reciprocate. It is my attempt to build a desegregated, rural,

Southern public school ethos or dwelling place sturdy enough to weather any perfect storms that hinder blacks from reaching their highest potential.

Each of the following policy implications, numbered 1–7, are justified with pertinent education research and supplemented by pertinent and archetypal narratives. Narratives chosen for this chapter include revisited descriptions from Ross Winston, retired County A school administrator; Debra Winston, former teacher of Counties A, B, and C; and Ross's eighty-one-year-old father, Woody Winston of County A. Other narratives of this chapter include the poignant words of Margie Hines, a semiretired, former County A school cafeteria worker. Margie is joined by her daughter Shelia Tibbs-Hines, a former elementary school teacher in Counties A, B, and C, and by her grandson, Mike Hines, former student of County A and current senior at a local university. All of their narratives are particularly useful here as they offer transferable information that spans (a) county school experiences representing the three northern mainland counties of the Albemarle area centered in this book, (b) three generations, and (c) at least eight different perspectives (school staff, student, grandparent, parent, teacher, administrator, male, and female).

1. Actively recruit black teachers (lead teachers, student teachers, and assistant teachers), administrators (at the principal and assistant principal level), and administrative assistants.

Noblit and Dempsey (1996) describe a strong wooden stool with three legs (religion, emancipation, and schooling) that existed among black families prior to desegregation. The sturdiness of the stool as an ethos or dwelling place forging possibilities for black families was compromised by the loss of the schooling "leg" after *Brown*. In one set of contemporary narratives from black former teachers who worked before desegregation, we find a "constructed set of virtues that allowed both wide participation of and benefit for the community as a whole" (Noblit and Dempsey, 1996, p. 145). The former teachers recalled a rather "large set" of constructed values in their community prior to desegregation: respect for others, responsibility for others, discipline as a community endeavor, struggle and suffering, excellence for its own sake, and standing firm with faith.

A recent (February, 23, 2003) conversation with a third-generation son of the pilot study reveals further evidence for this need. Mike Hines, grandson of Margie Hines, and current university student studying to become a teacher, graduated from Northeastern Albemarle High School in 2001. With a tone of discouragement on the telephone, Mike recounted an experience with his white principal when he was a student: "I asked the principal, 'Why don't we have any black role models, and especially black male teachers?' He didn't say anything. He started talking about the importance of diversity without directly answering the question. All we have for black role models at the school are custodians and cafeteria workers."

Today, former elementary school teacher, Shelia Hines-Tibbs works as a professor while also facilitating a recruitment and retention program for pre-service teachers of color at a local university. When she heard about my research from this book, she was concerned about the degree to which I was presenting a fuller picture than usually discussed when considering the current state of black teachers in northeastern Albemarle. She felt compelled to add to the story she heard me trying to piece together on the issue:

> In the 1990s, I was one of only two black teachers at the Elementary school in County B. I was treated well, I felt "white" so to speak, I mean, I felt like I was not separated at all. The assistant principal told me that black students were the least problematic of all students at the elementary, middle, and high school at the time.
>
> They tried a sort of colorblind school approach and it worked if they liked you, if your personality fit their norm enough. This fact didn't mean the black teacher was a sell out, I'm just more easy-going and willing to adapt and struggle for the kids to reach their highest potential while they are in my class. I had white parents take their child out of my classroom because I was finding gaps in the child's learning and working on it. Just when the child was starting to make progress they took the child out of my room and specifically to a white teacher— only to have the white teacher tell me, I know that she would have done better staying in your room, I'm having a heck of a time trying to help this child. With this type of story and the few blacks at the school teaching and administrative level in the year 2000 I can't recruit black students that want to teach in the rural districts of [County A, B, C, D, and E]. There is a lack of interest and there is a lack of black juniors and seniors aspiring to teach who actually have full-certification. You can't have black teachers if they refuse to work there.

I interjected (although I probably shouldn't have) and contended that there was "a concerted effort to shut the door abruptly to black school personnel and there should be a concerted effort to welcome them home again to teaching in the rural schools." Shelia Tibbs-Hines acquiesced. I feel that there was a lack of full recruitment planning and effort with incentives by the counties to remedy school desegregation's negative consequences and that a history of strong black teachers and administrators in these counties preceded the lack of interest Shelia Tibbs-Hines finds today.

2. Ensure comprehensive culturally responsive and effective teaching and mentoring of black students—training for white as well as black teachers.

When I worked at the North Carolina Education Research Council (NCERC), Thompson and O'Quinn (2001) edited a report titled, *Black-White Achievement Gap: A Summary of Research*. In this document, NCERC discussed the conclusions about desegregation in North Carolina. By their report, black schools are more likely to have less-qualified teachers and fewer teachers teaching in their field. NCERC highlight the longitudinal (1995, 1996, 1997) study of William Sanders and his associates (see Thompson & O'Quinn, 2001), where black students were less likely to have "effective" teachers than white students. Sanders' research suggests that having an "ineffective" teacher two years in a row puts a black student well behind his or her targeted highest potential for achievement even when the students is tested at the end of a third or fourth year with an effective teacher.

NCERC results are supported by those of North Carolina's Common Sense Foundation (personal communication, March 14, 2002) who also found that black middle-school students are 30 to 40 percent more likely to be taught by a first-year teacher in English or mathematics, and that number rises to 50 percent in urban areas of North Carolina (what Mickelson calls "second-generation segregation"). The percentages are not meant to suggest that first-year, white teachers cannot become effective teachers of black students, but they do suggest a cause for concern about the extent to which less-seasoned teachers disproportionately teach black students in mathematics and English. NCERC cautions North Carolina that the test-score gap can be closed without desegregation, but it would be nearly impossible. Without authentic desegregation, accompanied by sound preservice teacher education and in-service professional development, the gap in black–white test scores will persist, the Council explained. While black students in predominantly black schools may have the resources that matter for high achievement, white schools always do. There is some debate about the "true" existence of a gap in educational achievement, but there is clearly a gap in educational opportunities to learn and educational possibilities between black and white students.

Woody Winston's narrative explains how those black teacher-to-student "resources that matter for high achievement" might be transmitted. His experience in this matter is relayed through a vignette of a golden child, his granddaughter endearingly called "Sonja Babe." Sonja Babe is the youngest child of his eldest son. She was not expected, in Camden's desegregated grade schools, to be as successful as she became, by Woody's account. He suggested that high expectations, along with family support for Sonja's persistence, offer an example of what positive changes that struggle tempered by hope can create. Sonja's story is an important part of Woody's hope narratives, as she was the first to serve the ILA union, not as a laborer, but as an executive with an office, an attorney—a clear upward move in quality of life due to education.

> Well, I'll tell you. Now, when Jimmy's daughter finished school, she told her daddy that she was going to make the honor roll. . . . When you finished the school and there was something you got to be head of the class [valedictorian 1990 or '91]. And she was, and the teachers said she would never do it. But she did. I forgot what it was. Carl could tell you exactly what it was. But anyhow she

made the history on it [one of the first blacks to do so in desegregated school], because Jimmy bought her a brand-new car. It stayed down here two weeks before she finished school. After she finished, he gave it to her. Now she's a lawyer. . . . Yeah, she's a lawyer for the longshoremen there in Norfolk. . . . Yeah, that's the baby girl. . . . We call her Sonja Babe. . . . Yeah, she's a lawyer now for the longshoremen down. . . . Yeah, yeah. She would never make it. But she made it. It's something when you finish high school. And they make you over something there. Anyhow she made it. And when she made it, her daddy bought her a brand-new car. It stayed down here two weeks before she got it.

3. Diversify and expand school counseling, check and change disparities so that it extends to preparing all students for life during and after school.

The lack of sufficient counseling is, of course, related to case load, and the burden of counselors to adhere to national, state, and local pressures to maintain protocols for high-stakes accountability standardized testing. There is, however, another prong of counseling that emerges from the literature concerning the ability of the counselor to get support from families and primary caretakers of students in the school community. Arguably, counseling for rural, southern blacks of northeastern Albemarle experienced a breakdown that coincided with the loss of a more complete system of what Coleman (1988) calls intergenerational closure. A more complete system of closure involves school counselors and adult stakeholders in a given child's life in the school community "who see each other often, have expectations of each other, and develop norms about each other's behavior" (p. 106). Such closure in the black segregated school was replete with opportunities for spaces where all caregivers could discuss, to a high degree, a child's activities at school and come to some agreements about standards and sanctions with much fewer false pretenses or accusations of unethical practices, such as neglect or racism.

It is my adaptation of Coleman's work here that allows for a deeper understanding of Ross Winston's complaints. Although Winston attended a black segregated school, he missed out on the positive influences of intergenerational closure when his mother died. Ross's account of the paucity of "good" counseling comes from the perspective of a child in an otherwise nurturing school environment without a mother, without a key link in connecting school to home and community. Perhaps, from his narrative, we gain tools to better understand the current black child in a desegregated northeastern Albemarle school without counselors who are connected in genuine, loving, and obligatory ways to other integral adults in their lives. In this sense, this black child is without a mother or father figure at school, which is necessary to complete the delicate rectangle of intergenerational closure.

Key informant Ross Winston discussed the necessity of school counselors, to teach coping strategies and prepare students for life after school. Ross's mother died tragically during his school years, and he lamented the absence of adults at school, counselors who could have steered him in the right direction toward a finding a place after graduation. In his rural northeastern Albemarle county school there was no such help.

> Oh yes, yes. When my kids went, it was a lot better. It was a lot better, because they had like a school psychologist. They had like special programs. In school, when I was in school, what did they call it when they had somebody that was slow performer, what did they call that? I forgot what they even did then. But there was a program, but that wasn't until my later years in school that they started doing that. I pray for those slow kids now. It was like institutionalize them, you know.

If, for example, a child's mother or father had passed away, rather than try to offer something to try to help that child, Ross felt that school personnel often felt that they had to stay on them to get them back "right." There would be no sitting students down and talking to a counselor, from his narrative on the subject.

> Counselor? We didn't have no counselor. The counselor was the whip. The counselor was the whip. It wasn't the why you did something, it was what you did, and how you were going to be punished for it. Nobody looked at the problem that was causing you to do it, you know. They didn't know if you had problems at home, or they didn't look at none of that. There was no counseling at all in school.

Ross lamented the lack of a counselor and alluded to the fact that he would have welcomed such a paraprofessional in school as he matured along the key developmental pathways of life: physical, social, emotional, psychological, cognitive, linguistic.

> I can't speak for my wife, but I can say that a feel back, I feel like there was sort of a mourning here, because from '63 until '69, the time I got out of high school, I was still like in a mourning period, because I'm still trying to adjust life without a mother, and I think my wife was in a similar situation. I mean, you know, her daddy got killed the same year my mother did. So we, there were a lot of other factors that we had to think about or trying to adjust to, and so really some of the challenges and some of the other stuff that might have been going on, I probably was concerned, but I still probably had other thoughts of moving on in life.

Ross clearly believes in school psychologists/counselors as key adult stakeholders in the lives of young adults. His narrative was also driven by a strong faith in human agency or the ability to overcome barriers to reaching the educational outcomes one aspires to. It is clear from conversations with Ross that he also recognizes the inherent inequity of opportunity and difficult of being

resilient, when access to crucial school counseling information and resources
are denied to some marginalized students.

> So really, I don't see where that would really hold a kid back if they had access to
> all the information and everything that anybody else had, I don't see how that
> would hold them back. Now if they was denied access to let's say, like, to use the
> computer, and they couldn't, or everybody else had books and they didn't. So if
> they were denied access, because of that reason, yes, I would see it, but as long
> as they weren't denied access to information was available to them just like it
> was to everybody else if that child was determined, really in my camp, speaking
> for myself, that would make me stronger, to go ahead and go on. And I don't
> think anybody should use that as an excuse that somebody else held them back,
> you know what I mean?

4.   Document and change unfair black–white disparities in disciplinary
     actions.

Delpit (1995), a former teacher, recognized that the forms of discipline
used by white teachers was more indirect than what black students were used
to at home, thereby leading to less compliance by the students, and more
complaints about black students' behavior. In her highly acclaimed work, the
transferable thesis is that black students may be offered unfair opportunities to
"behave" when they are misguided by a predominantly white teaching force
caught in the trap of subtle mismatches in home and school cultures of
compliance.

Sometimes Ross Winston's discussion of school desegregation seemed to
ignore his experience as a black former administrator. There were other times
when his administrative standpoint was more in focus and it was clearly driving
our discussions. Several of the struggles he experienced as an administrator are
offered in the narratives below. These were struggles that took place during
the middle of northeastern Albemarle's transition into school desegregation.
Like Margie Hines, Ross abhorred what he interpreted as unfairness in school
disciplinary actions. While Ross's complaints related to his administrative
involvement in monitoring teachers, Margie's discontentment spoke to
inequities in the disciplining students.

> MARGIE HINES, black former cafeteria manager: And then there were some fights
> [school board] but they [whites] kept it quiet. One night they [whites] had Wil-
> ford Leir in the back of the building beating him up bad, a girl saw it and told
> the black kids and they all were fighting, but they kept it quiet, real quiet, you
> didn't hear about it much, it wasn't in the newspaper or anything. Some white
> boys messed another black boy's head up real bad. He's was walking from school
> and they threw something out of the truck and hit him in the head with it. They
> said his family drove right past him and didn't see him because he had fallen in
> the ditch bank. Somebody reported it, we think it was probably the boys who

did it, because they left him for dead. A few years later he died from that too; he was never quite right again. But, they [whites] kept it real quiet too.

Ross WINSTON, black former administrator: But even knowing that my student could see if a white teacher did something the penalty still wasn't quite as severe for them as for the black doing the same thing. I could see that. But when you've got one vote, you could voice your opinion. I might not have got no satisfaction on that one. But when they brought it back again, with a situation like that, they were making it a little bit different. One crime, one punishment. I did get them to do that. Instead of like saying, they just did this, or like a kid telling a white lie and a little white lie. A lie is a lie.

Ross Winston's unique lens also held context clues for understanding why he was one of only two informants who did not equate black student decline and corporal punishment in schools. His perspective on this issue of spanking in schools to discipline black students was markedly different from the other informants. Ross claimed that he wouldn't want white or black teachers and school personnel to have the privilege of spanking his own children. His agreement with the departure of corporal punishment in northeastern Albemarle public schools was accompanied by an undertone of volatility in race relations in the area. To further interpret Ross's comments, it seems that he is saying that discipline in the desegregated northeastern Albemarle schools is racialized and spanking students won't solve that ideological problem.

Man, some of these people that's in school, I look at their lifestyle, and I wouldn't want them touching my kid. You know what I mean. . . . No, no way. When I look at them, and I know what their lifestyle is and the things that they do, I wouldn't want them disciplining my kids. And I think the situations is that what's happening is, it's a responsibility that the parents today have, but they don't want to do. They want somebody else to do it for them. Spanking their child, they don't spank the kids at home, but then they feel like someone at school should have the privilege to spank them. And some of these people, I wouldn't want them touching my children. And they've got this thing now, you know, at that time it was black on black, you know. But now you've got you don't know what the person's racial thinking is, or I think a lot of people say things without even trying to you know address or even think about what they are saying, when they say they want people to discipline their kids. They wish it was like it was when they were in school.

It's just totally different. . . . Then, you see, you've got that thing about even with the punishment now, you know, a lot of black kids fall through a loophole of being more severely punished or privilege taken away . . . That's even here today, you know.

To further understand this disciplinary issue and why it needed to change, an additional question was posed: "Do you all think that there are still some black families that suffer today because of racist school decisions that were made in the past?" I heard a range of answers to this inquiry. Some families mentioned their feeling that certain black families, depending on their family names, were targeted for negative things or spared from them, or simply stereotyped, like the Biggs family for being student-athletes. I learned from the Biggs and Erskin families that they felt that whites cling to the black family name. If your black family had a good name, you were fine. If you were average and had no name, so to speak, with the school, then you may have gotten harsher punishment, and may have been more of a target or suspect whenever something happened. So that put some families, some people argue, behind other families.

5. Increase black parent participation (see Comer-type model [1996, 1999]) where the black parents of northeastern Albemarle schools have more representation and an active, legitimate voice).

In one set of contemporary narratives from black former teachers who worked before desegregation, we find a "constructed set of virtues that allowed both wide participation of and benefit for the community as a whole" (Noblit & Dempsey, 1996, p. 145). Blacks in the school community recalled a rather "large set" of constructed values in their community prior to desegregation: respect for others, responsibility for others, discipline as a community endeavor, struggle and suffering, excellence for its own sake, and standing firm with faith.

Another loss in Ross and Debra's narratives about integrated school was that lack of closure between black parents, school personnel, and the child. The loss of the adult stakeholders in the black child's life as collaborative, consensus, and no-fault teams was present in all of the stories of black participants. Ross discussed this loss in an anecdote about his interaction with the school as he attempted to address a problem with one of his daughters at school. Ross also offered his family's distrust of the school to see that the third generation of Winstons reached their highest potential in northeastern Albemarle's desegregated school.

> I really, one time I had a problem with a superintendent. And I went through the chain of command, and when that chain of command reached him, he was supposed to have gave me a call back, and as a matter of fact, I left word and asked him to call me back, and I know that that's a busy position, and he didn't return my phone calls. And so I got on the phone and I called one of the board members in and told him, "Looks like I've gone as far as I can go. I talked to the teacher, I talked to the principal, and I had asked the superintendent to call me back so we could set up something, and he wouldn't return my call." And that problem, it was taken care of. But really that's about the only thing, but I always, you know. . .
>
> Oh, no. Now, I had one daughter that was an A student and I had another daughter that was a C student. And my daughter that was the C student got all the help that she needed, you know what I mean, to don't care if some of them

might have been special classes or whatever. But you see, we was right on top of that, because we didn't take their opinion per se. We took our daughter and had her evaluated ourselves, too.

White families did not lose as much closure, at least not from the experiences conveyed by Ross and Debra. The typical white family has more allies within the school system. Sometimes those whites are old family friends, and other times they are actually family. In both situations, the white child has more of the intergenerational closure at the integrated school that mirrors what blacks once had in segregated black schools such as Marian Anderson. Ross explained:

> And you know for some, it's always a family that's, you know, got more people working in the school system than anybody else. It's always one family that's going to try to dominate anything that one of them get involved in, they going to try to dominate the whole thing. And off the record I'll give you their name, but on the record I won't give you their name. I just want you to check that out. And when that family, the first one that came here, and they weren't even qualified for the position that they had. But they got it because of the family name. And now sisters, cousins, nieces, I mean everything, the whole family is in there.

6. Address race and color in the curriculum. Use innovative and integrating texts, and lessons that address multifaceted issues of race.

Rosalyn Mickelson's work on Charlotte, North Carolina, post-*Swann*, discusses how the desegregated school systematically changed the status of black students. Mickelson spent fifteen years gathering research about the effects of first- and second-generation segregation in the schools in Charlotte-Mecklenburg, North Carolina. Mickelson's comprehensive quantitative study suggests that black students received disproportionately negative influences on their schooling due to first-generation segregation and that second-generation segregation also negatively influences their chances of college and university enrollment, especially at top schools, which thereby continues to afford whites more positive possibilities from educational experiences.

In light of this dismal information, Ross and Debra seemed to feel a special duty as black parents to educate their children about certain things they knew that they weren't getting in the desegregated schools of northeastern Albemarle. They sought to help prepare their children in ways that they may not have been compelled to by white teachers. Similar to Shujaa, Ross offered the notion that black students are schooled and not educated, but he uses the term "trained." He seemed also to be in the middle as a former school administrator who tried to effect change, and as a parent who feels that he could use his agency to educate his children at home to counterbalance the training they received at school.

No. 1, we had to let them realize, you know, although they were being edu-cated. I don't like to use that word, "educated." I like to use the word "trained." Yeah, I like to use the word "trained," because education to me comes within there [heart and home]. And I think we're sending our kids to be trained not educated. We should educate our kids ourselves. I think they're being trained. But anyway, you see, that's our [all adult stakeholders in a child's life at home and at school] fault.

I like to use the scenario, you take a dog and he jumps through a loop. Is that a trained dog, or is that an educated dog? I would say it's a trained dog. But I would say that's a trained dog. But a dog that takes a bone and goes digs a hole and buries it in the ground for later, that's an educated dog. That's just instinct.

Another example that I use: A lot of people holler about the Greeks and the Greeks. If they would dig back and really read their history, it was the Egyp-tians, you know what I mean. It was with the Egyptians that all this knowledge and stuff really came from. And you know there is the story told, and I read some books about how it was taken away or stolen by the Greeks. But a lot of people you know they, and that's why I have a problem with some of the Greek letter organizations, because I don't think some of them really did the research that really needs to be done some of these organizations. I don't . . . I mean, I like the organization, but I still think some of them have been leading us astray for a long time.

7. Eliminate negative strategic ambiguity about racialization in school. Begin schoolwide conversations about multifaceted issues of race. Stop pretending to be colorblind and stop waiting until negative con-sequences of race surface at school.

Mickelson (2001) indicated several crucial direct and indirect effects of desegregation on black students in some North Carolina schools. First, she found that end-of-grade tests (EOGs), end-of-course tests (EOCs), grade-point averages (GPAs), and Scholastic Aptitude Test scores (SATs) were all linked significantly to prior achievement. Second, tracking was the second highest predictor of SAT verbal and test battery scores and third highest pre-dictor of SAT math scores. Third, her results indicate that even when control-ling for prior achievement, effort, and self-selection, black students were significantly less likely to be in the higher tracks, what she calls second-generation segregation. Finally, she also found that the high and low tracks in high school English were heterogeneous, meaning that the classes were filled with students who had previously scored in the first-fourth decile and the first-tenth decile, respectively. The latter findings support evidence showing that prior achievement was not the sole culprit behind black students not being in the high tracks, but that track placement largely involved racial discrimination.

Retired school official Ross Winston is married to Debra, a current public school teacher in northeastern Albemarle. I wanted to learn about policy changes from their broad and deep perspectives on dealing with key race rela-tions. The idea was to pinpoint a place to start the conversation. It became evident yet again that race must be discussed as it pertains to recruitment and retention of school personnel. Initially, I asked them if they would talk about some of the feelings they have or have had about more overt racism in any of the decisions that were made by people in charge of policymaking in the northeastern Albemarle schools. To them, what was clearly racism in school decision making?

More explicit racial atrocities in decision making about school personnel emerged in Ross and Debra's dialogue about the plight of black substitute teachers. Debra took the forefront in the dialogue since as a substitute teacher, she could compare and contrast northeastern Albemarle versus other counties. Ross added to her story a cause from his administrative stance, racism among the secretaries, those in charge of assigning and calling in substitute teachers. Ross claimed that later in his service as an administrator, whites begin to complain to the new black secretaries that only black substitute teachers were being selected. The dialogue below suggests that this was a painful reminder for their family that race still matters and it matters most in northeastern Albemarle schools.

> RW: You know about racism here, man, you don't have to put this in here if you don't want to but. . . .

> DW: I worked for [inaudible] in northeastern Albemarle County B County. There's a big difference there between northeastern Albemarle County B and northeastern Albemarle County A and C, but northeastern Albemarle County A, of all three counties I've worked in, it is the most prejudiced county that I have encountered. And I'll tell you why I picked this up even before I started working in the City. I was subbing in both counties. Northeastern Albemarle County-B, it was often, very often. Northeastern Albemarle County-C was often. And many times they would call me, but I had already you know been asked to go to northeastern Albemarle County-B, and I always went to the first school. Northeastern Albemarle County-B, they would book full, if they knew a teacher was going to be out for two or three weeks ahead of time, if you happened to be there that particular day, they would go ahead and ask you could you come in at that particular time. Northeastern Albemarle County-A for blacks did a spur of the moment thing. I got to feeling as "If we can't find nobody white this morning, let me call and ask Mrs. Winston." And when I would go in there and look at lesson plans, I would also find that if a teacher knows that she's going to be out for two or three days, it would make better sense to keep that same sub. That's how we do it in the city. That's how it was done in northeastern Albemarle County B County. Northeastern Albemarle County A, you know they call you in that morning. You always had the feeling that they couldn't get anybody else. And you get in and you see that the teacher is going to be out all week. But they only asked for that particular day. So I mean, there's something wrong there. You know, and that put me out with northeastern Albemarle County A right from the start. But you don't have to write this because I know that Ross was an administrator [there], and he might be a little offended by it, but it's the truth is what I gathered.

RW: I'm going to add something to that. The reason that was happening is the secretaries controlled who comes in to do the substitute.

DW: That's right. So really the principal, he could care less, you know. All he wanted was someone there. So that was the secretary using her authority for her friends and everything. All right now, if you look at the way it's happening now, it's not happening that way no more in northeastern Albemarle County-A. You see, I don't work there anymore. You've got Paula, who's black, and she's in charge of calling in the substitutes now, and you've got Hanna at the primary school.

RW: I'm talking about the middle schools when there was a white secretary. And so, none of the parents . . . I understand what you're saying, but I'm looking at the reasons why it happened. Not saying that the reasons it happened was right, but why it happened was because the secretaries was white at that time, and they called their friends, and now we have got criticism since Paula and Hanna have been in there, that all they do is call black substitutes.

DW: I was treated nice. I didn't see any difference, but you know, in the back of my mind I kept saying, "You know, you know. The reason I'm here is because they probably couldn't find anybody else." And you know, that put me out with northeastern Albemarle County A I guess right from the start. . . . I guess they thought that nobody would pick up on the fact, but you know, I picked up on it, you know, right from the start. I picked up on it.

An additional point for the race conversation arose from a conversation at the home of Woody, Ross's father. In a short narrative, Woody relayed the need to discuss race to build stronger relationships between youth, between youth and school personnel, and between school personnel, and between school personnel and families of different racialized identities. Woody's story moves beyond mere racial discrimination to detail typical, contemporary displays of black–white school violence.

I've seen a colored girl tearing a white girl up and people walking right by. Because they know if they jump in, all them school children would jump on him. Understand?
        When they start to integrate the school, see they done it themselves. They didn't hire me to whip their children, but it'd be all right for them to whup ours. . . . That's right. See, a lot of people don't understand that. But that's so. They don't want you [a black man] whupping their children.

Woody's narrative about race foreshadowed a school incident that occurred one full year later. As recently as March 2004, a group of black youths and their families in northeastern Albemarle County B (noted initially by Debra Winston as being less racialized than County A) sought the services of the NAACP to handle complaints of racial discrimination against them at school. Policy change is past due.

References

Bempechat, J. (1991). *Fostering High Achievement in African American Children: Home, School, and Public Policy Influences.* New York: ERIC Clearinghouse of Urban Education, Office of Educational Research and Improvement, U.S. Department of Education and Institute for Urban and Minority Education, Teachers College, Columbia University.

Bloom, L. R. (2001). "I'm poor, I'm single, I'm a mom, and I deserve respect": Advocating in schools as and with mothers in poverty. *Educational Studies.* 32(3), 300–316.

Bourdieu, P. (1990). *The Logic of Practice.* Cambridge, UK: Polity Press.

Bourdieu, P., & Passeron, J.-C. (1977 [1970]). *Reproduction in Education, Society and Culture.* Trans. R. Nice. Beverly Hills, CA: Sage.

Coleman, J. S. (1988). Social capital in the creation of human capital. *American Journal of Sociology,* 94, 95–120.

Comer, J. P. (1996). *Rallying the Whole Village.* New York: Teachers College Press.

Comer, J. P. (1999). Prologue: Child by child: The Comer process for change in education. In J. P. Comer, M. Ben-Avie, N. M. Haynes, & E. T. Joyner (Eds.), *Child by Child: The Comer Process for Change in Education.* New York: Teachers College Press.

Comer, J. P., Ben-Avie, M., Haynes, N. M., & Joyner, E. T. (Eds.). (1999). *Child by Child: The Comer Process for Change in Education.* New York: Teachers Collegee Press.

Cross, T. L. (1998). Understanding family resiliency from a relational worldview. In H. I. McCubbin, E. A. Thompson, A. I. Thompson, & J. E. Fromee (Eds.), *Resiliency in Ethnic Minority Families: Native and Immigrant American Families,* pp. 143–157. Madison: University of Wisconsin.

Delpit, L. (1995). The Silenced Dialogue: Power and Pedagogy in Educating Other People's Children. *Other People's Children: Cultural Conflict in the Classroom.* New York: The New Press.

DuBois, W. E. B. (1903). *The Souls of Black Folk.* Chicago: A. C. McClurg & Co.

Eisenberg, E. M. (1984). Ambiguity as strategy in organizational communication. *Communication Monographs,* 51, 227–242. Reprinted in Hutchinson, K. (1991). *The Organizational Communication Reader.* Dubuque, IA: Wm. C. Brown.

Freire, P. (1996). *Pedagogy of Hope.* New York: Continuum.

Gutman, L. M., & McLoyd, V. C. (2000). Parents' management of their children's education within the home, at school, and in the community: An examination of African-American families living in poverty. *Urban Review,* 32(1), 1–24.

Hecht, M., Collier M., & Ribeau, S. (1993). *African American Communication.* Newbury Park, CA: Sage.

hooks, b. (1992). *Black Looks: Race and Representation.* Boston: South End Press.

Hughes, K. (2003). *4th Sunday in the Dirty [South].* Charleston, SC: Imprint Books.

Jencks, C., & Phillips, M. (Eds.) (1998). *The Black-White Test Score Gap.* Washington, DC: Brookings Institution.

Ladd, H. (2001). School-Based Educational Accountability Systems: The Promise and the Pitfalls. *National Tax Journal,* 54(2), 385–400.

Ladd, H., Chalk, R., & Hansen, J. (Eds.). (1999). *Equity and Adequacy in Education Finance: Issues and Perspectives.* Washington, DC: National Academy Press.

Lee, C. (1985). Successful rural black adolescents: A psychological profile. *Adolescence* 20, 129–142.

Linn, R. (2000). Assessments and accountability. *Educational Researcher*, 29(2), 4–17. Available: www.aera.net/pubs/er/arts/29–02/linn01.htm

Luster, T., & McAdoo, H. (1991). *Factors Related to the Achievement and Adjustment of Black Children*. Paper presented at the biennial meeting of the Society for Research in Child Development, Seattle, WA, April 1991.

Mickelson, R. (2001). Subverting Swann: First- and second-generation segregation in Charlotte schools. *American Educational Research Journal*, 38(2), 215–252.

Noblit, G.W., & Dempsey. (1996). *The Social Construction of Virtue: The Moral Life of Schools*. New York: State University of New York Press.

Scott, J. C. (1990). *Domination and the Arts of Resistance: Hidden Transcripts*. New Haven, CT: Yale University Press.

Scott-Jones, D. (1987). Mother-as-teacher in the families of high- and low-achieving low-income first graders. *Journal of Negro Education,* 56(1), 21–34.

Thompson, C. L., & Quinn III, S. D. (2001). First in America Special Report: *Eliminating the Black-White Achievement Gap*. North Carolina Education Research Council, June. www.firstinamerica.northcarolina.edu/reports/short_report_achievement.pdf

7

"Your Child"
Hope from a Past in a Present for the Future

YOUR CHILD
by Kent Hughes

Help me to be strong
Inspire, encourage and honor my thoughts
Push me forward when I fall behind
Pick me up when I'm down
Be my strength when I'm weak
My voice when I can't speak
Direct me when I'm lost
Show me how to, even when I think I know
Teach me when I want to learn
Teach me even more when I don't
Love and protect me forever
Because after all I am . . .
YOUR CHILD

Revisiting Family Pedagogy

Intergenerational Biggs Family Pedagogy

I was able to have discussions with Willis and Virginia Biggs and to observe them with their younger child, about whom they said: "My son minds. He really minds us." "Minding" came up often, meaning: "My son is disciplined; he follows our directions." I was again impressed by the Biggs family and how much this family worked. Willis works two jobs, usually doesn't get home until 8:00 at night, and leaves early in the morning. I believe that he is a good, responsive, active father. Willis is extremely proud of his daughter Kady and what she's accomplished.

I was also very excited about some things that Willis and Virginia mentioned. Virginia is a teacher and they talked about what is called "code-switching" in academics. The idea that in black families with black children have to change their speech to move back and forth between what we call mainstream American English, which generally means "white"—mainstream white American English—and black English, which, as some communication scholars (e.g., Hecht, Collier, & Ribeau, 1993) have noted, holds lingering patterns that come from the African heritage. That is, it is not just black Americans making up new things to say, but that some elements of black English came over along with the passage. Many of those patterns still exist, such as "he ben da." "He bend a go" is actually a Western African phrase that means, "He went." Similarly, we say, "He ben done gone." This is just one example of elements that linger in the language pattern. Virginia was explaining that one of her children said, "You know, you talk like a white woman when you're at school." And she explained to her that using the different tool, like the spoon for cereal and the fork for pasta, was how to approach ways to use changes in language to one's advantage. Virginia's argument to her daughter was that her family needed to use those different tools to accomplish whatever you need to accomplish as a good survival skill. It also leads back to a cultural response to teaching, as Virginia also alluded. Of course, there are trade-offs to this approach, as black English is continually accepted as incorrect by schools.

Not all black families are at this point in their language patterns, and in their ability to code-switch. Again, due to a history of oppression, I began to argue from what I had seen with these families up to that point that their education options were more limited than whites'. And so where they may have had option A (assimilate to white school) and B (hold on strongly to black identity and suffer consistently negative consequences at school), blacks acted upon those two consistent options. White families even in their same working-class and middle-class income bracket, perhaps had option A (reinforce white school standards), B (purposefully exercise white privilege in school), C (inadvertently exercise white privilege in school), and D (resist their own privilege). Whites acted upon those additional options. With that in mind, it seems that at least the Erskin and Biggs educational histories were largely dependent upon these options and actions which affect: (a) the chances and opportunities whites and blacks would act upon, (b) the options that would increase language capabilities or decrease the amount of mismatch between the language spoken at home or at school, and (c) the ability of the child to be able to code-switch back and forth.

Both generations of the Biggs family constructed a story of working well together. Their homes were immaculate. Willis and Virginia live in a double-wide trailer. They also live in a very rural area. Behind their home are fields, and in front of their home are fields, but they do live in an area where there are a lot of homes along their road. And they live immediately adjacent to a church, which said a lot to me about that family, because I believe they could have built their home anywhere. Yet, Christianity is a part of their under-standing of life and a major part of their understanding of education.

Their young child, affectionately called "Li'l Bruh," paid attention to what they had to say. During my second visit, I arrived as soon as Willis had gotten home from his second job, and he was extremely nice to me. When I walked in, Virginia was busy with what they call "tutoring time." The mother was tutoring the son in mathematics, and so I told her to take her time, to tutor him as long as she needed to. She said, "Two more problems and I'll come over," and she did and the child went to bed. This example is the type of family that we see here, with the second generation of Biggs and Erskin family members: an emphasis on homework and "you can do it" motivation.

This representation reminded me of another black mother, Candice Erskin Brown, for whom homework is also important. Both mothers even yell if necessary, to make sure that their children understand that they need to do their homework. Both strongly feel that they will help their children if they can, and if they cannot, another tutor will be found. Candice had already found an external tutor for her second-grade child. I was impressed. The Biggs family, like the Erskin family, was dynamic and fascinating. The nuances of their northeastern Albemarle school desegregation experience were distinct and specific enough to warrant a full chapter, to offer yet another transferable black experience of this complex educational space.

At the end of my final visit with the Biggs family, I was able to have a lit-tle tour of their home. I saw interactions between Ruth and one of her grand-children. As I was over this morning, Rena did participate. She apologized for not participating earlier; Larry must have shared excerpts of our conversation from the previous two days.

> RB: I'm sorry I didn't get in here to talk the other times I was asleep. He came in there and said, "Aren't you coming in?" I said, "I'm going to get up in a minute and put my housecoat on." Then I didn't know anything. I went and got in the bed. I went and got in bed last night. That's bad, isn't it?

There were possibly a hundred pictures of family members, children, and grandchildren on the walls. But I was surprised to see was a rather large photo, probably ten by sixteen inches of Joe Namath and his first wife, Debbie. Deb-bie May, as she was called, was actually the granddaughter of one of the white northeastern Albemarle farmers for which the Biggs family worked. Debbie grew up in the North, but often visited her northeastern Albemarle relatives for long periods of time. When Debbie was married to Joe Namath, Mr. Biggs said she sent money and gifts to Rena. They had known Debbie as a child, when she came to northeastern Albemarle to visit, all the way into her adult-hood. Debbie spent enough time in northeastern Albemarle to grow quite fond of "Miss Rena" Biggs. Although Debbie and Joe Namath are no longer together, the Biggs family still keeps that really large picture in their sitting room.

I respect the Biggs family tremendously. With Larry Biggs' positive comments about my grandmother, I realized the burden of living up to my family's reputation. The Erskin family and the Biggs families live within two miles of one another, and both families live within two to three miles of my parents. I felt sure that the information about my arrival would traverse family bounds. My mother later commented that Mr. Biggs said, "I enjoyed talking with your boy." The news did travel indeed. Before I left the Biggs home for a final time, I asked, "If you could go back and tell the young Larry and young Rena something about hope and education, what would y'all say?" Their answers spoke loudly and clearly about the origin of their pedagogy.

RB: I would tell them, go further. Go further.

LB: Reach for the stars.

RB: Yeah. Go further. Keep on. Just don't give up. I wouldn't go back. I wouldn't go back.

LB: Study hard and—

RB: Do better.

LB: Get that highest education that you can get.

RB: That's right. I couldn't get it. Didn't let anything. . . . I would just do all I could if I had it to do over again. I had it over again, umm. I'd probably be right here. I would be right here, but I would be better or something. I don't know where I would be. Thank the Lord I'm living, though. . . .

Intergenerational Erskin and Winston Family Pedagogy

The Erskin family narratives of struggle and hope reflected their experiences. Their constructions were dominated by the perspective of Dora, the mother, and her influence on the second-generation children. Dora acknowledged that her husband, Nolen, is part of the family's school desegregation story, yet her dominance often left him somewhat silenced during our meetings. I felt that I learned less about this generation of their family because I had unanswered questions about his points of agreement or dissent with Dora. Candice, their daughter, offered information that led to an understanding of the Erskins' construction of their educational experiences as transgenerational. The stories of tribulation and triumph, struggle and hope in desegregated education then became educative in themselves—educative in understanding obstacles that lie dormant and those that lie ahead, and hopeful tools for transcending the hurdles of attending predominantly white northeastern Albemarle schools.

Of course, the Erskin family members are more than a research project on struggle and hope; they are also a powerful unit of love. It is an evolving love constructed of displays of affection by Erskin mothers and grandmothers as well as young Erskin men. Candice's portrayal of her attempt to "degenderize" love for her boys seemed crucial to their growth and her own:

> Hugging and kissing. We have like a nickname. Every night we say, "I want a kissy face." That means, you know, "You didn't give me one." Then they'll come and give me a hug and say, "I love you, Ma." [I say]"I love you, too." That means a lot.
>
> How can they love their [own] families if you don't even have love here, if you didn't grow up with love. My boys hold babies up, and even animals. You would think the animals were babies. You don't see many males like that.

The Erkin family members live in one of the most rural parts of rural northeastern Albemarle areas of North Carolina. In the front of their homes are large fields, which look like corn was just harvested. In the back of their homes are wooded patches of pines. Their homes are approximately six miles from the high and middle schools, and about eight miles from the elementary school. Their narratives and constructions lead to a better understanding of the influences of desegregated schooling in northeastern Albemarle and the possibilities to ameliorate its residual harm to black families like theirs. I am proud to be part of their storytelling. Candice Erskin clearly foresees her sons as part of the fruit of her family's educational labor. Her comments toward the end of my time with her offered a fitting end to her family's narratives of struggle and hope:

> That's all I'm saying. Do the best you can. And like I tell my mother, "When my boys are grown, if they turn out to be something other than what I saw in them, at least I know I did my part. I did my part." To some of the black females I want to say, "Let's get away from the boyfriend that gets more attention than the children. You know, let's get away from that."

To some extent, one could argue that the white schools were "successful" for black families such the Erskins: (a) successful in stripping away most of their cultural contexts and understanding of schooling, (b) successful in schooling blacks to not question white power structures and black people's place in history, and (c) successful in schooling black children to achieve moderate "moving ahead" by white standards, while fooling many black parents into believing their children were being fully educated—that no child was being left behind. I was reminded of the fact that predominantly white schools such as those in northeastern Albemarle are skillful at schooling blacks, but not educating them. This is done in such a way that shows learned abilities to critique curricula, that presents the types of "good" jobs black students should expect, and that sorely lacks black cultural traditions and knowledge of those cultural traditions.

The Winston family conveyed the agency–structure tension that was offered in all of the previous family narratives, but their story also reflected a stronger understanding of limited change due to structural boundaries (likely due to Ross's involvement with northeastern Albemarle school administration). It was between this space of agency and structure that I found the Winston family stories of resiliency and efficacy. They were stories that involved unacknowledged conditions of actions on one side, and unintended consequences of action on the other side, with reflexive monitoring of action, rationalization of action, and motivation of action lying between the two (Giddens, 1979). The Winston family portrayed this tension in their narratives as they offered stories of being catalysts for change, while lamenting that not enough change occurred. They had hoped for an education but felt that they received what Ross called "training." The northeastern Albemarle school "training" of which Ross spoke seemed to connote black desegregated schooling as something that, unfortunately, led many blacks to merely reproduce oppression—a tactic the same blacks paradoxically argued against because it reflects white privilege ideology and practice.

Revisiting Entry, Role, and Reciprocity

A few months after packing up to leave northeastern Albemarle to inspect my complete collection of school desegregation stories, my mother called with a proud message:

> I saw Ol' Man Winston in town and he was smiling and he said, "I enjoyed talking to ma boy!" and I said, "Who?" and he said, "You know, your youngest boy." I said "Oh, Sherick." "Yeah," Ol' Man Winston replied, "I really enjoyed that boy."

Like other black men, I abhor most references to black males as "boys." Many of our families share the long historical struggle of our forefathers, who fought for the civil and legal rights to be acknowledged as men, and no longer as perpetually docile boys (Hughes, 2003), nor animals (Allport, 1954). However, I felt overjoyed and honored to fulfill the role of "ma boy" in the Winston family. It soon became clear to me that I am a boy, a child, their child of northeastern Albemarle, North Carolina. This clarity of vision was accompanied by conscientious reflection (or positionality and reflexivity). It was a new lucidity that seemed to demand of me a more in-depth exploration into the delicate, intricate necessities of entry, role, and reciprocity. Through reconsideration of entry, role, and reciprocity, I continue to contemplate how to be the best child for northeastern North Carolina, and in fact how to become a better young steward of desegregated schools in the area.

Entry

Emily Herring Wilson (1983) speaks of hope and dignity among black folks in the South. It is a hope and dignity that is so poignant that it becomes quite tangible as the school desegregation stories unfold. For the black school community of this book, a pedagogy of hope breaks down, climbs over, or digs around barriers of struggle that arise with each new educational opportunity. My entry point into this vibrant community hinged upon my ability to code-switch. Code-switching (Hecht, Collier, & Ribeau, 1993) is likely found in the repertoire of all native ethnographers. This communicative tool involves a sort of strategic calling upon of another identity, not only to "remember where I came from," not necessarily to "keep it real," but to return home with an understanding that my role is still to learn from the community as "Jessie Hughes' boy," while weaving in an out of a formal and casual register of language to suggest I have "made it" but haven't lost touch with my roots.

Role

In essence, it illustrates the concern of native ethnographers in my position to respond to the people who produced the role of black male—Dr. Sherick A. Hughes—only after metamorphosing into the role of rural, black, working-class "Shurrit Hughes" from "Nofe Riva" Road. Upon initiation of action, one iteration marks me as humble, respectful, and credible, while another suggests I am "uppity" and in need of being put in my place. So if blackness is part performance, such as whiteness, Latino-ness, etc., then I perform my native blackness through a delicate portrayal of two lived experiences: one experience of researcher and another as member of a researched community. Subtleties include accented "country" drawl words (such as "sho' nuff") and phrases (such as "ain't dat dah truf"), archetypal Southern etiquette (such as "Yes, ma'am"), and nonverbal behavior (such as the nodding that follows "You right, you right," standing or sitting in close proximity, and the touch to a shoulder or knee that often accompanies humor). There is a way of talking and listening that is brilliant and comforting to me, where points are taken and directions understood although neither party may have finished a sentence. I sometimes tease and say that I never finished a sentence until I was twenty-three years old!

I have mentioned only the details of communicative behavior of which I am cognizant. My details are not intended to be exhaustive or to be considered a "how-to" list for nonnative ethnographers. My information is only meant to be educative and to illustrate the complexity of native ethnography. My intent is not to suggest that I was "acting" to get what I wanted. I am professor and homeboy both; it is neither acting in servitude nor acting to participate solely with one audience or the other. It is playing my part in the theater I inherited—a company of multiple social contracts to fulfill my democratic rights as an individual and the democratic ideals that bind me to everyone else. I have also come to terms with the fact that I am not always good at being me. In attempts to explore or illustrate how history shapes our past, present, and future, I cannot always find the right communication tool for conveying my feelings of respect, beliefs about ethics, and passion for lifelong education at home and school. It is doubtful that anyone can.

All of the roles played by school personnel and families who experience school desegregation live these challenging roles and relive them with us through narrative. My job as a native ethnographer, trying to relive and recapture my own past, somehow helped me to understand likely challenges faced by all ethnographers seeking to "go native." Even the most sincere and altruistic among native researchers are sure to face difficulties conveying intentions and motives in communities that are to some degree no longer our own. I am reminded of Margie Hines' comments to me via telephone concerning a notably committed, competent, and caring white colleague of mine who visited the area when my ethnography was complete. Margie said, "I told her some things, baby, but I didn't tell her all the things I told you." The work of native ethnography may be an integral component of our future education policy efforts as we learn that participants, in their roles, do not always bring information across any perceived social borders separating their role from that of the researchers. Then, of course, there are the roles that are imposed upon us, as when I sought understanding and intellectual refuge in the homes of these familiar people and engaged their lived experiences of pedagogy.

Reciprocity

In the conclusion of Vanessa Siddle Walker's (1996) prize-winning book on segregated schooling, *Their Highest Potential,* the native of Caswell County, North Carolina, writes, "even under the oppression of segregation, teachers, principals and students could push to reach their highest potential. . . . This perspective too has a rightful place in educational history" (p. 219). David Celeski (1994), a native of Hyde County, North Carolina, summarizes a portion of his highly acclaimed account of the early transition into school desegregation in a manner that speaks to me about my role to convey and uplift the poor, rural, black experience of schooling: "Today a talented group of young scholars . . . have begun to explore and articulate the 'good qualities'" of blacks being schooled in the South (p. 173). As I sat in homes of black families of northeastern North Carolina, the fiftieth anniversary of the seminal 1954 *Brown vs. Topeka* school desegregation quickly approached. In the end, the families convinced me that another role I was to take on was that of continuing the families' school desegregation stories (largely 1967–2000), of honoring the legacy of their struggles, and of fulfilling the promises of 1954. The participating families made it clear to me that an additional role I must play is that of a vehicle for their stories, for bringing them their rightful place in history, for expanding possibilities for future generations, and for transforming relationships through their historical insights (Clark, 2002). This is an extremely important concept for me and required some depth of reflexivity and regard for my new positioning at my former home as a vehicle for the Biggs, Erskin, and Winston families. It also forces me to think and speak more about the issue of reciprocity. As I noted in the Chapter 2 of this book, Clark (2002) encourages researchers to be thoughtful about how we can (a) encourage participants to remember as a way of entering and transforming history, (b) support healing, reconciliation, and development within the cultural community of study, and (c) transform and build new cultural perspectives opening new dialogues about the past (pp. 91–95).

At the end of this study, I find my present position and ability to reciprocate as involving a negotiation of identities and brokering roles on the border of a rural, black working-class upbringing and a white academy that measures optimal, exemplary, and worthy citizenry. I am wearily and warily toeing the line, which separates my familial color of ethnic integrity from mainstream academic dignity and structural mobility. My early constructed reality led me to consider the working class not as a position of failure, but as an ethos of hard work, community, spiritual faith, and a thirst for pragmatic knowledge that provided a gateway for educational hope. Perhaps my educational experience is rooted in the "construction of meaning" that I "attached to marginality, not the state of being marginal" (Grant & Breese, 1997, p. 192). Similar to the "emissarial" black identity explained by Grant and Breese, I am well versed in the norms of achievement in the dominant culture and I have "used them to my advantage . . . even though there [were] several painful racist incidents" in my life before I entered college (p. 198). Despite the more public and internal identity politics, I "[am] comfortable with Anglo-Americans," and I have reached a university educational level that even most whites have not, but structural challenges of postdesegregated schooling render me somewhat of an anomaly; an anachronism among those with whom I share a collective racial identity (Grant & Breese, 1997, p. 198).

My life, like these participants' lives, is pedagogy, too, in which I push for black academic, economic, and moral success and where I pull open doors that expose the oppression and negative consequences of our inherited education/economic structure that precludes systematic black success. Hence I traverse borders of intellect and action with the belief that I am helping to expand possibilities for success for working-class blacks in a system that has defined success in ways that have disproportionately benefited white America. Are traditional white American successes what I want to pursue, where progress is a means of control over, rather than harmony with, organic and inorganic existence? In light of the complexities of my life, as a black, white-university-educated, "native" ethno-historian, I leave my work with black families as a brokering vehicle—colonizer/colonized, insider/outsider, mainstream and homeboy. Therefore, I find my entry, role, and ability to reciprocate bound by my ability to remain credible as both scholar and native son, to slip in and out of the formal, consultative, and casual forms of language (Gutman & McLoyd, 2000) and communicative behavior—all in one sitting. It is difficult, at times, to assume the role that best articulates my thoughts and feelings, while conveying an authentic sense of place and respect in both pedagogical settings. Even so, the mere fact that I was educated through black family pedagogy to code-switch without feeling "fake" or being consistently acknowledged as such suggests promise. So yet again, lived experience leads to school desegregation messages replete with cultural struggle and saturated with familial streams of hope.

A Need for "New" Pedagogies— Battling Symbolic Violence

As a mainstream, homeboy vehicle, I find my liminal moment in the spaces that allow me to unveil opportunities for hope. I intend for this book of stories and policy recommendations to work toward remedying the effects of school desegregation on the black families that let me into their lives. The silenced voices of northeastern North Carolina have now spoken here. The paucity of helpful educational policies is what these black families had to suffer immediately after school desegregation, and continue to bear at this stage of history; but these problems are social, not biological, and therefore they can be remedied through social change. I have suggested educational policy implications, but there is another arduous fight—the battle of change versus complacency with racialization.

This book is a commencement to initiate tasks that limit the negative consequences of racialization in schools that should have begun to do so in 1954. Yet, with some climate changes in the area over the last three decades, this is in a sense a new struggle. We need to construct a pedagogy of struggle and hope to address the implementation of sound desegregated school policies. It would seem wrong for me to propose a new pedagogy as a true outsider, solely from my tentative interpretations. However, as an insider/outsider, the question for the Erskin, Biggs, and Winston families is the same as the question for my own family and, arguably, for all of us: What is to be on our next pedagogical agenda, given all that has transpired in the last fifty years?

The new struggle for the third generation of black families to experience desegregated northeastern North Carolina schools is not likely to be for access, or even for equal access, but adequacy. Like their predecessors, later generations experiencing the legacy of white privilege after school desegregation and the history of symbolic violence need additional educational resources (Bourdieu, 1977). For Bourdieu, symbolic violence encompasses "every power which manages to impose meaning and to impose them as legitimate by concealing the power relations which are the basis of its forces" (p. 4). The later generations of black families in this book to experience desegregation in northeastern North Carolina schools are also likely to experience racism as symbolic violence in school. But contemporary racism no longer involves "nigger rhymes" and cross burnings, but an even more elusive form of symbolic violence in "pedagogic action," where white school power is arbitrary and white culture is imposed in ways that are not as easily exposed. And here is where the present and future struggle of racism lies, against this symbolic violence in the area's schools.

Another pertinent concept in Bourdieu's symbolic violence theory for later generations is "pedagogic authority," a requirement of social conditions that exercise pedagogic action. The relative autonomy of the agent with legitimated authority leads to the tendency for power relations to be reproduced in a manner that consistently puts the arbitrary culture into the dominant position. With this in mind, the idea that education is institutional racialization as symbolic violence in area schools suggests that such racism with enhanced illusionary tactics will likely reproduce black educational struggles. For example, the subtle yet strategic and continuous breakdown of intergenerational closure for black families could persist through the dominant culture's strategic limitation of blacks in positions of legitimate northeastern regional school authority.

Finally, Bourdieu argues that symbolic violence is realized over time through a history of what he calls "pedagogic work" (1977, p. 31). Pedagogic work is a process of instilling messages that must last long enough to produce durable training, i.e., Bourdieu's notion of habitus. The present pedagogy of struggle evident from the black family participants in this study offers narratives portraying a loss of intergenerational closure that has already traversed three generations and is moving toward a fourth. When such pedagogic work renders habitus, Bourdieu suggests, the state of education in places such as northeastern North Carolina, with its white cultural arbitrary control, is "capable of perpetuating itself after pedagogic action has ceased and thereby capable of perpetuating in practices the principles of the internalized arbitrary" white culture (1977, p. 31). In light of the evidence of symbolic violence in the pedagogy of struggles narrated by the participants, one could argue that there is a stronger need for another new pedagogy—a new pedagogy for the white decision makers in northeastern North Carolina schools to at least unveil more opportunities for black family pedagogies of educational hope.

It is important to note here that Bourdieu did not design his theory of symbolic violence to criticize any particular type of pedagogy, because he believed such violence to be inherent in the essential nature of all pedagogic communication (Morrow & Torres, 1995, p. 183). Bourdieu explains that one cannot liberate education from power relations, only reproduce power relations or someone else's pedagogy, albeit an attempt at antioppressive pedagogy (Bourdieu, 1977, p. 17). I interpret Bourdieu's point as admonishing researchers to remain value explicit and to avoid masking our pedagogic agendas through "the allusion that it is not violence" (1977, p. 183). My agenda and that of the participants of this study is clearly for a particular pedagogy of struggle and hope, one that criticizes the past and present pedagogy of the predominantly white desegregated northeastern North Carolina schools. Our pedagogic agenda, then, is a move toward unveiling more positive educational experiences and opportunities for the black families of the area. We believe this move to be good and just, although it speaks more to adequacy than to common understandings of equity and equality.

For adequate resources to be achieved, such as additional training for veteran teachers to be culturally responsive to black students and families, it is not inherently equal or equitable on one level for white students. On a second level, the narratives of this study suggest that such professional development is needed to offer an adequate education to black students. With an adequate education (more resources for blacks now to compensate for post-desegregation losses), black families can then survive and compete as a group on equal and equitable footing with their white counterparts in generations to come. Of course, this move is still not equitable to whites, as it requires a balance of educational privileges.

Advice for Future Studies:
Geneology of Educational Struggle and Hope

The Biggs, Winston, and Erskin intergenerational narratives of school desegregation have transferable historical significance in all the spaces where they remind us of the following points:

a. We are at a time in history where learning from the trials and triumphs of our elders is paramount, yet if they haven't written books, their stories of potential worldwide aid may be limited to their families, or lost altogether with their passing.

In fact, Mr. Walker Whitman passed away only weeks after sharing his school desegregation stories with me. A former school administrator, Mr. Whitman was a well-known emissarial black man, as well as a recipient of numerous honors and awards in northeastern North Carolina. He had written no books, however, his wife is over eighty, and the couple had no children.

 b. Family school desegregation experiences may evolve very little over a period of two to three generations; the major shift obviously occurred during the transition from segregated school experiences to those of the desegregated schools.

One example is in the experience of Margie Hines, whose grandson (like his father) lamented the greater number of blacks as cafeteria workers and janatorial staff versus teachers in one northeastern Albemarle school.

 c. Federal, state, and local school desegregation efforts addressing technocracy without addressing ideology may do little in the way of ensuring resources for families to reach their highest potential.

From teachers, administrators, and researchers, I am again reminded of my relation to other scholars through our shared concern for eradicating educational gaps.

Research suggests that overall, black families are less "prepared" by school standards to "prepare" their children for success as defined by state standards; which leads to another complicated question: "What do we mean by 'gap'?" Is it a gap in what we think black families should know, or what the predominantly white school system should know about black families in order to serve them the same as the white children for which the public schools were created? I think it means that there is a gap in both. For example, black families should be included in discussions about additional possibilities for motivating children, but the schools must help them think of viable alternatives, agreed upon by consensus, without "devaluing, deskilling, or infantilizing" of parents or school personnel at the meetings (see Bloom, 2001). In other words, researchers, families, and school decision makers should consider that there is still an "opportunity to learn" gap even in desegregated schools (see Mickelson, 2001) on second-generation segregation in Charlotte schools).

With the notion of black children not being as "prepared" as white children to enter kindergarten, we must further examine how "preparedness" is being measured in a school system that was created initially by and for the white middle class. In other words, there are ways in which the black student is prepared for age-appropriate civic participation that are often not explored.

Practitioners must recognize what talents each black child does bring to the school and work with the family to translate those talents into higher levels of preparation as defined by the school. Qualitative research on culturally responsive teaching, especially the teaching practices of African American teachers (e.g., Foster, 1995; & Ladson-Billings, 1992), suggest that when teachers explicitly honor and incorporate into the school language the styles, patterns of interaction, knowledge, and other forms of communicative behavior of racialized minority children, the children's learning increases (see Riehl, 2001).

> d.   Family pedagogy may evolve very little over a period of two to three generations, but a sound basic message may still help students reach their highest potential in school. Ontology, epistomology, and methodology of formal education may evolve little to inform the type of praxis that supplements families attempting to reach their highest potential.

A common family pedagogy of hope includes religious faith in northeastern North Carolina. Arguably, school desegregation and the modern civil rights movement in the United States would have been less effective without all parties rallying behind the major tenants of Christianity. With this project, I find my family tree of knowledge as bound by laypersons and scholars who have come before me. From the families, I (with help from my wife) rediscovered a family tree of struggle and faith (see poem below).

STRUGGLE FAITH HOPE
by Megan and Sherick Hughes

> Struggle: Lighting Bolt, rain, tornado, drought.
> Controlled burns smoldering, breathing for control.
> Faith: believing roots will hold;
> believing you are meant to be here,
> persevering in the face of struggle,
> sensing social justice as the natural order of things.
> You are being watched over, protected by
> believing that you will be protected; faith in things unseen.
> . . . we sing it in our Gospel Song—there is a balm
> in Gilead to heal the soul.
> Hope: for the best, while expecting the worst;
> as well as the impossible; surviving
> through growth, resilience, prosperity, and faith.
> Faith fuels hope, refuels hope, sustains hope in our struggling times.

The question of the degree to which authors should take ownership of ideas, or whether we should at all is an age-old concern. As an author of qualitative research, I am in fact expected to be value explicit about "my" claims and to use "I" and "my" rather than overuse the editorial "we" in my written work. At the same time, I am charged with writing against myself and recognizing that my ideas are triggered by my relationship with the narratives, spirituality, and human beings with whom I come into contact during my collection of school desegregation stories.

From a Foucaultian (1972) purview, understanding social theory is acknowledging the existence of a genealogy or family tree of ideas, but not necessarily new ideas (see also Noblit, Hatt-Echeverria, & Hughes, 2003). From this standpoint, no grand theory exists to soothe all of the educational woes of school desegregation. What does exist from Noblit's (1999) and Foucault's (1972) perspective is theorizing, an ongoing process where theory is not truth with a capital T, but is recognized as part of history. Our ideas are situated within a context of all the ideas that have come before us. This encounter is always a contradition. And it is understood as such in order to avoid "avenues that ignore the geneology of conceptions and claim a novelty that doesn't exist" (Noblit, Hatt-Echeverria, & Hughes, 2003, p. 324). To some extent, I am recycling, reusing, or reducing pedagogic actions within the confines of structure and agency (Giddens, 1979). In other words, I am sharing the stories of people who could tell you themselves, but without the authority afforded to me, the Ph.D.

I must also offer my credence to hope and the power of narratives to beat the odds, to realize the idea that my book can borrow from the elders of northeastern Albemarle as well as those of the academy to convince you to go hear the school desegregation stories for yourself. And after you hear them, you too may legitimize their telling of it en route to unveiling more educational opportunities for hope in the region. I cling to a belief in generative knowledge, the new "stuff" that may help us escape the mundane problems of the structures we call desegregated schools, with all their issues of racialization and educational gaps. Indeed, it is a millennial contradiction, as Noblit, Hatt-Echeverria, and Hughes (2003) explain: on the one hand, a stagnant structure, and on the other, a human capacity to struggle with a kind of educated resistance that can find cracks in desegregated school structures and fill them with hope.

Future historical ethnographies can be informed by my results suggesting the complexity of concepts like hope, struggle, and pedagogy as they exist in the day-to-day lives of black families after desegregation. My results suggest that black family–school relationships are extremely intricate phenomena and should be approached as such. My work indicates that inquiries into dynamic constructs such as resiliency, future orientation, and enlightened self-interest are likely to provide fuller pictures with relational rather than linear approaches.

This book also offers an understanding of the rural perspective of black families and their educational experiences, which is often missing from contemporary literature. Future studies could further explore the pedagogy of hope in tempering the black urban struggle for adequate education. Moreover, this study offers a foundation for historical ethnographies with North/South or other geographic comparisons of the pedagogy of educational hope and struggle. The critical theorists' concerns for injustice and oppression also offer possibilities for an expansion of my findings and interpretations of such pedagogy. It is my hope that my study will be a catalyst for future studies, and that future researchers will commit themselves as vehicles for subjugated black families and their allies as we find voices such as Woody Winston's in our own.

WOODY WINSTON'S FINAL COMMENTS

You stick right with it. Don't care what people talk about, you just stick right with what your doing. You'll make it. See, I didn't even have no education, and I made it. I just had enough education to get by. And use this here [tapping his pointer finger to the right side of his forehead].

References

Allport, G. (1954). *The Nature of Prejudice*. Boston: Beacon Press.

Bempechat, J. (1991). *Fostering High Achievement in African American Children: Home, School, and Public Policy Influences*. New York: ERIC Clearinghouse of Urban Education, Office of Educational Research and Improvement, U.S. Department of Education and Institute for Urban and Minority Education, Teachers College, Columbia University.

Bloom, L. R. (2001). "I'm poor, I'm single, I'm a mom, and I deserve respect": Advocating in schools as and with mothers in poverty. *Educational Studies*, 32(3): 300--316.

Bourdieu, P. (1977). *Outline of a Theory of Practice*. Trans. Richard Nice. Cambridge, UK: Cambridge University Press.

Bourdieu, P. (1990). *The Logic of Practice*. Cambridge, UK: Polity Press.

Cecelski, D. (1994). *Along Freedom Road*. Chapel Hill: University of North Carolina Press.

Clark, M. M. (2002). Oral History: Art and Praxis. In D. Adams and A. Goldbard (Eds.), *Community, Culture, and Globalization* (pp. 88–105). New York: The Rockefeller Foundation.

Comer, J. P., Ben-Avie, M., Haynes, N. M., & Joyner, E. T. (Eds.). (1999). *Child by Child: The Comer Process for Change in Education*. New York: Teachers College Press.

Comer, J. P., Haynes, N. M., Joyner, E. T., & Ben-Avie, M. (Eds.). (1996). *Rallying the Whole Village: The Comer Process for Reforming Education*. New York: Teachers College Press.

DuBois, W.E.B. (1903). *The Souls of Black Folk*. Cambridge, MA: University Press, John Wilson and Son.

Foster, M. (1995). African American Teachers and Culturally Relevant Pedagogy. In J. A. Banks & C. A. McGee Banks (Eds.), *Handbook of Research on Multicultural Education* (570–581). New York: Macmillan.

Foucault, M. (1972). *The Archeology of Knowledge*. New York: Pantheon Books.

Freire, P. (1996). *Pedagogy of Hope*. New York: Continuum.

Giddens, A. (1979.) *Central Problems in Social Theory: Action, Structure, and Contradiction in Social Analysis*. Berkeley: University of California Press.

Grant, K.G., & Breese, J.R. (1997). Marginality theory and the African American student. *Sociology of Education, 70*, 192–205.

Gutman, L. M., & McLoyd, V. C. (2000). Parents' management of their children's education within the home, at school, and in the community: An examination of African-American families living in poverty. *Urban Review, 32*(1), 1–24.

Hecht, M. L., Collier, M. J., & Ribeau, S. A. (1993). *African American Communication*. Newbury Park, CA: Sage.

Hughes, K. (2003). *4th Sunday in the Dirty [South]*. Charleston, SC: Imprint Books.

Hughes, S. (2003). The convenient scapegoating of blacks in post-war Japan. *Journal of Black Studies, 33*(2), 335–354.

Jencks, C., & Phillips, M. (Eds.). (1998). *The Black-White Test Score Gap*. Washington, DC: Brookings Institution Press.

Ladson-Billings, G. (1992). Reading between the lines and beyond the pages: A culturally relevant approach to literacy teaching." *Theory into Practice*, 31: 312–20.

Lee, C. (1985). Successful rural black adolescents: A psychological profile. *Adolescence*, 20, 129–142.

Luster, T., & McAdoo, H. (1991). *Factors Related to the Achievement and Adjustment of Black Children*. Paper presented at the biennial meeting of the Society for Research in Child Development, Seattle, April 1991.

Mickelson, R. (2001). Subverting Swann: First- and second-generation segregation in the Charlotte-Mecklenburg schools." *American Educational Research Journal, 38*(2): 215–252.

Morrow, R. A., & Torres, C. A. (1995). *Social Theory and Education: A Critique of Theories of Social and Cultural Reproduction*. Albany: State University of New York Press.

Noblit, G. W. (1999). *Particularities: Collected Essays on Ethnography and Education*. New York: Peter Lang.

Noblit, G. W., Hatt-Echeverria, B., & Hughes, S. (2003). The future of educational studies: Where identity meets knowledge. In G. W. Noblit & B. Hatt-Echeverria (Eds.), *The Future of Educational Studies* (p. 324). New York: Peter Lang.

Oakes, J., & Lipton, M. (2003). *Teaching to Change the World*. Guilford, CT: McGraw-Hill.

Riehl, C. (2001). Bridges to the future: The contributions of qualitative research to the sociology education. *Sociology of Education Extra Issue*, 115–134.

Scott, J.C. (1990). *Domination and the Art of Resistance: Hidden Transcripts*. New Haven, CT: Yale University Press.

Scott-Jones, D. (1987). Mother-as-teacher in the families of high- and low-income first graders." *Journal of Negro Education, 56*(1): v21–34.

Siddle Walker, V. (1996). *Their Highest Potential: An African American School Community in the Segregated South*. Chapel Hill: University of North Carolina Press.

Wilson, E. H. (1983). *Hope and Dignity: Older Black Woman in the South*. Philadelphia: Temple University Press.

Epilogue
Black Hands in the Biscuits
of Tomorrow

BLACK HANDS IN THE BISCUITS
by Sherick A. Hughes

White flour,
saturated and shortening.
Battered Black hands
rolling, needing, and covered in Whiteness.
baking in an oven of oppression—
Boiling Point!
Then, came another covered up,
buttered up, glaze-over.
White folks say,
"People of color cool-down your nerve,
keep your hands where they can serve."
"Yesterday," my Black folks say,
"but not today,"
my Black folks say.

Initial Thoughts

I thought, Where better to explore post-*Brown* hope and struggle in a black community than my family's home, my former home in northeastern North Carolina? It was set to be a homecoming of a precarious sort. As Thomas Wolfe, a fellow North Carolinian, wrote over six decades ago, "You can't go home again." I can, of course, physically go home again. My internal compass is always set for home, like a migratory bird that instinctively flies for the nesting ground of its birth. Such instinct-driven, mental, and emotional home-comings, however, can be quite elusive. My fledgling journey through acad-eme has been both a blessing and a trial, expanding my intellect and exposing me to further life possibilities, yet precluding visions of a romantic homecom-ing with its abundance of comforting routines, scripted conversations, and relentless nostalgia. In some ways, I have become an island off the coast of the northeastern North Carolina mainland of my birth—connected to the social ecology of the area and yet distinct from it.

It seems that one key to using any of the distribution of power I have gained since leaving northeastern Albemarle involves locating cracks in the structure in order to fill them with hope. By naming, checking, and critiquing this power, I may act strategically toward change en route to the end of humil-iation and suffering as it relates to racialization in desegregated schools. Part of my pedagogy of hope involves rendering black schooling struggles in north-eastern Albemarle nonreproductive by conveying voices from history. The nar-ratives presented in this text demonstrate those voices, sometimes regretful for lost opportunities, often frustrated for want of real change, always hopeful and yet haunting in their immediacy to our struggle today. The difficulty in return-ing home is facing the trade-offs of class and educational mobility—trade-offs I now understand better and that I must witness the moment I cross the threshold into my first home. Part of my dilemma in going home again also means acknowledging obstacles that stem from living as insider/outsider, col-onizer/colonized, mainstream/homeboy.

I imagined through the years that my research would allow me to empower my family and help more of us to succeed educationally and eco-nomically. The new catchword of those like me, who are deemed and self-proclaimed altruistic persons, is "empowerment." I currently struggle with the word empowerment, because it does not seem to encapsulate how I intend to implement my present and future elite status. Perhaps no one term can explain my future intentions.

Perhaps my dream seeks what oppressed members of society, such as Fred-erick Douglass, Harriet Jacobs, Harriet Tubman, Sojourner Truth, Sarah Grimke, Booker T. Washington, W. E. B. DuBois, Paulo Freire, Mahatma Gandhi, and Martin Luther King, Jr., eventually found: a way to maintain the dignity of my humanity, while helping other minorities like me maintain the dignity of their own; a way to build and sustain hope in myself and in educa-tion, while at the same time moving forward through post-*Brown* struggles. Through educational pedagogy and praxis and a combination of the concep-tual insights of Delpit (1995) in *The Silenced Dialogue* and Shujaa (1994) in *Too Much Schooling,* I work toward holding home and school accountable. Like Delpit (1995), I want to make power more explicit by critiquing conser-vatives as well as liberals who live under color-blind blankets where "acknowl-edging personal power and admitting participation in the culture of power is distinctly uncomfortable" (p. 123). Like Ross Winston and Shujaa (1994), I sense that blacks in northeastern Albemarle receive too much schooling or training and too little of the knowledge indicative of education. In education, not schooling, lies the tools for exposing the relativity of truth and how "white educators had [have] the authority to establish what was [is] to be considered 'truth' regardless of the opinions of the people of color. . . ." (Delpit, 1995, p. 123). Unlike Shujaa, I do not plan to seek an independent African-centered school as sufficient to eradicate oppression of the educational apparatus. Although I fully understand and respect Shujaa's impetus for a point of departure, I believe that if schooling is more indicative of education, as he argues it should be, there is hope for dismantling atrocities of the current learning infrastructure and home and at school. By adapting Shujaa's work (1994, p. 15), I hope to expand the possibilities for an antioppressive educational structure in northeastern Albemarle. I hope to contribute to change in our public and private schools that consistently fail to, but should:

1. Foster the development of adequate skills in literacy, number sense, the humanities, and technologies that are necessary to negotiate economic self-sufficiency in a global society (although NOT in a manner that is merely reproductive of oppression and competition).
2. Instill citizenship skills based on a realistic and thorough understanding of the political system, and support such critical citizenship skills by promoting questioning and critical thinking skills and teaching a balance of democratic rights and ideals.
3. Provide historical overviews of the nation, the continent, and the world that accurately represent the contributions of all human groups to the storehouse of human knowledge.
4. Educate to provide knowledge of self and the self's interdependent relationship with others to promote diverse social contracts within and between global societies.

When I move my argument for education over schooling as something that "should" become truth with a lower-case "t," then I also feel responsible for asking "truth of and for whom?" Maxine Greene discusses a Utopian truth that she calls "positive freedom"—a means to a beginning of life where I may posit and enact the possibilities of an alternative social reality, one without oppression in desegregated schools. Even if Greene's positive freedom is a plausible truth upon which a critical mass of past and present citizens in northeastern Albemarle can agree, how can we begin to implement this freedom? A good starting point for me was to follow the words of the Red Queen in *Through the Looking Glass*, "begin at the beginning," which means a beginning of self-exploration, of focusing more on how individuals come to see themselves in relation to the school community at large. So, how do I begin to see my place in the return to northeastern Albemarle?

I find myself fighting and yet embracing a membership with an elite group described by Judis (2000). Indeed, I am now "one of those" elite professors who can influence education policy within our spheres of influence, largely because we now have the luxury of legitimacy and the social space and time to do so. We may spend long hours debating educational outcomes, while many other northeastern Albemarle residents are either still living in survival mode or behind the veil of strategic ambiguity. I am now a burgeoning "native" ethnographer hoping his work will have some present impact on the positive freedom of "my" people.

In northeastern Albemarle, I often think of my place in the school community as betwixt and between, as a native son, a homeboy who has individual educational accomplishments for which the black community hoped and struggled. I also perceive myself as a source espousing and acting out new knowledge to my own family that sometimes confirms current family practices and sometimes challenges them, which can breed suspicion, defensiveness, questions about my naïveté, and their prayers that I have not gone too far in theoretical understanding to approach "real"-life situations productively. Perhaps I have learned to strive consistently for the ultimate democratic ideal of today, which moves me beyond a blinding past or futuristic idealism to question more openly dormancy, complacency, and mediocrity at this point in northeastern Albemarle's history of school desegregation. Perhaps I am plagued with the question of how the latest generation of my black family and others has been allowed to accomplish the same or less educationally with what seem to be, on the surface, more available legal and social resources.

Later Thoughts

This journey to positive freedom began on the pathways of struggle and hope trodden by a Southern rural black community. In many ways, it seems that we are the miner's canary for education in northeastern Albemarle—the more educated we become, the more sustainable living becomes in our region. Efforts toward antioppressive school desegregation must begin in the present if northeastern Albemarle is to build alumni to substitute for today's major players, when their time in the struggle for hope has passed. We have learned in the desegregated schools era that there is no sustainability of optimal education for all, production of honorable critical citizenship, or social contracts without such substitutability.

This journey is my attempt to maintain a conscience and a work ethic toward sustainable positive freedom in the eyes of God, family, and community. It is an attempt to implement the critical perspective necessary to question the creation and re-creation of school environments with elites that lead us to assume that all of our ideas and technical rationality are human progress. It is a beginning of a journey to not lose sight of my impetus to promote and seek knowledge that helps the social reality that produced me, a reminder to be cautious of my elite status, and an attempt to expose any shallow tributaries to the sea of knowledge about the educational success and failure of black folks from my community.

This journey has intended implications for those who identify themselves as black or African American and for those who identify themselves as white, Caucasian, or European American. For blacks in this particular scene, facing this particular context, where the conveyed messages of educational hope seep through the post-*Brown* struggle, the journey offers insight that can afford families more of the educational possibilities of democracy. I envision this ideal as a balance of democratic rights and ideals, where students in desegregated schools learn to engage a critical temper, but also to temper the critical by centering much of the critique upon the self. I take the advice of Paulo Freire quite literally, when he states that without hope the struggle in the desegregated school structure leads to further "hopelessness and despair." Therefore, I want this book to offer insight into the type of black family pedagogy that brings hope, a hope that transcends the barriers of desegregated, southern, rural schooling. Blacks in such contexts, we learn, can find messages of hope that generate knowledge and continue the struggle for optimal education.

This journey has no intended traditional policy implications, but instead it offers something of a critique of traditional policy logic. Traditional education policy scholarship has little to offer in the realm of nurturing the hope of the southern, rural, black working-class family struggling through a post-*Brown* school. Instead, as Shujaa alludes, even traditional education policy scholarship provides more schooling than education. And traditional education policies have not sufficiently transformed public primary and secondary schools into places that consistently and adequately serve students beyond the general white middle-to-upper-class family. How? Perhaps the educational policy apparatus, like the state apparatus, is controlled by majority decision making—a majority that does not include the diverse, critical, and educated voices of black families.

I do believe that some northeastern Albemarle area whites at the helm of the school policy making arena are genuinely concerned and compelled by authentic positive experiences shared with black family members. I have intended policy implications for those whites who view black mobility as important to better and lead us to positive freedom and a more perfect public education in our democracy. For those whites, my message is one that argues for increased opportunities to learn for black families and not merely equitable, or equal, but adequate community and school resource funding (see Ladd, 1999). The messages of struggle here indicate a history that is not overturned by simply balancing funding and equalizing investments in predominantly black and predominantly white communities. The family and school personnel narratives cry for the need for more funding in northeastern Albemarle schools to counter the ills endured by preceding generations and passed along to us. For example, a desegregated, high-poverty, rural, Southern school will not be able to attain the same performance levels as a low-poverty, suburban, largely segregated Southern school if those schools have the same resources (Ladd, 1999).

Of course, adequacy as the new equity standard may be viewed as an unfair proposal by many northeastern Albemarle whites with the current bulk of the distribution of power, unearned privileges, and feelings of entitlement in their favor. Yet the pedagogy of struggle and hope illuminated by the families in this book challenge all education policy analysts and policymakers to at least reconsider how we implement "equal educational opportunities" before we continue to blindfold ourselves with dismissal and denial.

This phase of my journey was not meant to offer generalized answers, but to present plausible, transferable information for helping black family members reach their highest potential in the northeastern Albemarle region of North Carolina. Without the exposure of narratives like those shared in this book, I fear that former cafeteria manager Margie Hines was correct in her haunting statement: "Nobody even knows [or cares] what goes on, about what happens to us in the rural areas." It is my sincere hope that this publication will support (a) efforts to acknowledge and address gaps in rural, Southern, black educational experiences; (b) efforts to fulfill the promise of *Brown* by education for racialized others, education about racialized others, and education to be critical of privileging through racializing others (see Kumashiro, 2000); and (c) efforts to redistribute the number of high-quality black hands, so that many more black hands may serve on legitimate school decision-making bodies and that only those who reserve the right to do so serve the biscuits.

References

Delpit, L. (1995). *Other People's Children: Cultural Conflict in the Classroom.* New York: The New Press.

Giroux, H. A. (1997). *Pedagogy and the Politics of Hope: Theory, Culture, and Schooling.* Boulder, CO: Westview Press.

Greene, M. (1988). *The Dialectic of Freedom.* New York: Teachers College Press, Columbia University.

Judis, J. (2000). *The Paradox of American Democracy: Elites, Special Interests, and the Betrayal of Public Trust.* New York: Pantheon.

Kumashiro, K. (2000). Toward a theory of anti-oppressive education. *Review of Educational Research, 70*(1), 25–53.

Ladd, H. F., Chalk, R., & Hansen, J. S. (Eds.). (1999). *Equity and Adequacy in Education Finance: Issues and Perspectives.* Washington, DC: National Academy Press.

Shujaa, M. J. (1994). Education and Schooling: You Can Have One without the Other. In M. J. Shujaa (Ed.), *Too Much Schooling, Too Little Education: A Paradox of Black Life in White Societies* (pp. 13–36). Trenton, NJ: Africa World Press.

Appendix

Notes on Methodology

Design

The approach to inquiry in this book is termed native "historical ethnography" because it transcends the research traditions of the two distinct methods. It is a methodology brought to the academic spotlight most recently by seminal work of Vanessa Siddle Walker (1996) in her book *Their Highest Potential*. Like historical inquiry, which includes oral and archival histories, it focuses upon recounting the chronology of events through various periods of a school's history. In pursuit of educational history, this approach is also concerned with putting events into context in order to understand the "how" of school activities. Similar to historical methodology, it is concerned with what people represent for others to get a sense of experiences from past generations. Within this methodology, however, is the concomitant exploration of the meaning of those educational experiences in the context of participants' daily lives. Consistent with ethnographic methodology, it is concerned with not only apprehending educational history, but also the recognition of how people construct the story from the past, in the present, for the future. Thus, stories relayed here move beyond reliving events of black education in the northeastern Albemarle area of North Carolina to comprehend how the events are socially constructed, which reveals the poignancy of the story told as well as the values of the families.

Noblit and Dempsey (1991) also discuss "ethnohistory" in their book *The Social Construction of Virtue: The Moral Life of Schools*. From my reading, there is little difference in the conception of ethnohistory and historical ethnography. For Noblit and Dempsey (1991), the historian differs as she or he seeks historical meaning in context, while the historical ethnographer attempts to understand what participants seek to accomplish with their histories. My work, similar to Siddle-Walker's, has then dual concerns: "it is ethnographic in its effort to provide a cultural understanding of an environment from the perspective of the environment's participants" (Siddle Walker, 1996, p. 221). And it is historical in that, at least to some degree, part of the dynamic culture under study no longer exists and had to be recollected. I attempt to pull both methods together, focusing on how the families constructed hope amid struggle during the transition from segregation to desegregation to the present.

Initial Study Processes

I began this research with a pilot study of members of my own family's school experiences in northeastern Albemarle to comprehend whether there actually was a poignant story to be told and a silenced voice to share, one not previously acknowledged by authorities. The results of this pilot revealed a story of hope. It led to an understanding of pedagogy of educational hope that was there all along, waiting to be explained—to be contextualized. Snowball or chain sampling was the strategy used to locate those information-rich cases, stories and voices, from other black northeastern Albemarle families.

Since I attended northeastern Albemarle schools from kindergarten through twelfth grade, I began the snowball process by interviewing people who I remembered to be well known and widely respected among blacks in northeastern Albemarle: two retired black teachers; two retired black school administrators; one retired black school counselor; one retired black cafeteria worker; and two white teachers, one current, one retired. Each of these initial encounters involved one-time interviews that ended with, "What families should I talk to?" Or, "Who else knows a lot about desegregation in northeastern Albemarle?" As the snowballing list of black families, potential information-rich cases, became quite sizable, a few names or incidents were mentioned repeatedly. The family names mentioned or those involved in the events noted as intense or valuable by a number of different initial informants would become the cases for this research. As Patton (2002) describes, "the chain of recommended informants typically diverge initially as many possible sources are recommended, then converge as a few key names get mentioned over and over" (p. 237).

Thus, the cases of interest were identified from purposefully sampling the teachers, administrators, and school staff or "people who know people who know people who know what cases are information rich, that is, good examples for study, good interview participants" (Patton, 2002, p. 243). This sampling technique led to the historical ethnography of three black families whose names have been changed to protect their anonymity: Biggs, Winston, and Erskin. I found that a working definition of the recommended families included (a) current black grandparent(s) or first-generation adults, all of whom were parents and/or school personnel during the early transition into northeastern Albemarle school desegregation and (b) child(ren) of those grandparents or second-generation adults, who were students during the northeastern Albemarle school desegregation periods examined and who are themselves parents with children who attended the consolidated, desegregated northeastern Albemarle schools. Participants sometimes included only one black grandparent, because the other was deceased. The second-generation participants (forty to sixty years old) were narrowed by (a) availability, (b) a first-generation grandparent's suggestion, and/or (c) whether they had children who attended northeastern Albemarle schools. In addition, this book's design for historical ethnography has three components: (1) oral history, (2) archival history, and (3) ethnography.

Collection of Data and Triangulation

Historical Ethnography: Oral History Interviews

In light of previous literature and my pilot research, which included two black grandparents, two of their daughters, and one son-in-law, the historical ethnography seemed to require three visits each with the first and second generations of the families. At least one of the three visits was at a home; usually all three were. Other visits took place in workplaces or leisure spaces for one to four hours. Sometimes, the two visits occurred early and later during the same day. The interviews generally took place over two to three days. In some instances, more than one generation was interviewed during one visit (see Phillipson, 1999). Several members of the black family unit from the first and second generations were present on two separate visits during the pilot study. The oral history component of the historical ethnography brings sustenance to the research by grounding it in well-documented, multiple accounts of events experienced by the generations. I argue, like Clark (2002), that oral history and cultural community development for the generations are linked in at least three distinctive ways (p. 91):

1. Oral history restores the subject to history by documenting the history of communities that have been excluded from historical accounts and encouraging individuals to see themselves as historical actors. It is possible through oral history projects to encourage people to remember as a way of entering and transforming history (Clark, 2002, p. 91).

2. Oral history is a dialogical encounter based on rapport between the interviewer and the narrator. At best, it can support healing, reconciliation, and development within the cultural community (Clark, 2002, p. 94).

3. Oral history is an artistic practice that can transform relationships and build new cultural perspectives opening new dialogues about the past (Clark, 2002, p. 95).

Historical Ethnography: Observation

As with interviewing, the observational component of this historical ethnography also involves considering the relationship between the researcher and the researched community. Glesne and Peshkin (1999) in *Becoming Qualitative Researchers* offer insight into the distinct observational moves practiced by those concerned with this relationship. Their book describes researcher–researched concerns for observations through the lens of postmodern ethnography where translated experiences are then transformed into understandings that consider closely the intersubjectivity of all of those involved (Glesne & Peshkin, 1999).

The oral history interviews of black family members were hence supplemented observations that included concerns for issues of race, social justice, and intersubjectivity. This work involved concerns for the nonverbal environment (home and neighborhood condition, preferences, etc.) of the black families, my own reflexivity, and the intersubjective nature of my relationship with the family members. The observations were never unobtrusive, because I was in the families' intimate spaces—their homes and places of leisure. The observations of their neighborhood's condition, their home décor, and their meaning making and strategic use of language afforded me some necessary tools for understanding how they have socially constructed educational struggles, hopes, and the relationships that embody their struggles, hopes, and school experiences.

Historical Ethnography: Archival History

Perhaps the most helpful method was the use of historical documentation to triangulate interviews and observations (Siddle Walker, 1996). Archival history was the third component of this historical ethnography. During the last two years, I have spent forty days in the North Carolina state historical archives gathering documents general to the state and specific to northeastern Albemarle's school desegregation. Initial archival research focused on general correspondence from the state superintendent's papers to get an understanding of North Carolina's early transition into school desegregation from 1959–1970. This research revealed documents with information about the Pearsall Plan and Freedom of Choice, both plans initially approved by state legislators to stall school desegregation after *Brown*.

The next phase of the archival history research delved into more local educational history of northeastern Albemarle schools during desegregation. No history books were found that are written about this time in northeastern Albemarle County schools. Thus, the local school history research began in the state historical archive papers and archival microfilm from northeastern Albemarle school board minutes. This archival search began with the time northeastern Albemarle schools were segregated at the time of *Brown* (1954) to the Freedom of Choice period of desegregation (1967) to the present. Other local historical and demographic information about northeastern Albemarle was obtained from the North Carolina Department of Public Instruction. Finally, demographic change through northeastern Albemarle history was obtained from the U.S. Census Bureau's online database.

Interview Questions

The interview questions are based on Dr. Jacquelyn Hall's work on the desegregation era of schools in Chapel Hill, North Carolina. Her work has been an important addition to the desegregation collection in UNC-Chapel Hill's Southern Oral History program. Hall's specific questions were adapted to my concern of educational hope, struggle, and relationships. Two separate question sets were created to parcel out those appropriate for the first generation from those more pertinent to the second generation. The questions also correspond to the number of visits with families. In one case, however, questions for visit one and two were done in one sitting due to the work and child-care constraints of second-generation single-mother Candice Erskin Brown. In this case, a third home visit was conducted to observe and pursue more informal inquiry.

Methods Used in Analysis

Narratives and themes in of the book chapters emerge from three years of collecting data that included documents, interviews, and observations. This historical ethnography research analysis involves several elements: coding field notes, narratives and stories, searching for themes, writing, and theorizing (Coffey & Atkinson, 1996).

Data Management

Two transcriptionists were hired to transcribe interview data. Along with handwritten running notes, and field notes, spoken and recorded on audiotape were also transcribed. Such efforts helped me to compile more than 500 pages of comprehensive data for this book. Once the field notes and interview transcripts were in document form, there was an analysis of the meaning-making that participants conveyed and the contexts of the meaning making process. First, data were grouped by creating and recreating codes from the field notes. The latter coding process is closely followed by an initial search for themes and tentative interpretations.

A second element of the analysis involves the narratives and stories obtained from participants. Coffey and Atkinson (1996) suggest that qualitative researchers can probe for who, what, when, where, and why of the narratives shared. The more complete the narratives and stories, the better they are contextualized and allow more possibilities for a deeper understanding of themes. During the process of analyzing narratives and stories from participants, I again searched for themes and issues of contrast and comparison of narratives and stories across families, within families, and between first- and second-generation participants. During this analysis stage, I searched not only for patterns, but also for particularities of the observed family contexts. It was during this stage that I began to find the transferable information this historical ethnographic methodology had rendered.

Third, I attempted to develop a final set of themes that represented the recounted experiences of the families. Some of the themes are "emic" (from their words), others are "etic" (from my perspective or from relevance to the literature). Some of the emic themes are relatively simple, and others complex, but they always are considered as particular to a black family's culture, generation group, or even individual behavior. I found emerging consistencies, which involved the location of themes, which allows the stories of individuals, groups, or cultural contexts to be translated across one another.

Along the lines of Coffey and Atkinson's notion of qualitative writing, the writing that follows my analysis includes, but is not limited to (1) general statements about black families, (2) general statements about settings and contexts, (3) general statements about situations in black families and themes, (4) specific statements about the black family culture in northeastern Albemarle, (5) specific statements about a particular scene, or incident, in a black family, and (6) summary statements regarding particularities of scene situation, and contexts in relation to general black family cultural statements.

Potential Threats of Methodology

While I spent a great amount of time observing families' living, working, and lounging spaces, I am cognizant of how my previous northeastern Albemarle experiences and personal biases might affect my translation of those experiences. I ponder how my taken-for-granted understandings and assumptions cloud my judgments. How does my movement in the families' spaces involve the mediation of values and interpretations? And how may these black families buffer or bolster interpretations of the past and present as a sort of catharsis as they perceive me as a vehicle to translate their experiences for others within and outside the community?

Thus, in the attempt to illuminate the families' assumptions about certain themes, or consistencies in education struggles and hopes, I illuminated my own. As Siddle Walker (1996) explains, however, my closeness to the community is also an advantage. I know that I could not have achieved rapport and entry as quickly in the small northeastern Albemarle community without my past as a "good" northeastern Albemarle student from a "good" family. As in Siddle Walker's account, much of the most important document or pictorial "finds" were located in the families' homes. Hence the advantage of my intimate relationship with the community was undoubtedly influential. To address these threats, an informant was used for a reality check and a home-base check-in person was used when I felt (a) really sure and (b) really stuck. Moreover, as mentioned, I kept an audiotape diary of interview data and field notes, which were transcribed word-for-word by two hired transcriptionists.

A second threat was the reliance on interviews to find and tell the story. This crutch brought a serious threat to recounting this story, and is what Siddle Walker names "the influence of nostalgia" (1996, p. 223). The analysis of documents offered historical reference points, which were important for adding substance to the themes, as well as their confirmation or denial. It is highly possible that the sentiments of education struggles and hopes offered may not be shared by the white community in northeastern Albemarle— although the consistency of narratives and themes across time, families, and generations indicates that this is a narrative that needs to be understood. The triangulation of sources, interviews with black and white former teachers, principals, and other school officials also shored up this potential threat.

A final threat is related to the accurate interpretation of events by participants. This threat, too, was addressed in several ways. First, several key informants with great knowledge of northeastern Albemarle, who were not members of the observed families, were chosen to help throughout the project to sort out conflicts in details. Second, each of the three families of this book and the respective generations read the transcripts and initial drafts of my chapter of their story, thereby presenting further triangulation of analysts. Their substantive comments have considerable weight for noting the appropriate points of interest and the accuracy of narratives and themes. They were also asked what had been omitted; their comments show up in the final draft of their story. Even with these self-checking tools, I have not written myself out of the ultimate story. These tools are useful for creating a dialogue, and for chronicling my subjectivity as well as intersubjectivity. As Michelle Fine (1994) poignantly argues, too often we write essays about subjugated others, as if we are neutral transmitters of voices and stories. We tilt toward a narrative strategy that reproduces an "us" telling an objective story about a subjugated "them." This strategy denies the fact that the shaping and retelling of narratives is never an objective process, and the final product is always a production of the researcher (e.g., me) and the researched (e.g., present and past school personnel and families).

The final threat comes from any attempts by me to make essential or make absolute the participants' narratives of their experiences. Because this study suggests that there are myriad of feelings and responses to school desegregation that may change even within individuals, multiple perspectives/theories are incorporated to understand shared experiences. Thus, a triangulation of perspectives and theories are used in opposition to grand theory. This move is anticipated to offer a more complete picture of the complexities of school desegregation. For it seems to be a complex story that exceeds stories of an all-happy, segregated black school, and an all-harmful, predominantly white desegregated school, in the eyes of the beholders.

I am not separate from these ideas. They helped make me a scholar today. Despite threats of my methods, I returned, in the end, to understand better how the three families did what they did with their education histories. I continue to learn from them.

References

Clark, M. M. (2002). Oral History: Art and Praxis. In D. Adams & A. Goldbard (Eds.), *Community, Culture, and Globalization* (pp. 88–105). New York: The Rockefeller Foundation.

Coffey, A., & Atkinson, P. (1996). *Making Sense of Qualitative Research: Complementary Research Strategies*. Thousand Oaks, CA: Sage.

Fine, M. (1994). Working the Hyphen: Reinventing Self and Other in Qualitative Research. In N. K. Denzin & Y. S. Lincoln (Eds.), *Handbook of Qualitative Research* (pp. 70–82). Thousand Oaks, CA: Sage.

Glesne, C., & Peshkin, A. (1999). *Becoming Qualitative Researchers: An Introduction* (2d ed.). White Plains, NY: Longman.

Noblit, G.W., & Dempsey. (1996). *The Social Construction of Virtue: The Moral Life of Schools*. New York: State University of New York Press.

Patton, M. Q. (2002). *Qualitative Research and Evaluation Methods*. Thousand Oaks, CA: Sage.

Phillipson, M. (1999). *Values-Spoken and Values-Lived: Race and the Cultural Consequences of a School Closing*. Cresskill, NJ: Hampton Press.

Siddle Walker, V. (1996). *Their Highest Potential: An African American School Community in the Segregated South*. Chapel Hill: University of North Carolina Press.